This book evaluates the major debates around which the discipline of international relations has developed in the light of contemporary feminist theories. The three debates (realist versus idealist, scientific versus traditional, modernist versus postmodernist) have been subject to feminist theorizing since the earliest days of known feminist activities, with the current emphasis on feminist empiricist, standpoint and postmodernist ways of knowing. Christine Sylvester shows how feminist theorizing could have affected our understanding of international relations had it been included in the three debates. She elaborates a feminist method of empathetically cooperative conversation which challenges the identity politics of international relations, and illustrates that method with reference to the Greenham Common Women's Peace Camp (in the UK) and the efforts of Zimbabwean women to negotiate international funding for their local producer cooperatives.

FEMINIST THEORY AND INTERNATIONAL RELATIONS IN A POSTMODERN ERA

Cambridge Studies in International Relations is a joint initiative of Cambridge University Press and the British International Studies Association (BISA). The series includes a wide range of material, from undergraduate textbooks and surveys to research-based monographs and collaborative volumes. The aim of the series is to publish the best new scholarship in International Studies from Europe, North America and the rest of the world.

Series list continues after the index

FEMINIST THEORY AND INTERNATIONAL RELATIONS IN A POSTMODERN ERA

CHRISTINE SYLVESTER

Northern Arizona University

CAMBRIDGE
UNIVERSITY PRESS

Published by the Press Syndicate of the University of Cambridge
The Pitt Building, Trumpington Street, Cambridge CB2 1RP
40 West 20th Street, New York, NY 10011–4211, USA
10 Stamford Road, Oakleigh, Melbourne 3166, Australia

First published 1994

Printed in Great Britain at the University Press, Cambridge

A catalogue record for this book is available from the British Library

Library of Congress cataloguing in publication data
Sylvester, Christine, 1949–
Feminist theory and international relations in a postmodern era /
Christine Sylvester.
        p.   cm. – (Cambridge studies in international relations: 32)
Includes bibliographical references and index.
ISBN 0 521 39305 1 (hardback). – 0 521 45984 2 (paperback).
1. Feminist theory.   2. Women in politics.   3. International relations.
I. Title.   II Series.
HQ 1190.S95   1994
305.42'01 – dc20   93–10251   CIP

ISBN 0 521 39305 1 hardback
ISBN 0 521 45984 2 paperback

To Jean Bethke Elshtain and Cynthia Enloe
– two exemplary "women" who subvert IR

CONTENTS

ACKNOWLEDGEMENTS

This manuscript has developed over several years as flashes of color and movement in my head, and I am grateful to a number of people for helping me to meld the hues and to choreograph the text. I am particularly thankful to Steve Smith for encouraging me to write this book under the auspices of the Cambridge University Press series on studies in international relations. The Center for International Studies at the University of Southern California invited me to campus as a Senior Visiting Scholar in 1991 in order to begin the manuscript, and the insightful comments of many USC colleagues pushed my thinking in useful directions. Northern Arizona University was generous in providing the leave of absence that enabled me to take up the USC invitation as well as a summer grant in 1992 that made it possible to finish the book in a timely manner.

Rob Walker read this manuscript in its entirety as did my extraordinarily talented graduate assistant, Ellen Taylor, and an anonymous reader from Cambridge University Press. All provided enormously helpful comments, and, in addition, Ellen did a professional job of editing the entire manuscript and checking bibliographic references. Sandy Anthony then did the formal copy-editing for Cambridge University Press and provided considerable long-distance support and comfort, for which I am grateful. Graduate students in my 1993 seminar on International Relations Theory also read the manuscript and offered glimpses of how the book may be received "out there." Moreover, portions of the argument, which have surfaced over the years in various conference papers and book chapters, were scrutinized to good effect by Jean Elshtain, Steve Rosow, Adam Lerner, Marysia Zalewski, Linda Rennie Forcey, Steve Smith, David Campbell, John Odell, and William Connolly.

The Dali photograph was supplied by the Musées Royaux des Beaux-Arts of Belgium. The painting by Ruby was generously offered by Dick George, the publications manager for the Phoenix Zoo, a kindred spirit who takes the matter of elephant talent very seriously.

I wish to express general gratitude to colleagues who contributed to two stimulating conferences I attended – on "Man, the State, and War" at the University of Southern California (1989), which Spike Peterson organized, and on "Gender and the State" at the Wellesley Center for Research on Women (1990), the brainchild of J. Ann Tickner. In addition, the Feminist Theory and Gender Studies section of the International Studies Association has warmed my heart and jazzed my thinking by boldly churning the waters of the field. There are also the "women" of Zimbabwe to remember for their contributions to chapter 5, and the Department of Economics at the University of Zimbabwe to thank for inviting me to be a visiting research associate for 1987–8; without that extended time in Zimbabwe, I would have met far fewer of the "women" who appear here. Finally, I offer heartfelt thanks to my mentor from graduate school, Karen Mingst, for showing me that "women" can do IR too.

No section on acknowledgements could possibly end without bringing to the fore the dedicated patience of a very special friend, Kevin Pyle. Not only has he suffered with grace a decade of my never ending work schedule, he has helped to lug my books, computers, and printers to the far corners of the United States, the United Kingdom, and Zimbabwe, and he has done so time and time again. Indeed, as I write this, we are ostensibly on Christmas break in Taos, New Mexico – so go most "vacations." Kevin shakes his head, smiles good-naturedly, and softly mimics the sounds of a computer and printer until I laugh and laugh.

Among our stops together has been the lovely town of Cape May, New Jersey, where we spend as many long summers as possible. I finished most of this manuscript in Cape May in the summer of 1992, and I must thank Carolyn Dietrick for her usual welcome to town and the staff of Body Mechanix for keeping me fit despite my passion for the farfalle con pesto at Frescos.

Painting by Ruby (Phoenix, Arizona Zoo, courtesy of Dick George)

INTRODUCTION: CONTESTATIONS AND EL(L)E-PHANTS

Paul Viotti and Mark Kauppi (1987) identify three mainstream approaches to studying international relations – realism, pluralism, and globalism. Sandra Harding (1986a) writes of three feminist epistemologies – empiricism, standpoint, and postmodernism. Neither list of approaches exhausts the possibilities of analysis in its respective field, as each writer notes. But silences fill most spaces at the fulcrum of academic international relations (IR) and feminism.

Those silences can be discerned in the nearly feminist-blank pages of mainstream IR journals published in the United States, notably *International Studies Quarterly*, *International Organization*, and *World Politics*. In less charitable moments, a feminist reading those journals might suspect that IR bears a relationship to feminism like elephants do to aesthetics, and it is a relationship of impossibility. But then one would take some solace in knowing there are some international presences in the US-based feminist journals of *Signs* and *Feminist Studies*, and many such presences in *Women's Studies International Forum*. The British international studies journal *Millennium*, we remember, gave us a special issue in 1988 on women in international relations.[1] Across the Atlantic, in this other stronghold of IR scholarship, there is now a counterpart – a special issue of *Alternatives* on the theme "Feminists Write International Relations;" it is edited by a feminist rather than by the usual editorial team.[2] As the IR/feminist divide holds fast, the feminist IR challenge mounts.

In a Phoenix, Arizona zoo, an Asian elephant named Ruby single-footedly decenters conventional wisdom about the (seemingly non-existent) relationship between visual arts and elephant proclivities. She paints abstract expressionist works.[3] She is an aesthetic elephant. Her "strange" behavior partially transforms her keepers into epistemologists who ask: "What does Ruby think or feel as she selects different colors from the paint palette offered by her caregiver? How does she know when her newest creation is finished and stops painting?"[4] All around her there are now imaginative reworkings of

1

seemingly fixed identities: "elephant" becomes "elephant-painter"; "zookeeper" becomes "zookeeper-art philosopher;" visitors to the zoo become momentary art critics. Ruby, and those who appreciate her unexpected creations, are homesteading the art world and the meaning of "elephant."

"Homesteading" refers here to processes that reconfigure "known" subject statuses – such as "elephant," but also the commonplaces of human "men" and "women" – in ways that open up rather than fence in terrains of meaning, identity, and place. As I detail in upcoming chapters, this type of homesteading rests on empathetic cooperations across odd and seemingly incommensurable positions and statuses. It entails recognizing that certain spaces have been marked out as homes for certain bodies, activities, and talents and not for others, and it entails taking seriously the possibilities to homestead those turf-bound homes with the knowledges gleaned from infidels at the fences.

This is not the way the term "homesteading" is usually used. In the United States, the term conjures up images of settlers in wagon trains moving west once a variety of Homesteading Acts opened large tracts of Indian lands (renamed federal lands) to US citizens. By the terms of the 1862 Act, for instance, as long as you paid a small fee per acre, built a homestead on specified parcels, and occupied it for usually five years, the land was yours (usually his).[5]

Double images of emancipation and exclusion mark this common-place understanding of "homesteading." The more romantic, emancipatory side is memorialized in official memories of government-sponsored programs that provided a cheap, labor-intensive way to occupy new places and identities as landowners, farmers, cattle ranchers, wool producers and so on. In order to homestead in this way, however, previous inhabitants had to be evacuated, literally or figuratively, from their places. Often they were pushed to new locations reserved for them, where, safely out of sight, they were then evacuated from or denigrated within the authoritative accounts of the time.

Today the term "homesteading" can apply to individuals who acquire rural farms without much prior experience in agriculture or who take advantage of various government programs to improve blighted urban neighborhoods (urban homesteading). Again one purchases independence cheaply through hard work while someone else moves off the land, out of the farmhouse, away from the old neighborhood and into an uncertain, perhaps, and often less desirable place.

To recognize that homesteading is Janus-faced is to become aware of the thrills and dangers of associating certain places – lands, phenom-

2

ena, theories – with certain people and experiences and not with others. Not only can injustices occur when one tames an only seemingly vacant "out there" by homesteading, but naturalizing categories edge into place through the repetition of exclusions, until we can fail to recognize the historical claims of evacuated others.[6] At the same time, we cannot fail to see that the homesteading acts of evacuators can be homesteaded in ways that rearrange nostalgic notions of who belongs "naturally" where doing what.

Recuperating "homesteading" as a means of expanding knowledge and potential requires that homesteaders from the past and those looking to the future show willingness to cooperate in revealing the stories, identities, variables, and perceptions that were rooted out and evacuated so that some could roost where others were refused homes. It requires also a certain ability to occupy a variety of landscapes simultaneously rather than defend one homeplace as the true site of all identity. Kathy Ferguson (1993: 154) uses the term "mobile subjectivities" to refer to the process of

> moving across and along axes of power (which are themselves in motion) without fully residing in them. [Mobile subjectivities] are relational, produced through shifting yet enduring encounters and connections, never fully captured by them. They are ambiguous: messy and multiple, unstable but persevering. They are ironic, attentive to the manyness of things. They respect the local, tend toward the specific, but without eliminating the cosmopolitan.

Most importantly, they are "politically difficult in their refusal to stick consistently to one stable identity claim; yet they are politically advantageous because they are less pressed to police their own boundaries and more able to negotiate respectfully with contentious others" (ibid.: 154). With mobile subjectivities, "elephant-keepers" can be "elephant art appreciators" and analysts of IR can hopefully move to feminism-sensitive research that enhances everyone's vision and knowledge.[7]

Empathetic cooperative homesteadings do not leave the farm, the neighborhood, the old and new inhabitants, or the theories undisturbed. But neither do they promote mass evacuations of preexisting knowledge. Rather, the process induces varying degrees of unease with the statuses and theories we have come to think of as commonplace in their authority and truth.[8] How we become creatively homeless in ways that enable us to homestead ourselves as we homestead IR differently is what this book, in large part, explores.[9]

It also probes the homesteads that already mark the field of IR as it has developed across three field-defining debates, paying attention to the gender content of those homestead walls and the range of phenomena that have been included and excluded. While recognizing some intriguing new-style challenges currently being framed for conventional IR, it is my contention that the field's attachment to exclusionary homesteads has not slipped sufficiently to permit us to achieve positions of empathetic cooperation with those whose faces, experiences, and assigned places have been established as other so that IR can be what it is.

The trouble with IR

IR is implicitly wedded to an unacknowledged and seemingly commonplace principle that international relations is the proper homestead or place for people called men. I say implicitly, because one of the characteristics of mainstream IR is that it presents itself as gender blind, as a realm of objective human knowledge. Nonetheless, across three debates in the field, there is a recurring sense that "men" have coherent homes in IR and "women" are suited for other places from which they may venture forth to visit international relations, only in order to provide support services for "men's" politics.

When speaking of "men" and "women," it is important to establish from the outset that I do not pose these gender categories as permanent, immutable, determinant, and essential. Rather, I see "men" and "women" as socially constructed subject statuses that emerge from a politicization of slightly different anatomies in ways that support grand divisions of labor, traits, places, and power. By "socially constructed," I mean that men and women are the stories that have been told about "men" and "women" and the constraints and opportunities that have thereby arisen as we take to our proper places. I signify indeterminacy by wrapping the two gender categories in inverted commas (or by saying, people called men, people called women) whenever possible. When a storyline takes men and women as natural categories, however, I also signify that by leaving the two gender words unadorned.

In contemporary IR theory, there is hardly a surfeit of women or "women." IR theory does not spin any official stories about such people or evoke "womanly" characteristics. Some say the field has no stories about people at all, telling only of abstract balances of power, national interests, regimes, trade flows and the like. Feminists, however, find evocations of "women" in IR as the Chiquita Bananas of international political economy, the Pocahontas' of diplomatic practice, the women companions for men on military bases (Enloe, 1989),

4

and the Beautiful Souls wailing the tears of unheralded social conscience at the walls of war (Elshtain, 1987).[10] Moreover, "men" are in IR too, dressed as states, statesmen, soldiers, decision makers, terrorists, despots and other characters with more powerful social positions than "women." That "men" and "women" usually stay in their designated places and engage in the behaviors presumed by the theories, does not mean that the assigned places are true, and therefore in no need of theorizing, or that they reflect inherent talents rather than strivings for fulfillment within assignments.

I am concerned with the theoretical moves that have evacuated the people and traits of "women" from IR theory, and seek to offer a feminist method that can disturb the train of gender stories that touts a certain homesteading experience at the expense of others. I argue that the early debates in the field, and the pretheoretical discussions about international relations that preceded them, helped to establish IR as a "man's" realm of politics.

Think, for example, of Jean-Jacques Rousseau telling us in *Emile* that women are permanent slaves of their sexual passions and cannot, therefore, develop the reason necessary to shape and participate in formal political culture. All women belong to the private places of households and all men have public responsibilities: Emile is to be free by "controlling his desires and passions to the end of realizing his true will, [and so] Sophie's job is to make sure he is successful in this task; for only if her husband is virtuous can the general will be realized" (Hirschmann, 1992: 70).

Think of Niccolo Machiavelli before him, writing in the *Discourses* about "How States are Ruined on Account of Women," because women tempt men to mix private affairs and public matters in ways that reduce rationality, sometimes through seduction and sometimes through open scheming and corruption (Pitkin, 1984). Think of Thomas Hobbes assigning (unproblematized) women mother-rights in the state of nature, thereby nearly guaranteeing that some would be conquered when they tried to defend themselves and children against others who did not have to assume similar involuntary obligations to weaker parties (Pateman, 1988). Then think of the here and now, and the fact that people who are not "men" can succeed in public office only as exceptions to the commonplace cultural understanding that "men" rule, which means that "women still have an anomalous place in politics and not a usual [place]" (Hirschmann, 1992: 19).

With "women" safely stowed away in private places outside of politics, "men" are left as the inhabitants of (unruined) states, socially contracted Leviathans, and the general will. Linked with their territories in a symbiotic identity that denies the homesteadings that removed some from politics, these citizensandstates gaze out on one another and declare sovereignty. Since sovereignty must be recognized, or it can be violated, "men" and their "states" fight for it in acts of international relations that are, says Jean Elshtain (1992: 143), "the definitive test of political manhood." This iterated process of pronouncing self-sovereignty and fighting for it recreates a Hobbesian state of nature in places beyond civilized governance. But it does so with a twist: Hobbes's state of nature featured stories about two genders; the IR state of nature remembered is a place where one gender seems naturally in charge. Cosmopolitans, like Abbe de St. Pierre and Immanuel Kant, tried to tame the state of nature by proffering universal standards of politics to replace or dilute interstate relations. But standards of maternity, food preparation, and other activities associated with "women" were marginalized in these early plans for perpetual peace.

Think next of the two official debates in IR that established certain identity parameters for the field. The first debate, staged between realists and idealists, raised the general question: Will IR be the study of self-interested territorial entities called states operating in an environment of anarchy, or will it be about states and nonstate actors developing webs of interdependence, cooperation, and rules of peace? The second debate, over methodology, queried whether IR would be about developing testable theory or about the pursuit of legal reasoning and moral judgment concerning whether, for instance, a state enjoys a right of intervention in the internal affairs of another. Both debates confined the field to matters of statecraft, system rules, and either/or methodologies. Were these the only burning questions that could delineate relations international from other types of relations? Or were the first two debates in IR dialogues among "men" from western industrialized countries about issues of concern to them that were projected onto all of us? If the latter, we cannot conclude that those issues were strictly masculine, with no resonances for people glimpsing the world through nonmasculine, nonwestern, or nonprofessional lenses. But we can ask questions about how and where variously situated "women" were evacuated from our usual notions of the international and from its relations. We can ask why no one in the fledgling field spoke of this evacuation or theorized gender aspects of power.

The evacuators of longest standing in the field have been the realists. They tell us that: (1) states are the main actors in international relations; (2) states are unitary and rational in their behaviors; and (3)

6

states pursue power defined as national interest (Holsti, 1985).[11] There are many tensions in realist IR, but gender conflict is not acknowledged as one of them. There are statesmen and (male) decision makers and (mostly male) soldiers in international relations; ordinary "men" and "women" are "secure" within the "home" territories states control. There are founding fathers of realism but no recognized founding mothers gazing down at us from the Mount Rushmore of sacralized progenitors. There are nation-states but there are no households in realist IR. There is national interest, but that interest is only vaguely and jingoistically related to the interests of "women" inside nations. There is rationality but often only unitary understandings of what that means and of who exhibits it.

Idealists railed against realism during the first debate and sought to mold international relations to reflect the supposedly cooperative standards of domestic politics in liberal states. In emphasizing peace and altruism, the idealists appropriated for international relations certain traits commonly assigned to nonpolitical western "women," and they did so without offering gender attributions for their ideas. This particular evacuation of "women" through plagiarism was possible in a culture of politics that had long established "women" as nonautonomous from the understandings of us that "men" pronounced, even though "men" (and other dominant categories) actually relied on the invented other for definition and identity. In this type of relationship there is approach and avoidance, need and the assertion of independence, distinctive costuming on both sides of the gender divide and, as illustrated by idealist writings, elements of furtive cross-dressing by the dominant side (when the weaker side cross-dresses, this can be taken as a good sign of emulation, as when a third world country beams western television to its viewers – unless "women" decide to "wear the pants" in the family).

The more contemporary scientific school of neoliberal institutionalism, one of the by-products of the second debate over methods, barricades itself from idealism by accepting the notion that the international system is anarchic, while arguing that states must cooperate in IR or risk suboptimal outcomes. Successful instances of cooperation, some claim (Keohane, 1989a), can expand initial contracts and prompt states to step into a potentially system-transforming region of generalized commitment to the fortunes of the group. "Reciprocity" is the key process that can enable states to move from specific agreements (I will lower tariffs if you will) to more diffuse forms of cooperation (we will commit to free trade for the good of the group).

However, when "women" in the US Navy, an institution on the

FEMINIST THEORY AND INTERNATIONAL RELATIONS

cusp of what the field usually delineates as national versus international relations, behave professionally for the sake of the group and ask the same in return, they have been known to suffer repeated failures of reciprocity and some overt moments of sexual harassment.[12] Reciprocity describes how statesmen and their states relate to each other. "Women" do not figure into the lexicon of states and so they may only visit international relations for the purpose of providing support services for the cooperative clubs that statesmen form. The good they may do while working in a military branch of the state, or while serving as a secretary in an international organization, is not reciprocated by promotions into international relations. Only "men" and their sites of politics reciprocate each other, and this means that our understanding of reciprocity is gendered.

IR now faces a new set of field-delimiting questions posed by postbehavioralists of various hues. Yosef Lapid (1989) summarizes the third debate as encompassing moves to develop new research programs, research traditions, and discourses in IR (e.g., Banks, 1985), efforts to probe thematic premises and assumptions of old theories (e.g., Rosenau, 1990, 1986; Jervis, 1988), and concern to explore historically contingent and socially mutable knowledge (e.g., Ashley, 1989; Alker and Biersteker, 1984; Halliday, 1985). This debate is porous enough to hold the hope that the usual monopolizers of IR dialogues will have to reckon with an even larger number of dissident critics striking unexpected poses in disheveled landscapes. No more impermeable lines of white "men" in ties shooting can(n)onical wisdoms our way.[13]

Yet the third debate can sound like its predecessors in one key respect: despite thirty years of feminist theorizing, "women" do not appear in the citation list of third debaters and gender is not among the categories of contestation that Lapid notes.[14] In silences we read the minutes of a debate that has shaped up as far more in-house than those who feel challenged by it recognize. There is a groaning table of genealogical research that points out the ways we have built a canon that misses or flatly exiles social, economic, and political identities, institutions, and aesthetics that do not fit into the official debate categories of IR (Ferguson and Mansbach, 1991; Ashley and Walker, 1990a). There is a call within the third debate for assigning blurred genres, ambiguous identities, and widely disparate sites of struggle "a location in a scholarly culture, a place and function in political life, a range of possibilities allowably explored, and a set of standards by which their merits and claims of seriousness must be proven or shown to be lacking" (Ashley and Walker, 1990b: 367). Yet feminist writings

8

can be marginalized or preempted by those who plead for a more inclusive IR.[15]

Why exile our iconoclastic paintings from the major and minor exhibition halls? Is there yet another sovereign voice singing IR, this time with dissident-sensitive lyrics that hint at but do not belt out a feminist message? Could our would-be allies expand their awareness of cacophony to the point of becoming more empathetically cooperative and active in unpacking, rearranging the knowledge of the field, and adding to it through new homesteading practices? To my mind, it depends on whether all of us can recognize the gender, class, race, and institutional privileges we may share with mainstream analysts and enter empathetic conversations that cause those positions to slip, to hyphenate "oddly," and to become "politically difficult."[16]

The possibilities in feminist epistemologies

Given the evacuation of "women" from IR, it is time to stalk the shadows of the field and subvert and enliven, destabilize, disorder, disenchant, insecure, and homestead a field whose internal differences are so tied up with the voices of mainstream and dissident "men" that they smack of debates within the hierarchy of one church. Feminist theory is about studying gender – its stories, shapes, locations, evocations, and rules of behavior – usually in tandem with other modern subject statuses such as class, race, age, religion, region and so on. That there are many feminisms will become clear as we probe first the feminist voices that emulate science, then those that give sound to feminist (and women's) ways of knowing, and then those that seek to deconstruct "women" in order to provide all of us with more breathing space for ontology and action.

There are also many "women worthies" whose names crop up in feminist stories of history. These people did not keep to their assigned places "at home," did not leave well enough alone, did not, in some cases, hide from statist wars or, in other cases, countenance those wars. For those reasons, we know only a little about the contestations, challenges, and complicities they posed to IR. Their words have been lost, or covered-up and stored in the basement, or simply ignored because they are the views of people called women and "women" have no place in the political places of "men." Part of my project entails locating and unveiling various shelved goddesses, sages, and oracles who could have made contributions to IR had we been inclined to take note of their ideas and actions.

At the same time, it is important to bear in mind that if "elephants"

9

can be "artists," "women" and "men" can be any number of things. Hence we cannot become obsessed with the effort to exhume women worthies at the expense of exploring the possibilities for identity hyphenations, metamorphoses, and mobilities that can homestead IR in new ways. The identities of women and of those who peg "women" as being of some qualities and not of others, can slip most creatively, *sans* psychosis. We must consider various ways of knowing that help us to slip and slide around identity-constituting subjectivities in theory-useful ways.

Chris Brown (1992b) argues that normative IR, the type of theorizing that is always implicated in feminist exercises, should not just be about the moral dimensions of theory – thus whether gendered stories of IR are just or not – but about questioning the meaning and interpretation generated by the field. Feminist theorizing presents us with at least three ways to contemplate women, "women," and other gender issues in various disciplining canons. The boundaries between the ways are not always sharp, nor is each way of knowing coherent within itself and recognizable by its users as "a" school. Tendencies, however, are discernable. Positions have been taken and specific types of homes for "women" have been sought or rejected within the canons of academia.

Feminist empiricist epistemology suggests that women (we are usually in an uncontested category in this tradition) have yet to roost in IR because science is contaminated by the gender biases of the societies that house it. Instead of offering value-free and objective research, scientific IR – and all philosophies that separate the knower from the known – takes the masculine condition as the defining human condition because that is what we tend to do in our societies. It then poses questions, devises methods, and collects and interprets data in skewed, women-eclipsing ways. (We will have occasion in the following chapters to consider the case of an analysis that draws conclusions about what the average US citizen prefers in the post-cold-war era without breathing a word about the sex and gender of that statistically average (or unaverage) citizen (Yankelovich and Smoke, 1988)). Feminist empiricism generally calls us back to the mission of science as a bias-reducing philosophy and method, thereby providing a way to give women homes within scientifically based fields.

Feminist standpoint ways of knowing harbor the suspicion that even good science invalidates women – and standpointers are also certain that women exist as mothers, household food preparers, agri-culturalists, caretakers, and so on. Women's activities sustain the species and provide fertile ground for developing particular knowledges about human relations and relations with "nature," about

10

struggles for voice, recognition, and status as autonomous beings, and about the intricate ways that societies dominated by people with other assignments can block those knowledges. In a scientific culture – whether realist or idealist, traditionalist or behavioralist – women's characteristic activities and ways of knowing are denigrated as "instinctive," "intuitive," and "emotional," even as certain appropriations of "women" for mainstream knowledge occur. Through feminist struggles for respect and dignity, our ways of knowing can develop into epistemological and political standpoints that are less distorted than the canons that shore up and reproduce the standpointed knowledge of sovereign privilege – the world according to those who create and win wars. These standpoints can become guidelines for scripting women's homes in IR once the debris of a gendered canon is cleared.

Feminists who speak of a postmodern era in which women become problematized as "women," find much to support and to critique in the aforementioned feminist approaches, and offer devastatingly "strange" insights into the world of international relations. Many of these feminists suspect that "science" and "women" are texts of dominance on the one hand and subordination on the other that have been naturalized in modern societies. The modern world is one in which western people called women have a domestic script to follow, a household place in which to follow it, and a set of vapid aesthetic and cultural guidelines for success that "scientific" studies help to bolster. If we listen uncritically to "science" stories and to "women" stories, we hear in them the sounds of conditioning, the sounds of rule-governed subjectivity. The postmodern turn in philosophy enables feminists to question the social constitution of modern womanhood and the scientific criteria by which claims to gender knowledge have been legitimized (L. Nicholson, 1990: 3).

Within the postmodern movement in feminism, however, there are two streams of thinking (in a diverse literature) that I discuss in the chapters ahead: feminist postmodernism and postmodern feminism. The first, often thought of as an off-shoot of French poststructuralist philosophy, tends to emphasize the deconstruction of authority, including the authority of a coherent Self that is often posed as sovereign man (e.g., Foucault, 1982; Derrida, 1981). Poststructuralist feminists, who are commonly described as "French" (e.g., Irigaray, 1977, 1985b and Cixous, 1976), often look to language as a force in the construction and reconstruction of phallocentric symbolic orders. Their analysis entails, among other things, changing language and meaning by writing from the woman's body as an entity that has been least influenced by patriarchy (see discussions in Butler, 1990; Tong, 1989); or they can seem to "see sexual difference constituting itself discursively through inscribed meanings ... the feminine [i]s that which is repressed, misrepresented in the discourses of western culture and thought" (Dallery, 1989: 52, 53). US-based feminists who take on board aspects of poststructuralist philosophy tend to be somewhat more interested in refusing to reify what Teresa Ebert (1988: 22) refers to as "'female experience,' 'woman', or the 'feminine' (whether as the 'natural' body or as the 'body' of the writing, as in [some French feminist fascination with] *l'ecriture feminine*) nor does it essentialize the binarism of male/female."

Responding to a postmodern era of uncertainty as well as opportunity to see, hear, and dispute "women," feminist postmodernisms append themselves to a multifaceted poststructuralism that tends, nonetheless, to be perceived as "a" "particular intellectual style" (C. Brown, 1992b: 319) or as "an" unfortunately cast "emergent ideology demanding partisan allegiance, with the narrative figuration of 'postmodernists' as its doctrinaire adherents" (Ferguson and McClure, 1991: iii). This poststructuralism is known to "resist or deconstruct common assumptions of culture" (Jencks, 1989: 16), and since men and women (and maybe even feminism) are examples of "common assumptions of culture" efforts are made to render "questionable the possibility of locating a place from which to speak and act as a woman knowing that all such places are socially and historically constructed, not given by nature" (R. Walker, 1992: 192). This can have the effect, as a critic like Seyla Benhabib (1992: 229) points out, of leading a 'retreat from utopia' within feminism, not in the useful sense of scrapping the "modernist vision of a wholesale restructuring of our social and political universe according to some rationally worked-out plan." It is the sense, rather, that we jettison "the longing for ... that which is not yet," for which "utopian thinking is a practical–moral imperative."

Postmodern feminism is emerging as a position of negotiation between standpoint feminism, with its conviction that real women exist and lean toward practical–moral imperatives, and feminist postmodernist skepticisms. The point of respectful negotiation illuminates the question: "how can we simultaneously put women at the center and decenter everything including women" (K. Ferguson, 1993: 3)? How can we bring women into view and valorize their experiences while casting a skeptical eye on gender identities worn like birthday suits? Can we have meaningful identities and question them too, or must we chose between identity and resistance to identity? Can we theorize "the subject as *produced* through signifying practices which

12

precede her" (Ebert, 1988: 23), while also granting personal and social significance to some of those produced practices?

Kathy Ferguson (1993: 28), for one, thinks we can make many "strange" identity stews. She argues that whenever we reinterpret the world through a forgotten lens, as one does when posing a woman's way of knowing, we open the door to a "subjectivity that might be less colonized by and more resistant to the disciplinary strategies of modernity." Indeed, rather than discovering "a" woman's way, research using feminist standpoint has found many locations of women and many local standpoints from which to question many disciplining strategies (e.g., Steady, 1987; Mohanty, et al., 1991; Anzaldua, 1990b; Sylvester, 1993b; 1993c; 1993d). The realization of multiplicity means that we can be skeptical of the assignment "women" while searching for treasures that lie in women's rooms (or spaces of life) before rushing to torch the modern house-apartment-studio-hut-hovel-shanty of gender. Each space gives us a different location of subjectivity, a different element of identity, such that to have meaningful identities and to query them too situates us as appreciators of the ways we stand in one space and regard another space with an empathetic–critical gaze that defies ready colonization.

Thus, at once a postmodern feminism questions the possibilities for reforming various canons simply by flipping them over to expose the usually hidden instantiations of women, for the reason that "women" is marked in important ways by "men." One is also skeptical, however, about abandoning "women" as a false invention of sovereign "man" without checking for the knowledges of life that these evacuated ones have learned and that we have ignored all along. Put differently, in this time of change (about which more is written below), we can think of "women" as stick figures that legitimate the existence of dominant "men" while also realizing that we cannot talk to stick figures. To reject gender as another oppressive and oppressing social construct is all well and good on an abstract intellectual level. In practice, it means erasing people who do not agree with our interpretation of gender as the futile, the fleeting, or the fatuous. And out with those people – these painterly el(l)e-phants – go many possibilities for empathetic forms of cooperation with difference. "Women" can be erased once again and homesteads can be built once more by those with "delusions of purity – delusions that are particularly galling (and self-contradictory) when they claim to be 'beyond' dualisms and hierarchical thinking" (Bordo, 1992: 161). Those deluded ones are utopian, but so are those who refuse to erase potential knowledge. Utopian gazes are multiple.

13

Postmodern feminism homesteads through a radically empathetic conversational politics that helps us to learn the strengths and limitations of our inherited identity categories and to decide our identities, theories, politics, and daily concerns rather than continue to derive them from, or reject them out of hand because they come from, established authority sources.[17] We need a method of empathetic cooperation to elicit the subjectivities of "women," which have always been considered to not-exist in public authority, and to provide a sanctuary for the usefully homeless condition that results when our sense of identity becomes mobile as a result, not only of appreciating the many spaces we inhabit in our assigned and created places, but of "really listening to what others say, ... attempting to incorporate those views into [our] own [so that we] become somewhat transformed by that incorporation" (Hirschmann, 1992: 252). Much of this book is about the challenges and horizons of interaction and theory writing that a feminism for a postmodern era, rather than a feminism or nonfeminism as "postmodernist" doctrine, partisan allegiance, and ideology, makes possible.[18]

Why the postmodern?

Proliferations of feminist epistemologies and IR debates are symptoms of the extraordinary late-modern or postmodern era we are living, an era in which certainties of knowledge and identity are shattered daily by realities that were not supposed to be. The superpower United States carpet bombs the tiny peripheral country of Vietnam and loses the war. The US space program that took "men" to the moon in 1969 cannot take a school teacher and NASA astronauts safely into space in the 1980s. The Soviet bear comes up tame while the Europeans force a return to the drawing-board of discredited integration theory as they move backward and forward around economic unity. The white South African government turns back from its historic stand on apartheid without being forced to do so by the mass uprising so many people expected. Just to the north, drawing far less attention, the Zimbabwean government of Robert Mugabe turns away, more reluctantly than governments of Eastern Europe, from the promise of a single-party state in the future. The French build Disneyland. Former East Germans find that freedom means unemployment and second-class citizenship in Germany. The list of strange believe-it-or-nots goes on and on.

What is happening, opine many analysts, is that the age of modernity is showing signs of wear and tear-down and so are the theories fashioned to celebrate or condemn it.[19] Precisely when this began to happen is subject to debate. Was it during World War II, when the Holocaust "deliver[ed] an unhealable wound to Enlightenment notions of human perfectibility and rationality" (Bordo, 1992: 160)? Did that war explode the hierarchies of the world by moving us more and more into an information era that diluted the possibilities for lengthy hegemonies? Are postmodern origins discernible in the OPEC shocks or the Vietnam syndrome of the 1970s? Does postmodernity trace back earlier to the global depression or to the first war to end all wars?

Establishing the characteristics and chronology of modernity poses fewer quandaries. Anthony Giddens (1990: 1) speaks for many when he locates modernity in "modes of social life or organization which emerged in Europe from about the seventeenth century onwards and which subsequently became more or less worldwide in their influence." Included in the litanies of things modern are manufacturing industries triumphant over crafts, capitalism triumphant over feudalism (later spawning its "opposite," socialism), wars with clear winners and losers. Modern also is the tendency to separate time from local spaces, breadwinners from keepers of the hearth, humans as the historic species from "dumb" animals, the life world of the private sphere from the technical systems of the public, international from domestic politics. In the modern era, knowledge becomes enamored with science; progress becomes the route to ever-increasing levels of mass consumption; modernization is equated with development; curative professionalized medicine tames disease; and the male wage earner is the optimal worker in a rational division of labour.[20]

There are eithers and there are ors in the modern era. Rarely are there both-ands except in the sense that modernity totalizes and incorporates the "eithers," "ors," "boths" and "ands." These and other indications of modernity have been linked, argues Jean-Francois Lyotard (1984), through grand narratives of continuous betterment in social engineering. The dark past is conquered by modernity. The social contract strikes down despotism and early patriarchy. Life improves. Evolution is at its apogee.

Postmodern tendencies – to the degree that we accept their existence as "post" rather than as part and parcel of modernity's capacity to generate change – often reveal the undersides, the cases that never really fit, the discontinuities that subverted the orderly narrative, the dissidences and dissonances that belie a story line, the homes that the ostensibly homeless build, the painterly talents lurking in the wrong bodies. Postmodern tendencies can also reveal the complicities that enable the old order to persevere. Women's "rights," "progress," and "movements" fit that two-sided mold as parts of and, at the same time, victories over modernity. And yet "[t]he post-modern condition," Giddens (1992: 21) also says, "is modernity emancipated from false consciousness, from unrealistic aspirations and unrealisable objectives"[21] – such as keeping people called women homebound in the domestic service of others by appeals to romantic love and housewifery or by sheer force of law.

Ironically for modern would-be controllers of women, "women" always figured into modern social theory awkwardly. Classical Marxists said that "women reproducers" labored in ways that were not susceptible to technological modernization and so this category of person was outside history. Contractarian liberalism excluded "women" from the originative myth of civic society and installed a notion of democracy that put an imprimatur on preexisting conditions of sexual (and, for awhile, racial) slavery (Pateman, 1988). "Women" still does not fit the image of combatant citizens in most western societies and our minds can still be deemed "irrational" and "disorderly" (Hartsock, 1985; K. Jones, 1990). Modern critical theory would emancipate all of us through processes of competent communication that reveal the false constraints on our autonomy (Habermas, 1987; M. Hoffman, 1987); but emancipating "all of us" can be a recipe for the continued marginalization of "women" and feminists and people who disagree with "us" in a "new" humanist project.[22]

Our awkward sitings in the modern world of social theory mean that when contemporary feminisms of all forms – all born in the crucible of modernity – come knocking at modernity's door, entry is partly blocked, partly open, and less than satisfying when offered because of hidden gender messages in the milieu. As Jane Flax (1990: 23–4) puts it, "[i]n a wide variety of cultures and discourses, men tend to be seen as free from or not determined by gender ... [thus w]omen are left with the responsibility for thinking about gender, but because we do it, such work is devalued or segregated from the 'mainstream' of intellectual life." In our status as outsiders within (Collins, 1990) modernity, even the mildest of our challenges situates us as postmodern (although not necessarily as postmodern*ists* wielding the analytic tools of construction, genealogy, and textual analysis), for "feminist theory reveals and contributes to the growing uncertainty within Western intellectual circles about the appropriate grounding and methods for explaining and/or interpreting human experience" (Flax, 1987: 624). Accordingly, all feminisms can be thought of as postmodern and I do so in this book. Postmodern feminism is the label I put on efforts to negotiate the borderlands of

16

feminist and other theories in a postmodern era so that we neither get lost in the shuffle nor find ourselves confined to separate, politically wrent, feminist homelands.

Looking backward and forward

It is important to provide a context for one's work in the often-denied politics of the personal; because, in a postmodern era, we simply cannot take refuge in our previous certainties of objective vision. A sketch of my "homes," therefore, from gelatin silver prints and pastels on paper.

I am sitting at my desk (so often), a late modern subject whose hyphenations of identity and empathy and place, whose physical and psychic mobilities, impart a relished sense of always being on a 747 to somewhere. It is not a fully secure sense, but it is satisfying. Born in the last year of the World War II decade and raised in the goody-two-shoes atmosphere of the 1950s – although my working-class family was a little too rough at the edges to fit the Betty Friedan (1963) model, and I had no idea what a suburb was – I remember civil defense shelters in local schools and homemade bomb shelters in basements (ours was lined with discarded newspapers and stocked with Velveeta cheese and Spam). I remember feeling secure through air raid drills at primary school – "duck and cover, children" – and only insecured by the determined gender emphasis teachers placed on acting like good girls (tripping over baseball bats) and good boys (picking up those bats and swinging for home). Erased by these rules and brought to visibility by refusing them, I spent a lot of time in the "cloak room" with overripe bananas, bologna sandwiches, and rubber boots.

I remember thinking John Kennedy was "neat" but that Robert Frost's halting reading at the Kennedy inauguration was far neater; I assumed all US presidents had favorite poets around all the time to punctuate important moments. I thought my father was neat too, and then he took off with another woman and her children. Kennedy died: no more poets, but plenty of revelations on his sexual opportunism to come. My father's personal opportunism would go unchronicled. Security was ebbing. My mother was in a panic.

I thought the Cuban Missile Crisis was a moment of high excitement rather than fear; something was happening "out there." Indeed, I was never afraid of nuclear attack. I did not believe it. In this I was the quintessentially protected citizen of the United States and the blasphemer who thought all the talk about the Iron Curtain and the evil Cubans denied average people their lives in accidental spaces.

17

Vietnam: another moment of high excitement of a very different type. Awful. I protested. But I did not bake a single loaf of bread during the 1960s nor join a commune.

I did go to boot camp, though, in a way.[23] Earlier. I was pushed into intellectual shape by nuns dressed in body-denying outfits as they did housewife-denying jobs. I never thought they were especially "neat," but I liked the quiet, contemplative, madcap years of Catholic schooling, high school through university. I remember daily camaraderie, intrigue, and power among (little) women; my schooling, you see, was all-star all-girls. There were lessons on doubleness in that context too (they were admittedly simple and trite back then): develop your brains and confess something called "sins" to always male forever priests. An incomprehensible ensemble of messages led to memorably gargantuan rebellions.

I slipped and slid through geospaces, living a time in Germany, England, Zimbabwe (a remarkable and recurring home space), on the east coast of the US, the west coast of the US, and now in the (regrettably coastless) southwest. Places and people I hold dear, but I do not seem to know my place. Never have. "I" am happily transient and fixed on feminism as the keeper of tensions and the progenitor of conversations that enable further tensions and shifts in my life. In the following chapters I revel in postmodern feminism while trying to give other feminisms their due, because I like them too. I criticize IR, sharply at times. But like my memories of Catholic boot camp, I cannot deny IR.

These are some pieces of my dynamic objectivity.[24] Some may call them biases or think them superfluous. I include them because they link up with some of the choices made in this book.

The first short essay ahead considers the sweep of feminist-resonating concerns now being reinserted into history and some of the bearers of the news. Chapter 1 focuses on the wave of feminist epistemology and practice that began in western countries in the 1960s, and brings us briefly to the memory of worthies and their causes far back in a linearly painted past.

Chapters 2 to 4 enable some IR worthies to speak through exemplary texts chosen to illustrate discipline-marking trends. There, I do not know my place and intervene regularly, dressed in all the feminist costumes sequentially and in an irreverent mix, to offer critiques and reinterpretations of a field's formative topics. Throughout, postmodern feminism nudges to the top table and feasts on IR follies.

In chapter 5 I look IR's "security" promise in the eye and, in a fit of postmodern feminist journeying or "world'-travelling" (Lugones,

1990), I dream of Greenham Common in England and fly off to Harare, Zimbabwe in search of unexpected places, people, and actions that can insecure our sense of a field. The final chapter points in the direction of homesteaders who are equal partners in conversations designed to rethink the places captured and obscured in IR's three debates. It is a moment in which el(l)e-phants paint relations international.

SKETCHES OF FEMINISM'S FIRST WAVE IN ANTICIPATION OF CHAPTER 1

Only recently have scholars begun to consider the possibility that there may be at least three histories in every culture – "his," "hers," and "ours." "His" and "ours" are generally assumed to be equivalents. (Jane Flax, 1987:629)

Sexism as a system of domination is institutionalized but it has never determined in an absolute way the fate of all women. (bell hooks 1984:5)

In 1963 Betty Friedan's *The Feminine Mystique* articulated for many North American "women" "the problem that has no name," that being that the "natural" vocation of housewife is unfulfilling.[1] The women whose lives Friedan recounted wondered what was wrong with us that we could refuse the comfort of our natures. How could the promise of modern happiness elude so? How could it be that children and husband and house were not enough? Some had wondered such forbidden things before, as they contemplated Simone de Beauvoir's (1952) broad-gauged discussion of women as other. This time, the process of questioning developed staying power, momentum, spreading out and politicizing a world of otherizing experiences.

One component of the feminine mystique was the suburban household, a vessel of homesickness for meaning in life. Friedan writes that in the 1930s, "[t]he majority of heroines of the four major women's magazines [in the U.S.] (then *Ladies Home Journal, McCall's, Good Housekeeping, Woman's Home Companion*) were career women ... happily, proudly, adventurously, attractively career women" (ibid.: 32). During the preceding era, "women's" identity had been given a boost by the successful campaign for the vote. The return "home" in the 1950s, she implies, was one symptom of and response to late- or post-modernity: "After the loneliness of war and the unspeakableness of the bomb, against the frightening uncertainty, the cold immensity of the changing world, women as well as men sought the comforting reality of home and children" (ibid.: 174). But the household was clearly not "women's" home so much as it was a nostalgia for a "place" that "could be imagined as a real possibility for the future" (Connolly, 1991:463).

Still to be trekked was the gender terrain that made the nostalgic household look like a true site of emancipation for "women." There were new appliances marketed for the home and thus for "women," quick foods that hastened "women's" work in the kitchen but that laced our bodies with sugar, fat, and chemical additives, and immunizations that protected against ravaging diseases like polio while nuclear weapons protected against the Communist disease (enemies within the United States were already neutralized just as "women" were neutralized within suburbia). Against the uncertainties of an age, Friedan's light flooded the corners of consciousness and revealed an ostensibly progressive era giving some of "us" only half-a-loaf satisfactions.

"To take the emancipation of women as a vantage point," Joan Kelly (1984:19) would later write, "is to discover that events that further the historical development of men, liberating them from natural, social, or ideological constraints, have quite different, even opposite, effects upon women." Kelly, speaking from an implied feminist standpoint position, recounted the inequities of the European Renaissance. The post-World War II period of progress also had its "opposite effects," and Friedan's bold rendering of one of them – feminine housewifery – helped to inspire a social movement that is now in its fourth decade of existence. We discovered other sites of broadcasted femininity through our participation in anti-war and civil rights activism in the United States and in student movements in Europe – all "progressive" and all led by "men." Whether our activities situated us within national politics or at the cusp of politics national and international, we learned that "men are everything, women their negation, but that the sexes are equal" (MacKinnon, 1982: 29). "Women" began to want equality at home and some also wanted equality of political expression in nebulous places abroad, where "our" forces were blocking local initiatives. Few of us thought about making homes in the policy-making realm of international relations, and few thought systematically about our relationships to "women" whose daily experiences were nothing like ours.

In this, the western feminist movement of the 1960s confused its eras and sought, for a while at least, to apply one logic of modern emancipation, the logic of liberal certainty, to late- or post-modernity. We narrated the historically specific experiences of white middle-class

21

"women" as the experiences of Everywoman. We sought equality with "men" in societies dominated by "men" and by masculine knowledge without fully questioning the emperors' epistemology. We thought of our homes in the narrow sense of households and nations and did not worry that states*men* were at home with the cold war, deliberating over Soviet missiles in Cuba and sending troops to far-flung places across the globe.[2] In this liberal moment of the women's movement, "women" figured theoretically into a sex class undergirded by the individualist sense that we were each part of the order that male political theorists painted for us – all sufficiently isolated and suspicious that we needed "rights" to protect us (Z. Eisenstein, 1981; Firestone, 1970; Delphy, 1977).

Dissident "women" helped to reveal some of our oversights and to deepen our recognition of the complexities of the era by reminding us that "we" were not the "us" of all experience. According to hooks, (1984:5–6), the "feminist emphasis on common oppression in the United States was less a strategy for politicization than an appropriation by conservative and liberal women of a radical political vocabulary that masked the extent to which they shaped the movement so that it addressed and promoted their class interests." We learned that nonsuburban "women" were oppressed by the very conditions that made the pastiche of suburbia possible for cranky privileged "women." Many African-American "women" were left in squalor as affluent suburbanites took their tax dollars and raced away from – and during the women's movement's early days, stayed away from – inner cities. (Their exodus had ironic parallels in the South African policy of removing Africans from areas whites wanted for themselves, which, in that case, *were* the cities (and areas with fertile land.)) "An" oppressive-for-some "problem that has no name" was a condition unknown to "women" who joined national liberation struggles in Algeria and Cuba, for those in South Africa's shanty towns seeking to maintain family life with migrant worker husbands, and for all "women" who participated in workforces and knew that the wonderland outside the household, where some suburban "women" craved to be, was not always worth the entrance fee. We saw difference and began to glimpse the international implications of "our" feminism.

We learned other lessons. Lesbian "women" pointed out that life in the suburbs was a sham utopia for "women" because it rested on society's love affair with heterosexual power relations and patriarchal authority. The suburban model of conventional marriage was simply a new take on an old problem of institutionalized domination and subordination based on a pervasive and "women"-controlling sexual division of labor. In societies grounded in "a political structure that privileges men [and] uses much more complex forms of political manipulation to do this than mere biology" (Z. Eisenstein, 1981: 8–9), biological differences between "men" and "women" could slide into a comfortable ideological niche of naturalness. To change such a script would require a fundamental challenge to patriarchy and its sexual-institutional props. Equality under patriarchy was oxymoronic.

These lessons helped move the contemporary western women's movement into a second wave characterized by debates over solidarity – were we Woman or women – and by political struggles to determine whose experiences were the most oppressive and/or liberated, and who, therefore, had the greatest claim to leadership of a true feminism – lesbians, poor women of color, white theorists, liberals, Marxists, socialists, radicals, anarchists, ecofeminists, third world women and so on. Heaped on this equally outmoded search for certainty in unity around one correct understanding of feminism, were efforts to establish fundamental otherness from men in talents, bodies, and proclivities. This approach smudged one line of division (woman/women) by drawing another.

Now a third feminist wave is finally comfortable with postmodernity. It affirms difference (women has triumphed over woman) and is also skeptical about whether women exist as a meaningful identity and type of person or whether "women" is a set of socially assigned characteristics and evocations. Are "we" merely the receptacles of qualities society does not wish to promote as public virtues? If "women" do not exist, or if we exist only as a residual expression of material relations of inequality, then the anchor of the "women's movement" – feminism – becomes a tool of the gender status quo. The used-to-be markers of a movement – woman/women and feminism – are now mulled over the way one might consider ambiguous shards unearthed in an archeological dig, and many from around the globe are doing the mulling. "His" and "ours" remains a problematic conflation and now "ours" is a possible conflation of biological woman with gendered, classed, raced and otherwise subjected "women."

Remembering those who came before

We must remember that late twentieth-century feminisms do not mark the initiation of waves of struggles by people called women for recognition, agency, and authorship, rights and obligations, respect and advancement. "Feminism," write Bonnie Anderson and Judith Zinsser

23

(1988: xvii), "originated as a rejection of traditions which limited women, and ... this process of rejection led to the creation of a feminist view of the world which is still being elucidated and realized." That "view" was always more plural than singular and more differentiated cross-nationally than unified.

At the beginning of the modern era, in that long sixteenth century of which Immanual Wallerstein (1974) writes (initially without much gender sensitivity),[3] European "women" rulers and educators – Queen Elizabeth (1558–1603), Marguerite of Angouleme, Queen of Navarre (1492–1549), and Lady Jane Grey (1537–54) – enhanced their personal power by converting to Protestantism, a religion that allowed aristocratic "women" to partake of the new emphasis on learning and take a position in religious debates. Less powerful middle-class converts could also use religion as a stepping stone upwards by learning to read the scriptures, thereby improving their literacy skills. The efforts of these two classes of "women" to "reject traditions which limited women," however, were taken out on others. The space-opening Reformation reduced the power of Catholic nuns, downgraded the significance of "women" saints and abbesses, and elevated the male-headed family to the position of social exemplary in societies newly celebrating family life over the previously glorified state of celibacy.

The scientific revolution, which blossomed in the seventeenth century, was largely an affair of "men." However "[a] few women took part ... [and] proposed restructuring domestic authority in order to improve the position of the female sex" (Boxer and Quataert, 1987: 21). That these early feminists did not attain their goals is evidenced in social preoccupations of the time with women's premarital virginity and marital chastity, preoccupations that deflected "women's" productive and intellectual contributions to western society. Witch hunts decimated some independent-minded "women," such as midwives, whose monopoly of gynecological knowledge threatened the emerging profession of scientist-physicians (Mies, 1986; French, 1985), as well as "women" who led unconventional lifestyles by refusing, for example, to confine their sexuality to marriage. The hunts were ostensibly aimed at thwarting pacts with the devil, and yet they were "directed and organized by governmental elites for political purposes" (Boxer and Quataert, 1987: 33). The emergent state institutionalized marriage and gave "men" legal authority over property, including wives.

Seventeenth- and eighteenth-century social contract philosophers glorified the powers of the sovereign leviathans and then the fledgling democracies, and helped popularize the notion that the realm of state was separate from a civil sphere lodged within a more visible and important civil sphere. "Women" were in a household-based civil sector and "men" were in the significant civil sphere of commerce, science, arts, and politics. "Women" were part of the support structures of the nation and "men" were the nationals on whose behalf the state conducted international politics. Since "men" were also the legal heads of households, they had a foot in each possible demarcated sphere. "Women," by contrast, were sequestered in the texts of these philosophical authorities.

This inequitable and arbitrary ordering of social space now looms to some feminists as revelatory of a sexual contract that was struck before the mythically foundational social contract created western politics. According to Carole Pateman (1988:47–8), the sexual contract created families in the image of master–servant relations:

> Hobbes states in *Leviathan* that in the war of all against all [the state of nature] "there is no man who can hope by his own strength, or will, to defend himself from destruction, without the help of confederates." But how can such a protective confederation be formed in the natural condition when there is an acute problem of keeping agreements [owing to the isolation and mutual wariness of all]? The answer is that confederations are formed by conquest, and, once formed, are called "families" ... In *Leviathan* ... a family "consists of a man, and his children; or of a man, and his children, and servants together; wherein the father or master is the sovereign" ... [If] one male individual manages to conquer another in the state of nature the conqueror will have obtained a servant ... [If] a male individual manages to conquer a female individual [t]o protect her life she will enter into a contract of subjection – and so she too becomes the servant of a master.

Here is the place of memory for "women," an originative site of that nostalgia that so irked Friedan and so hamstrung the supposedly fulfilled women she interviewed in the 1950s.

Nostalgias for "women's" place were troublesome to early feminists too. As the notion of sovereignty expanded at the hands of John Locke and Jean Jacques Rousseau to include the collective acts of average citizens, Abigail Adams was sufficiently skeptical about women's place in property-tied definitions of western citizenship to warn her constitutional conference-bound husband in 1777 that "the ladies" of the new United States would not be bound by laws in which they had no voice or representation. In Britain, Mary Wollstonecraft took on Rousseau's presentation of women as unfit for inclusion in the general will, by virtue of natural limitations and disorderly tendencies, claiming in rejoinder that only when (middle-class) women are deprived of education do they preoccupy themselves with the trivialities associated with their station. These voices, like that of the Marquis de Condorcet, who made similar points in France, were overshadowed by the social tendency of the time to see "women" as ornamental caretakers of citizen "men" and citizens in training.

Some "women" were able to homestead their commonplace assignments. With respect to black "women" in the US bell hooks (1990:42) writes:

> We could not learn to love or respect ourselves in the culture of white supremacy, on the outside; it was there on the inside, in that "homeplace," most often created and kept by black women, that we have the opportunity to grow and develop, to nurture our spirits. This task of making a homeplace, of making home a community of resistance, has been shared by black women globally, especially black women in white supremacist societies.

These homeplaces were historically warmed and made into locations of resistance by "women" who took up their assignments with care and social conscience.

By contrast, Aida Hurtado (1989:849) writes of certain homesteads that could exist in name only because they were publicly homesteaded by racism in a way that took them out of the private sphere of contracted societies: "the political consciousness of 'women' of Color stems from an awareness that the public is *personally* political." Under the weight of today's welfare programs, policies to control the reproductive rights of minorities, and a penal system that jails disproportionate numbers of nonwhites in democratic societies, "[t]here is no such thing as a private sphere for people of Color except that which they manage to create and protect in an otherwise hostile environment" (ibid.: 849). The Janus faces of homesteading are revealed.

"Women" in Europe and North America were also appropriated to, and sought their own homes in, the industrial revolutions of earlier times. As capitalist firms proliferated, many "women" lost their historical control over weaving and food processing and their earlier status as master artisans in return for access to (some) waged jobs (a few escaped to the colonies and metamorphosed into homesteading "ladies" who did their bit to oppress "women" of color). "Women workers" sought to join labor unions and to partake of higher education, trying to win acceptance in male-dominated working fields. Working-class "men," however, resisted the affront of "women" working outside the home, and education tracked "women" into sex-linked occupations that foreclosed what society often saw as "a crisis of impending feminization" (Rossiter, 1982: xvii). By specifying apprenticeship training or requiring certain education for professional opportunities, society further disadvantaged "women" in the market vis-à-vis "men" (Boxer and Quataert, 1987: 44). Henceforth capitalism relied on "women's" noncirculating production and nurturing of producer "men," or on their lower-paid factory work, while defining "women's activities" as external or incidental to the economic realm of real social significance.

European and North American "women" were not pushed so far that they could not organize bread riots, follow Henri Saint-Simon's New Christianity disciple, Enfantin, to North Africa and the Middle East in search of the lost Female Messiah, form suffragette and socialist movements in the 1840s, or stand behind the Ida B. Wells's of the early US civil rights movement (Moses, 1984; Liddington and Norris, 1978; Dubois, 1978). Until World War I, however, vocal opponents of "women's" rights controlled the discourse. In 1872 a US Supreme Court Justice declared in Bradwell vs. Illinois that the female sex was too naturally timid and delicate for many of the occupations of civil life. Thirty years later, US President Grover Cleveland maintained that sensible and reasonable women did not want to vote. Not until some "women" made significant image-challenging contributions to World War I was the longstanding cry for women's suffrage finally heeded in Europe and North America. But this was by no means the end of the struggle in societies where "women's" worth was measured by the number of children they bore and raised as proper married women.

One can go back further in linear time to find examples of European "women's" struggles, slim victories, and many defeats. Michele le Doeuff (1991) writes about the resistances of Hipparchia of Thrace to the domination of male theorists of her time. Christine De Pisan's *The City of Women*, written in 1404, a time when secular intellectual ferment mixed Christian scholasticism with inherited Aristotelian dualities, bitterly records her discovery that there is "scarcely ... a volume, whoever its author, without ... some chapters or sections blaming us" (De Pisan, in Kelly, 1982: 21). Pisan drew attention in her writings to individual "women" achievers, a focus that persists in the more contemporary feminist efforts to bring to light "women worthies" omitted from the official canons of knowledge (like Hipparchia). Unfortunately, "women" like De Pisan, "learned, articulate, and politically astute, may have threatened but never destroyed a widespread acceptance in Italy of 'women's' natural political incapacity and historical invisibility" (Hughes, in Kelly, 1982: 25–6). Moreover, she, like others elsewhere, questioned the rules that anointed "men" as the framers of

27

civilization while accepting the rules of public achievement set by the sovereigns.

One can also travel back to nonwestern settings to discover early feminist-resonating activities that counter some contemporary claims that feminism is strictly western. On the continent of Africa alone we encounter nineteenth-century Nigerian "women" in revolt against British marketing policies, "women"-led military revolts against white settlers in Southern Rhodesia and against colonial policies on the copper-belt in Northern Rhodesia, and "women's" protests against colonial expropriations of land and labor in Kikuyuland (Van Allen, 1976; Aidoo, 1981; Parpart, 1986; Ranger, 1979; Presley, 1986). An anguished world of feminist-like activities permeates the history of apartheid South Africa (C. Walker, 1990) and reveals cases of "women's" valor that slide backward and forward around the labyrinths of class, race, place, and gender identity.

Consider the British writer Emily Hobhouse's double-sided honor of being designated keynote speaker for the 1913 dedication of a monument commemorating the many Afrikaner "women" and children who died during the Anglo–Boer war. The honor of speaking at the ceremonies (actually she was ill and sent an address) indicated to Hobhouse that the scripts of gender were changing in her society. She said: "I think for the first time, a woman is chosen to make the commemorative speech over the National Dead – not soldiers but *women* who gave their lives for their country" (quoted in Brink, 1990: 278). She does not mention the thousands of African "women" and children who died in the Anglo–Boer and other colonial wars and whose scripts of otherly identity were rigidly fixed in the minds of Afrikaners and English alike. She does not foresee that the monument to white "women" of war will become embedded in *volksmoeder* myths immortalizing "the concept of Boer women as mothers of the nation" (Brink, 1990: 280). Little does she know, in other words, that for the white colonial "heroines" of the early twentieth century, time would come to a near stand-still around a Victorian trope of motherhood enshrining white "women's" "true" occupation while manifesting fear of "racial decline from white fatherhood to a primordial black degeneracy incarnated in the black mother" (McClintock, 1990: 100). Hobhouse sends Africans around her into exile by affirming through silence a sense of their unspeakable otherness "out there" relative to "our" home spaces of valor.

We can then slip irreverently forward in geospace and compressed time to 1983 and a conference at the University of Illinois on "Common Differences: Third World Women and Feminist Perspectives." The

28

conference was pathbreaking in international relations, although greeted in silence by the field's gatekeepers, in that it brought together US "women" and "women" from third world countries around a discussion of institutionalized sexism and the application of western feminist theory to third world contexts. Some of the participants subsequently wrote about third world "women's" resistance to the western feminist idea of common experience, much as refugees, migrants, and black groups in Britain would later protest the "disenfranchising effects of Europe 1992 on third world communities in Britain" (Mohanty, 1991: 5). Others emphasized the potential of building feminist alliances across international borders and between different worlds within nation-states (Harrison, 1991; Wong, 1991). The general health of feminism was affirmed by acknowledging the importance of theorizing "from the point of view and contexts of marginalized women not in terms of a victim status or an essentialized identity but in terms that push us to place women's agency, their subjectivities and collective consciousness, at the center of our understandings of power and resistance" (Alexander, 1991: 148). "We" were recognizing the historical "construction of whiteness in relation to the construction of a politicized gender consciousness" (Mohanty, 1991: 12). We were grappling with our era.

Women's struggles against identity-limiting nostalgias of place are nothing new; they are historically variegated and linked to dynamics of class, race, and gender, and appear in many territorial locations and home-sites. It is nonetheless the case, however, that contemporary support structures for feminism, in academic Women's Studies programs and journals, in national lobby groups like the US-based National Organization of Women (NOW) and the British cross-party 300 group, and in international regimes such as UNIFEM, are new and vital to the diffusion and power of feminist knowledge and strategy. These organizations bring the words of IR-isolated "women" to our shores and the words of western feminists to nonwesterners. Indeed, communication is central to the new wave of feminist thinking that queries, in a variety of settings, "women's" "existence and specificity ... simultaneously asserted and denied, negated and controlled" (De Lauretis, 1990: 15). It is to these queries that I now turn.

1 THE PALETTE OF FEMINIST EPISTEMOLOGIES AND PRACTICES

Communication and debate in contemporary feminist circles now revolve around issues of epistemology – ways of knowing – and practice – ways of acting and doing – in an era of uncertainty and opportunity. The activities discussed in the preceding pages, that resonate with what we think of today as feminism, link to issues of contemporary epistemology and practice by revealing to us where we have been, what we have come to know and overlook, and what we have or have not done for "women." Teresa de Lauretis (1986: 10) expresses something of that link when she says:

> Feminism defines itself as a political instance, not merely a sexual politics but a politics of experience, of everyday life, which later then in turn enters the public sphere of expression and creative practice, displacing aesthetic hierarchies and generic categories, and which thus establishes the semiotic ground for a different production of reference and meaning.

We might say that to our foremothers we owe that "semiotic ground" for our varied and different productions of feminism today and to postmodernity we owe the context for our most recent forms of "expression and creative practice."

To focus on epistemology is to consider "what knowledge is, what makes it possible, and how to get it" (Harding, 1991: 308). At this second-to-third wave juncture in feminist history, there is increasing agreement that the usual or

> traditional epistemologies, whether intentionally or unintentionally, systematically exclude the possibility that women could be "knowers" or *agents of knowledge* ... the voice of science is a masculine one; ... history is written from only the point of view of men (of the dominant class and race); [and] ... the subject of a traditional socio-logical sentence is always assumed to be a man. (Harding, 1987: 3)

That basic sense of agreement, however, does not preclude contests from emerging in feminism over the existence and content of woman's/women's ways of knowing and acting in the world and over the interrelationship of feminist epistemologies to movement politics in the present era. We shall see that the feminists who occupy positions in these debates refuse tidy confinements, their arguments spilling over into each other and tumbling through geopolitical space like the runny colors on an elephant's palette.

Empiricism and Liberalism: The Assimilationist Feminisms

Feminist empiricist epistemology starts from the premise that modern science provides a valuable way of knowing the activities of women (no inverted commas here; empiricists believe in real women) in the world and, therefore, it is a potentially helpful tool for recovering, publicizing, and valorizing "our" contributions to civilization. Science, however, has let us down, owing to the contamination of its knowledge by the social biases against women (and other subordinate groups) that mark most modern societies. Science can correct these biases by incorporating more feminist women and problematiques into research enterprises. But even to make this small point – and other feminist empiricist points are less "small" – is to speak a taboo about science, to reveal the sacred cow of modernity as simply "politics by other means" (Harding, 1991: 10). It is to show "a column of elephants holding up the earth ... that prevents the observer from asking questions that would quickly come to mind were the elephants not so solidly in view" (Harding, 1991: 78).

Feminists of the empiricist persuasion argue that there is something called good science – that asks the right questions, that allows for both classically understood elephants and el(l)e-phants to hold up the world – and much that can be called bad science. Bad science brings into laboratories, surveys, and regression analyses the gender biases rampant in society at large, such that, as the US National Institutes of Health have admitted, to give just one example, females figure into medical research less frequently than do males, with dire consequences for our health. Bad science is "blinded to the ways in which [its] descriptions and explanations of [its] subject matters are shaped by the origins and consequences of [its] research practices and by the interests, desires, and values promoted by such practices" (Harding, 1991: 15). Good science, by contrast, can be thought of as "a subfield of the critical social sciences" in that it would expose the "culturewide interests, values, and assumptions that end up functioning as evidence 'behind the back' of the natural and social sciences" (Harding, 1991: 15–16).

If we think of science as "the direct generator of economic, political, and social control" in the modern era (Harding, 1986a: 16), then the controllers of control have been "men" who take other "men" as prototypes for all humans, not for thought-out or scientifically validated reasons, but because the societies in which they are embedded assume that "men" compose the active portion of the species. We remember Jane Flax (1987: 629) telling us that "[i]n a wide variety of cultures and discourses, men tend to be seen as free from or as not determined by gender relations ... [m]ale academics do not worry about how being men may distort their intellectual work, while women who study gender relations are considered suspect (of triviality, if not bias)." Thus Jean Piaget (1965) and Lawrence Kohlberg (1981, 1984) generalize about the standards of human moral development from samples of male subjects without asking how gender training influences the content of morality and how that content enters into the very questions one asks to ascertain moral outlooks (Gilligan, 1982).

Despite the usual claim that scientific method eliminates social biases through rigorous hypothesis testing, many scientists are isolated from the activities that sustain them, and "[m]en who are relieved of the need to maintain their own bodies and the local places where they exist can now see as real only what corresponds to their abstracted mental world" (Harding, 1986a: 156). This tendency to not-see gender bias can intensify under the convention of scientific immunity from outside criticism. Seemingly rigorous in the effort to find truth, the scientific establishment is nonetheless loathe to air its dirty laundry by rigorously examining shortsighted problematiques and methodological failings. Sandra Harding (1986a: 35) attributes this reluctance to:

> the unusual notion that science enthusiasts have of the proper way to understand the history and practices of science: this kind of social activity alone, we are told, must be understood only in terms of its enthusiasts' understanding of their own activities – in terms of the unselfconscious, uncritical interpretations "the natives" provide of their beliefs and activities. That is, scientists report their activities, and philosophers and historians of science interpret these reports so that we can "rationally" account for the growth of scientific knowledge in the very same moral, political, and epistemological terms scientists use to explain their activities to funding sources or science critics.

Feminist empiricist efforts to study women's presence and agency stem not only from a simple fairness argument but from the belief that research incorporating feminist awareness is more reliable and supportable than research based on the experiences of one group of isolated people. This strategy leans on the notion that feminism is the type of revolution in social history that, like the bourgeois and feudal revolutions before it, enlarges social perspectives in profound ways. Conventional scientists usually deny the revolutionary content of feminism and counter that feminists merely introduce bias into their studies by politicizing the identity of the investigator, the knower. Feminist researchers re-counter that politicized research can actually improve objectivity by revealing "the covers and blinders that obscure knowledge and observation" (Millman and Kanter, 1975: vii). From "our" locations we are able to see the importance of such questions as how women and men compare in asserting authority (West and Zimmerman, 1983), how they may differentially command the attention of others in public (Eakins and Eakins, 1976), how women's self-concepts and ways of knowing interrelate (Belenky, Clinchy, Goldberger and Tarule, 1986), and how aptitude tests for mathematics rely on puzzles geared to the interests of "properly" gendered western boys (Fausto-Sterling, 1985). None of the corrective studies features the issues most scientist men find puzzling in the world. But, when feminist empiricists participate in processes of peer review along with men, their voices give scientific rationality a missing social context. Moreover, the very participation of people called women corrects the widespread impression that "woman scientist" is a contradiction in terms because "man scientist" "name[s] far too perfect a union" (Harding, 1991: 19) of rationality and gender, far too cozy a home. Awareness of context, so vehemently denied by the science establishment, is what minimizes bias (Longino, 1989) and the perpetuation of gender nostalgias.

Feminists alert to the questions science does not ask often hear that the "context of justification," the testing of hypotheses and interpretation of evidence, and not the "context of discovery," where problems are identified and defined, fall under the "laws" of scientific methodology (Harding, 1986a: 25). Harding (1987: 184) points out, however, that:

> traditional empiricism does not direct researchers to locate themselves in the same critical plane as their subject matters. Consequently, when nonfeminist researchers gather evidence for or against hypotheses, "scientific method" – bereft of such a directive – is impotent to locate and eradicate the androcentrism that shapes the research process.

Hence, there is already a conflation in scientific practice of discovery and justification. Indeed, the urge to ignore this can call to mind "an unpleasantly exaggerated masculine style of control and manipulation" (Millman and Kanter, 1975: xvi) that appears in the speech of

33

prominent scientists of past and present: Francis Bacon hounded nature and did not shy away from "entering and penetrating holes and corners" in his scientific quest (quoted in Harding, 1991: 43); Richard Feynman saw his early scientific ideas take shape as an "old lady, who has very little that's attractive left in her ... [nonetheless] we can say the best we can for any old woman, that she has become a very good mother and has given birth to some very good children" (quoted in Harding, 1991: 43–4).

There is also much within science's usual "justificatory strategies" to question – although the feminist empiricist might not be at the fore-front of this criticism. Probabilistic statistical procedures require researchers to think in terms of separate and isolated variables that may or may not correlate at an acceptable level of significance to specific observable behaviors. What if dependent and independent variables are figments of the scientific imagination? What if the meanings accorded the term "state," when taken as a dependent variable, for example, are deeply embedded in the gendering experiences of male theorists and of masculine-deifying society and thus are inseparable from a range of masculine independent variables? What if key behaviors defy crude measurement, as is the case with intersubjective under-standings of politics or of international relations? When one sees discrete and independent categories of being – a world of "orphans" out there with their institutions – one needs statistical bridging mechanisms to bring them together. Feminist attempts to reform bad science bring to our attention "empirical inadequacies in empiricist epistemologies" (Harding, 1986a: 26), even though feminist empiricists themselves focus only on the ways that science can correct gender biases in research.

Consider some "empirical inadequacies" in empiricist IR thought. James E. Dougherty and Robert L. Pfaltzgraff (1990: 1) argue that:

> [t]he international relations theorist rejects the tendency to substitute for careful analysis such superficial bumper-sticker slogans as "Make love, not war" ... [t]hose who ... take a responsible approach to international affairs must go beyond emphemeral opinions and shib-boleths to a systematic study of the global system. Anyone who tries to make some sense out of the apparent incoherence of the world scene, so that discrete events, instead of being purely random, can be explained within an orderly, intelligible pattern, is a theorist at heart.

Here in one brief statement is the equation of responsibility with systematic, orderly analysis – followed, in their ongoing text, by a litany of "men" who have indeed accomplished this feat. Here also is the pronouncement of exile for those who traffic in a predefined "ephemeral" or "bumper-sticker" sphere of IR. The emphasis is on placing discrete events in an intelligible pattern rather than suffering the only other option thought to be available – pure randomness. The lines are drawn. There is no theory worth recording that lies outside the order of the scientist.

This audacious view has suffused much of the research in the field since the days when the behavioralist/traditionalist debate, which will be detailed in chapter 3, set the stage for the sweeping entry of physics-envy into US IR. In the retreat to value-neutrality came the notion that "the underlying concepts of International Relations could be rendered in a purely abstract form ... assembled into generalizations possessing the explanatory and predictive characteristics of powerful theories in natural science, and ... suitable tests employing quantitative methods could be derived from the logical entailments of posited theoretical relationships" (Olson and Onuf, 1985: 7). This view appealed to relatively few "women" in IR: Jean Elshtain (1987: 89) tells us that her "graduate school bibliography, over 250 titles, include[d] only 4 entries by women – hopeless idealists all, who sneaked onto my list as examples of what to be avoided."

Value-neutral IR reinforced the idea that the state was an abstract entity when, in fact, states are stuffed and bristling with male decision makers who only theoretically restrict their IR-relevant relationships to other decision makers. No scientific analyst who believes in separating the decision maker from the wide contextual elements of knowing that surround him, however, could seriously investigate the possibility that decision makers draw insights from "wives." Foreign policy "acts," "diplomacy," "interactions," and "interdependencies" that produce and change important balances of military and trade power – all give the appearance that there are no "gender-specific consequences" (Halliday, 1988: 420) of IR for "women's" activities and of "women's" activities for IR.

James N. Rosenau appears to provide some space for "women" by telling us to look closely at micro-level activities for clues about the sources of postinternational politics. But, given the cultural context of that admonition, there is great potential for researchers to assume that "micro-level" has to do with the political activities of people called men or people called the public. "Women," having long since been evacuated from international politics and publics, do not come to mind as micro-level political actors. Hence there is a dearth of research interest in the "women" who pushed baby carriages through the Berlin Wall in 1989, thereby helping to change the configuration of power in the international system, relative to interest in what appears to be mostly male-led attacks on "foreigners" in the new eastern Germany. Because it is not obvious, feminists must point out time and again that "if we employ only the conventional, ungendered compass to chart international politics, we are likely to end up mapping a landscape peopled only by men, mostly elite men" (Enloe, 1989: 1). Even as feminists indicate where "women" figure into the micro-levels of this "men's" place for politics (Enloe, 1989; Stiehm, 1989), we run up against the possibility that these revealings fall in the category of "discovery" and not of "justification." In Michael Nicholson's (1985: 56) words, "[c]ertain methods are appropriate for answering certain kinds of questions, but if these questions are themselves thought to be illegitimate for some reason or another, the methods become superfluous." Peruse the mainstream IR journals to see how much questions of gender in IR count.

Among the questions and justifications that do count, there are innumerable examples of bias having to do with unproblematized gender assumptions about the puzzles investigated. War casualty figures, for instance, are not known to include "raped women" and "sodomized children." The hypotheses taken seriously in professional IR do not proffer relationships between masculine leadership traits and war-proneness, even though the notion of hegemonic leadership, for instance, is rife with such unexplored implications. (Are disorder and war more likely when a hegemon is in decline because rule-governed order diminishes or because a new generation of "decision makers" has an opportunity to flex its muscles unfettered by the gang leader? Are there not racist and sexist "wars" ongoing within hegemonic peaces?). The ability to not-see gender affirmations and exclusions, the el(l)e-phants in mainstream IR, is truly reflective of politics by other means.

Feminist empiricism strengthens science by reinforcing modern claims that science is *the* route to knowledge. It weakens science by discounting its claims to splendid isolation from social practices and by implying that even if one were to follow the norms of science more carefully, those norms "have been constructed primarily to produce answers to the kinds of questions men ask about nature and social life and to prevent scrutiny of the way beliefs which are nearly or completely culture-wide in fact cannot be eliminated from the results of research by these norms" (Harding, 1987: 184). Feminist empiricism not only brings some ambiguity to science, it also draws attention to paradoxical components of contemporary feminism – the simultaneous desire to be heard and heeded by respected segments of society and the desire to resist mainstreaming into a manstream, the desire to fit into science and also "to invent modes of thought ... that will enable women to get more control over the conditions of their lives" (Harding, 1991: 5).

Absent new social relations in the broader societies that encrust science, it is difficult to see how feminist arguments for reformed science and reformed IR can gain the thoroughgoing acceptance required to resist cooptation. Indeed, as Harding (1991: 3) reminds us:

> The "indigenous peoples" of the modern West – those most at home in Western societies – have culturally distinctive belief patterns in which scientific rationality plays a central role. These "natives," like all others, have trouble even recognizing that they exhibit culturally distinctive patterns of belief; it is like discovering that one speaks a distinctive genre – prose.

The feminist empiricist approach, therefore, can seem to be more compensatory than transformational of the modern scientific world view. The same has been said of the liberal feminist politics that are closely associated with empiricist epistemology.

Liberal or Equity Feminist Politics

Harding (1991: 3) says that "[f]rom the perspective of women's lives, scientific rationality frequently appears irrational." But not always or even often. The desideratum of liberal feminism is to bring (real) women into sociality as individual agents with rights equal to those that individual white and privileged adult men enjoy on principle in liberal societies, and the method relies heavily on the type of rationality that fuels the politics of science.

Political liberals in general, echoing some scientists, believe that the generically rational human has particularities of "race, class, and gender [that] are ultimately irrelevant to questions of justice because 'underneath we are all the same'" (Offen, 1988: 123). Liberal feminists, however, echo their empiricist brethren by cataloging many practices of liberal societies that run counter to this equality narrative, owing to bias, discrimination, and gender unrepresentativeness among philosophers and liberal legislators. They seek to show – rationally – that where the active, culture-defining human is the man, women have been denied rights and opportunities and the home bases outside the household that they deserve on the basis of law and equal capabilities.

Echoing Friedan's early emphasis on the middle-class-with-a-problem, liberal feminists in the United States have been especially concerned to provide ways for (unproblematized) women to escape

37

the irrationality of the private home to enter rational arenas of science, government, foreign policy, industry, commerce, and education without suffering pay and status discrimination or sexual harassment on the job. Women who want to remain in private spaces, they say, should be recognized as workers, and their work should be remunerated, esteemed, and/or shared. Women should also enjoy the full political fruits of citizenship through legal control over person and property and by having the right to protest inequalities. By extension of this logic, women who work in the institutions of international relations, such as the United Nations, should have full rights within those organizations and the opportunity to enter into male-marked domains of high-level, high-paying jobs.

Liberal feminists of the 1960s painted the state as an agency that only monitors gender-neutral laws, as in "[t]he Archimedean observer of good science is the impartial ruler or administrator of Liberal political theory and the disinterested moral philosopher – the good man – of Liberal ethics" (Harding, 1989: 274). Lately, there has been a shift in emphasis to the state as an active protector of women's rights, an emphasis that can bring potent results. In the United States, the battle for an Equal Rights Amendment to the Constitution was lost but, temporarily at least, some state-protected abortion rights were gained; this right has also been achieved in most European countries, where the women's liberation movement has often been nearly synonymous with the push for reproductive rights. Federally-sponsored daycare facilities are still wanting in the United States, but affirmative action guidelines have (at times) helped ensure that at least blatant discrimination against women in professions historically reserved for men diminishes. In countries that were once victims of liberal western polities, such as Zimbabwe, postindependence legislation often establishes women as legal adults from the age of eighteen, protects them from dismissals owing to pregnancy, provides some maternity benefits, and enables women to divorce husbands without automatically forfeiting the children to their fathers (Sylvester, 1991a). All of this has made our assigned homes more palatable in nation and in household. At the international level, the liberal United Nations sponsored international conferences between the 1970s and 1980s that brought western and third world feminists into relations of greater equity. We still only visited international relations when we attended such meetings, but they were moments of honor for women.

There are problems with liberal feminist politics, however, that drive feminists of other persuasions to distraction. First, liberal feminism accepts the role and rights of the individual to the point of subverting "notions of attachment and loyalty associated with noncontractual family relations" (Fox-Genovese, 1991: 16). The notion that people may have connections that exist prior to and that influence political relations is difficult for most streams of liberalism to accommodate. The liberal individual is a disembodied, egoistic, and isolated chooser who has few *public* interdependencies, outside of those voluntarily assumed, and few structural constraints inherited from past contracts. That individual is systematically blind:

> to the range of effective arguments used to combat male privilege in the Western world during the past few centuries, and even to arguments put forth today by women and men in economically less-privileged countries, where women's aspirations to self-sovereignty are often subordinated to pressing short-term political and socio-economic necessities (Offen, 1988: 138).

Second, the individual rights orientation can lead liberal feminists to overlook "social and economic changes that can ensure decent lives for all people ... [and this means] that the rights of women collapse into privilege for the few and exploitation for the many" (Fox-Genovese, 1991: 19). The emphasis on women being not-different from men and, therefore, entitled to men's rights, can shield us from what it means to be a woman in various parts of the world and in various classes, ethnic groups, and religions. It can, in other words, shield us from difference and amalgamate us into a humanist feminism (I. Young, 1985). One result is that an African feminist like Filomina Chioma Steady (1987: 8, 20) finds it reasonable to posit a profound difference between "the frameworks of dichotomy, individualism, competition, and opposition, which Western feminism fosters," and African "values stressing human totality, parallel autonomy, cooperation, self-reliance, adaptation, survival, and liberation." Her voice is a powerful reminder that sisterhood is not necessarily global, but at the same time it is ironic that to make this point entails accepting received categories of "scientific" analysis – western/non-western and white/black – as true.

In short, just as feminist empiricists accept certain premises of science, even as they critique other premises, liberal feminism basically accepts liberalism in a state activist form and critiques its applications to women. For this reason it has become something of a fashion to accuse liberals of shallow feminism when they "come close to celebrating male paradigms as human paradigms" (Tong, 1989: 13). Nancy Hirschmann (1989, 1992), however, is determined to rehabilitate liberal theory and politics by infusing them with a set of feminist epistemological considerations that are usually thought of as strikingly antiliberal.

39

She makes a feminist liberal-standpoint-postmodernist reconstruction of liberal theory work by showing that the basic human situation is one of social connection rather than individual isolation. Following from this, we can investigate and theorize about the situated standpoints that our various connections condition.

Hirschmann's point of departure is liberal consent theory – the variety that celebrates contracts as guarantors of women's rights and that generalizes to society at large "his" notions of autonomy and obligation, as in the chant that people are inherently and naturally free and that "[t]he only legitimate limitations are those imposed by the self" (1989: 1227). In such constructions, nonvoluntary consent is an oxymoron and autonomy is "a separateness and independence that is a reaction against others" (ibid.: 1230–1).

Hirschmann argues that this reactive model of individual autonomy rehearses the creation of the male subject in the socially-determined process of gendering. It is undergirded by the fact that boy babies and their female mothers have different bodies, a simple and not necessarily crucial difference, that, under the impact of social lessons, sets in motion a sense of differentiation as a proper social stance. The gist of the process is the struggle of males to gain a proper gender identity by rejecting the model of relationship encrusted in the mother–child dyad. Patriarchal messages in society tell boys that real men are defined in terms of what they are not, and they are not-women. Accordingly, boys learn to abstract "individual will (the ability to make choices and act on them) out of the context of the social relationships within which it develops and within which it is exercised, because [they see] those relationships as threatening by definition" (ibid.: 1231). Their self is established defensively against others who threaten to revive their submerged longings for original connections.

Mother is a physically similar self to girls and few social messages suggest that properly gendered women are unlike their mothers. Accordingly, "the girl comes to see herself as connected to the world through her connection with mother; self and other will constitute a continuum for her" (ibid.: 1230). She individuates from mother, to be sure, but her adult autonomy "derives its strength from its context of relations, not from the absence of others" (ibid.: 1231). Differentiation is not distinctness and separateness, but a particular way of being connected to others (Chodorow, 1978: 107).[1]

The reactive autonomy that carries the day for most men becomes a concealed justification for behaviors that leave women far behind in the homes of childhood. Men deal with men "at discrete and controlled points of contact, only through rule-governed and role-defined structures" in public society (Hirschmann, 1989: 1238). Women, on the other hand, are marginal citizens whose socially determined seques-terings in the household seem, tautologically, to prove their fitness for the "private" sphere. If women were brought into the public, the "hysterical animal within [them]" (Boxer and Quataert, 1987: 24), the uterus, would disorder and irrationalize society.[2] Thus it comes to pass that the "public" cannot be the preserve of women, which means that "voluntaristic theories of obligation can be read, at least in part, as theories of power, with power conceived as domination" (Hirsch-mann, 1989: 1240).

A different approach to knowledge-power emerges when we combine women's different lessons on autonomy and obligation with the connected relationships that mark boys' initiation into sociality. That is, relational autonomy, which posits that "the autonomous self is already connected rather than also connected" (Di Stefano, 1990: 36), provides a more plausible start for liberal political theory and action than the reactive autonomy of consent theory. This more plausible starting point undermines correlative norms of scientific practice, such as "social autonomy, transcendence of the socially concrete and par-ticular, and epistemic and moral decision making on the basis of impartial methods, rules, and laws" (Harding, 1986a: 229).

Of course, just as liberal contract theory is alien to many, one can argue that these mother–child relations are alien beyond the psy-chology-minded, nuclear family-oriented experience of the West. It could be that in dethroning contractarian dogmas the alternative ends up failing "the diverse forms the family takes inter-culturally as well as intraculturally" (Tong, 1989: 158). It is also problematic to counter the tendency of modern political theory to see "women" as threats to order by overordering early child–parent relations. Not only, says Harding (1987: 7), do "gender experiences vary across cultural cate-gories; they also are in conflict in any one individual's experience." Hirschmann does not dispute any of this. She says that "[b]y identifying individual development as in part the product of created institutions, [we] can translate individual experience into cultural phenomena, or at least explain the institutional and cultural aspects of a supposedly individual experience" (1992: 169).

In a somewhat different double-edged defense of liberal feminism, Zillah Eisenstein (1981: 6) argues that:

> [l]iberal feminism involves more than simply achieving the bourgeois male rights earlier denied women, although it includes this. Liberal feminism is not feminism merely added onto liberalism. Rather ... [in

41

its] recognition of women as a sexual class lays the subversive quality of feminism for liberalism because liberalism is premised upon woman's exclusion from public life on this very class basis. The demand for the real equality of women with men, if taken to its logical conclusion, would dislodge the patriarchal structure necessary to a liberal society.

Hers is the same type of argument that feminist empiricists make about their relationship to science; namely that inclusiveness disables the old enterprise and radically changes it. Perhaps including women in IR theory would similarly change the enterprise. Perhaps more feminist scholarship would show that states are not simply "the primitive individuals of the international system" in the sense of being "the social atoms or constituent units of which the international system is composed" (Wendt and Duvall, 1989: 55). They are primitive, rather, in the sense of encapsulating the struggle of their creators to maintain distance from identity-threatening relationships. Perhaps, as well, feminist scholarship would reveal the reactively autonomous contract that binds representatives of states to liberal–reformist international regimes while failing to reform the conditions of "women" who work within them. Harding (1991: 61) warns us that "[t]he perceived radicalness of this apparently modest principle of equal opportunity becomes evident the minute one looks at the heroic struggles that have been necessary to eliminate the formal barriers against women's equality in science, mathematics, and engineering."

But there are doubters. The degree to which empiricist–liberal feminism can correct the problem of bias in theoretical and practical IR without liberating "women" from liberalism itself is explicitly questioned by standpoint epistemology. Standpoint disables received knowledge and practice by enabling (real) women to set the standards of inquiry.

Standpoint(s) and Radical-Cultural Politics: Difference-Between-Women-and-Men Feminisms

Feminist standpointers agree with empiricist feminists that women have either been housed in "man's" world, out of a humanist–liberal sense that "underneath we are all the same," or we have been labeled "different" as in "inferior," owing to the conflation of our customary activities with the sum total of our capabilities. Where the two epistemological-political traditions of feminism part company is over why this is so and what should be done. Feminist empiricists believe that elevated feminist consciousness can correct the gender biases in science by seeing to it that women are integrated into all phases of studies. Standpointers contend that research should begin from the perspective of women's lives, not simply because such a starting point corrects for bias but because it "leads to socially constructed claims that are less false – less partial and distorted" – than claims that privileged men can socially construct (Harding, 1991: 185). In other words, although women's lives may seem limited, there are "positive products of this unjust situation" (Black, 1989: 67) in the form of superior insights that can lead to superior conduct of personal and world affairs.

One begins but one does not end the analysis with women's lives. Hirschmann (1992: 167), who conjoins aspects of liberal, standpoint, and postmodernist analysis, maintains that "[t]o the degree that a particular group of people share socially and politically significant characteristics ... they will share a standpoint." Yet *feminist* standpoint is not a simple and straightforward extrapolation of women's shared experiences to social theory because, as Harding (1991: 123) tells us:

> it cannot be that women's experiences in themselves or the things women say provide reliable grounds for knowledge claims about nature and social relations. After all, experience itself is shaped by social relations; for example, women have had to *learn* to define as rape the sexual assaults that occur within marriage ... Moreover, women (feminists included) say all kinds of things – misogynist remarks and illogical arguments; misleading statements about an only partially understood situation; racist, class-biased, and heterosexist claims – that are scientifically inadequate.

Feminist standpoint is an epistemological achievement that entails working through the thorny issue of women having assigned ways of knowing that may be distorted by patriarchy. To articulate observations about nature and social relations that start from the location of women's lives but that do not fetishize those received lives, we must bear in mind that standpoints of the subjugated "are preferred because in principle they are least likely to allow *denial* of the critical and interpretive core of all knowledge" (Haraway, 1988: 584 [emphasis added]).

Analysts who contribute to standpoint theorizing draw on a variety of analogies to make the point that feminist standpoint is achieved. They ask us to think in terms of parallels with proletarians triumphing over bourgeoisies, slaves bettering masters, and handmaidens dismantling God's-eyed kingdoms. Each case illustrates in a different way that there is no such thing as unmediated knowledge. Everything we know reflects someone's very situated sense of a correct story that all of us must repeat and heed. One must work hard – both mentally and politically – to free oneself from the constraints of authority in order to uncover "a reality [that has been] distorted but not destroyed by the power of those able to construct the appearances in the first place" (K. Ferguson, 1991: 324).

Nancy Hartsock (1985) makes this point by arguing that the proletarians of Marxist thought are like women in feminist thought: both are sites of superior vision into the workings of tyrannies, owing to their subordinated positions in material life. Proletarians and women are each assigned "natural" material activities as laborers and as reproducers, respectively, vis-à-vis the culture-producing activities of bourgeoisies and most men. In both cases, they inhabit a world characterized "by interaction with natural substances rather than separation from nature, a world in which the unification of mind and body is inherent in the activities performed" (Hartsock, 1983: 290). Moreover, despite their separate task assignments, women and proletarians share a space of meaning and knowledge that is socially constituted as inferior to the spaces occupied by more privileged segments of society – bourgeoisies and men. Indeed, sometimes "women" become "proletarians," in which case their social location is the lowest of the low, and the richest in possibilities of insight.

In Marxist thought, the development of "science to see beneath the surface of the social relations in which all are forced to participate and the education that can only grow from struggle to change those relations" (Hartsock, 1985: 232), enables the proletarian to realize how false consciousness and alienation operate to stupefy victims of capitalist accumulation processes. Through learning the mechanisms of exploitation, the proletarian can struggle with others for justice. The effort results in the transformation of a class-in-itself into a class-for-itself. Similarly, achievement of a feminist liberatory standpoint requires a social effort to reveal gender foils and blandishments of capitalist society, the deeper "problem that has no name" that is easily hidden in the presumed normalcy of daily life and in concerns thought to be personal. Learning that one's experiences are held in common sets the stage for the struggle to realize the alternative politics embedded in experiences of interaction rather than separation, unification of mind and body rather than abstract transcendence.

One could say that in following "an ontology of discovery," standpoint feminists hope to achieve "an epistemology of attunement" (K. Ferguson, 1991: 327). This "attunement," however, rests on more than deductive discoveries. It rests on "democratic, participatory politics" that enable people who have been evacuated from knowledge production in the past "to decide how to start asking their research

44

questions" (Harding, 1991: 124). Feminist politics is part of that demo-cratic process because it gives megaphones and paintbrushes to those denied expression within epistemologies that showcase dominant groups. Expressive political struggles impart a strong objectivity to the process of knowing by refusing to turn away, as objectivism does, "from the task of critically identifying all those broad, historical, social desires, interests, and values that have shaped the agendas, contents, and results of the sciences much as they shape the rest of human affairs" (Harding, 1991: 143).

Mary Hawkesworth (1989: 536) tempers the feminist standpoint claim of strong objectivity, however, by pointing out that:

> [a]lthough they repudiate the possibility of an unmediated truth, feminist standpoint epistemologies do not reject the notion of truth altogether. On the contrary, they argue that while certain positions (the oppressor's) produce distorted ideological views of reality, other social positions (the oppressed's) can pierce ideological obfuscations and attain a correct and comprehensive understanding of the world.

The maternalist version, for example, can seize on "truths of life" that flow from the body-specific tasks women are assigned. Women mother by physically bringing children into the world and caretaking them thereafter, or by extrapolating from their physical capabilities and usual roles in reproduction to the realm of caretaking in general. This line of thinking tells us that we are socially defined by a material capacity and tend to nurture rather than to ravish and destroy life (O'Brien, 1981; Ruddick, 1989a; Elshtain, 1981). The epistemological implication of being assigned reproduction is that women safeguard the values that modern society often honors in the breach. These lessons from our experience provide resources that can be used to ground theory and society in women-mediated truths about the many ways that our species requires caretaking.

An extreme and essentialist form of this argument emphasizes that truth actually does lie in our bodies. Robin West (1988: 1–3),[3] an advocate of feminist jurisprudence, argues that there are four quin-tessential female experiences that mark our difference from men and our worth as:

> essentially, necessarily, inevitably, invariably, always, and forever ... connected to life and to other human beings ...: the experience of pregnancy itself; the invasive and "connecting" experience of hetero-sexual penetration; the monthly experience of menstruation, which represents the potential for pregnancy; and the post-pregnancy experience of breast-feeding.

45

West tells us that these biologically-linked experiences affect our identities and ways of interpreting and responding to the world around us. Yet only the biological experiences of men count as object lessons for the law and these experiences do not typically impart a strong sense of connection to life and other humans.[4]

Moving to a less embodied and yet still materialist and truth-seeking understanding of standpoint, we can consider the Hegelian master/ slave relationship as the key metaphor for describing gender relations in an unliberated context. The slave is a materially-embedded extension of the master's will. The master, however, thinks this relationship is co-determined, as in slaves creating masters and masters simultaneously creating slaves. When one looks at the world from the slave's standpoint, the notion of co-determination is ridiculous: who, after all, put whom in chains? The master, however, cannot see the flaws in his thinking because "the nature of privilege is to obscure the ways it exists at others' expense" (Hirschmann, 1991: 230–1). The only way for the truth to surface is if less false visions come to the forefront of common-sense knowledge. Again, this entails a change in the slave's sense of self and a struggle to valorize experiences that defy the image of co-determined oppression.

Mary Daly (1978) joins biological arguments with images resonant with masters and slaves to promote authority-reversing practices of truth. She probes the ancient, often theological texts of male dominance and finds women there as lusty wanderers weaving and spinning the connections in the universe that threaten and annoy men; hence their terms for us – nags, shrews, whores, scolds, spinsters, and worse. Daly argues that patriarchy – male dominance or colonization of all life – is the original oppression in the human species and is today omnipresent because "[e]ven outer space and the future have been colonized" (ibid.: 1). Escaping this original oppression entails leaving his world, a world that often stands as God's world, the father's world, or God the Father's world, for places where women can explore their nature, desires, and alternative perspectives relatively free from a relentless patriarchal gaze. Daly's views resonate in the works of Sonia Johnson, a former Mormon excommunicated for her mild feminist challenges, who admonishes the audiences she addresses to walk out from under patriarchy and it will collapse from nonrecognition and neglect.[5] To walk away, one must first achieve a sense of patriarchy as false, fragile, and dependent on recognition to persevere, and a sense of the truth one is walking toward.

A different, less rigid sense of who owns truth informs Nancy Hirschmann's work. Attempting to recuperate liberal theory through extensions of object-relations theory that are at once standpoint-based and irreverently postmodernist, Hirschmann knows that standpoint epistemology can homogenize the diversity of women's experiences in the world and thereby corral differences into one proclaimed truth. She knows that the realm of biological difference can be the bottom line of standpoint thinking, the path to an ultimate foundation for truth. She knows as well that women respond to relative powerlessness within the culturally determined exclusiveness of gender by striving for meaning and integrity in the activities they have been assigned in child care, nurturance, and affection; thus our jobs are not "true," albeit they may be meaningful. By keeping her eye on the notion that feminist standpoint is socially achieved and not something that can simply be excavated and displayed by all people called women, she argues that a method of mutual recognition is necessary to extend the struggle for standpoint beyond an immediate circle of people with similar bodies, tasks, senses of the meaningful, and approaches to politics. People who are not usually called women, and "women" who reside far from our circle of knowledge and meaning must be considered along with people who are not initially sympathetic to feminism or to the notion of socially located knowledge.

Hirschmann's sense of standpoint is not at odds with Steady's (1987) portrait of African feminism as reflecting the particular struggles of Africans with racial, colonial, and capitalist institutions. It also suggests that one can maintain those particularistic experiences and subjectivities while conversing together to find some new, tangential points of identity hyphenation that become, to use the idiom I prefer, powerful tools to homestead the stories told about and for people like us. This is different than theorizing sympathetically with the other. In an environment of what I call empathetic cooperation, it makes all of us "other" to the places we are assigned by social theory, so that we can recognize and work through the distortions and partialities that mark those theories. "Recognition," says Hirschmann (1992:251), "does not have a unitary meaning; rather, the inclusiveness it requires means that recognition is and will be negotiated in an ongoing way by the very process of conversation that it establishes."

The emphasis on ongoing conversations about the always unfolding potentialities of negotiated experience not only corrects for the feminist standpoint tendency to become attuned to a discovered truth. It also departs from the implication that women's situated knowledges are always superior to those of privileged men and, therefore, if we won a war of epistemologies we would be the new hegemons of social order. As well, whereas some standpoint thinking can embroil us in trying to locate the most authentic voices of oppression among women – something the women's movement in the West did during the 1970s, when some lesbians called heterosexual "women" "breeders" as a way of discrediting their standpoints, while heterosexual women tried to keep lesbian "women" out of the public eye, out of major posts in "women's" organizations – the emphasis on negotiated experience draws attention to borderlands of identity. Thus, we avoid the conclusion that "those who are differently located socially can never attain *some* understanding of our experience ... " (Narayan, 1989: 264). We can recognize mutually that all of us, including "third world" or "African women," are marked by heterogeneous multiplicities, such that "[t]here is no way to 'be' simultaneously in all, or wholly in any, of the privileged (i.e., subjugated) positions structured by gender, race, nation, and class" (Haraway, 1988: 586).

Hirschmann's work raises all of these points and to them we can add the consideration that masculinist standpoints, which we often think of as amalgamating into patriarchy, may also be multivectored and hyphenated (Yaeger and Kowaleski-Wallace, 1989). We are thereby made aware of the tendency in feminist standpoint thinking to realize that "expressions of women's voice usually call for respect for differences among women (and sometimes among men as well)," while searching "for a founding experience [that] tends to elide difference nonetheless" (K. Ferguson, 1991: 323). Relinquishing that foundation, we recognize that struggles informed by achieved standpoints about nature and social relations are not automatically emancipatory and that "[a]ccounts of a 'real' world do not ... depend on a logic of 'discovery' but on a power-charged social relation of 'conversation'" (Haraway, 1988: 593).[6]

Tensions and controversies in feminist standpoint epistemology notwithstanding, the approach makes us aware of people called women as agents of knowledge and theory. It draws attention to the incompleteness and failure of objectivity in any project that purports to be generalizable while giving voice and agency only to a privileged few. It also tells us something about the ways that subject statuses are imbued with meaning by those who inhabit them. It even tells us something about the homes that subjects can build for themselves by embracing a status, hyphenating it with another, or rejecting it. Moreover, it does not require us to think in terms of abstract "individuals" who have no characteristics in life except rationality and the drive to be free of involuntary obligations. Indeed, it brings flesh and blood, diapers and nursing, and women as thinkers into focus.

For these reasons, feminist standpoint is an especially popular mode of disabling masculine IR theory and practice. J. Ann Tickner (1988), for instance, rewrites Hans J. Morgenthau's six principles of political realism from a feminist standpoint perspective that departs from objectivist notions of wary autonomy among states and monolithic pursuits of power. Rebecca Grant and Kathleen Newland offer a collection on *Gender and International Relations* (1991) that has strong standpoint overtones: "Women as a category, gender as a topic and the impact of feminism as an ideology are three powerful sources of ideas which can contribute to a new, feminist epistemology of international relations" (ibid.: 4). Robert Keohane (1989b) tells us that when aligned with feminist empiricism, feminist standpoint is the only feminist approach of any value to professional IR. He invites feminists to find a home in standpoint, in part because he hears resonances in it with neoliberal institutionalism (for example, a sense of power as the ability to act in concert), which is his favored approach.[7] Keohane specifically wants us to mix together empiricism and standpoint to form a different starting point for empiricism. Hirschmann also asks us to combine epistemological premises, but she works through the logic of the combination by arguing that our empirical observations are informed by our standpoints, which may or may not be positions we wish to maintain.

The threads of this preliminary IR-standpoint story line will be picked up in later discussions, as will the elements of feminist standpoint theorizing that are conducive to postmodern feminism. First it is useful to consider the ways feminist standpoint epistemology makes its way into contemporary feminist practice, because this too impacts on IR.

Radical and Cultural Feminisms

Radical and cultural feminisms take feminist standpoint, often understood in the limited sense of woman's way, into the realm of practice. Some form of this thinking has characterized contemporary feminism since the 1960s (Echols, 1991; Eisenstein, 1981), when some claimed that women made up an oppressed sex class under patriarchy. Indeed, the consciousness-raising groups of that era were implicitly dedicated to the hermeneutical project of stripping away "false consciousness" through collective discussions of many "problems that have no names." Heated discussions about lesbian separatism were expressions of standpoint; so was and is lesbian nonseparatism (see B. Smith, 1991).

Among some women of color, the womanist position, eloquently

49

individualized by Alice Walker (1983: xi) as a woman who "appreciates and prefers women's culture, women's emotional flexibility ... [but who is] committed to the survival and wholeness of entire people, female *and* male," is yet another form of cultural feminism. This woman commits to "a valorization of women's works in all their varieties and multitudes," and yet recognizes that "the negative, stereotyped images of black women" can best be understood both by celebrating the voices of black women and by turning "to what black men have written about themselves" within a context of the "impossibility of being the (white) patriarch" (Williams, 1990: 70, 71). (What the men have written and done subverts patriarchy when it refuses to rehearse the story of black men as wife-beaters lusting after white women; and it reinforces patriarchy when it is taken on board by white canonicals who leave the black woman an insider–outsider of "our" and "his" making, just as African women are double-outsiders at "home" in colonized societies.) In this manifestation of radicalism, solidarity is allegiance to sisterhood and to race: identity is hyphenated into an achieved standpoint.

Central to radical and cultural feminisms, however defined, has been the belief that women initially, strategically, and perhaps permanently need space to define oppression for themselves and to formulate emancipatory strategies in solidarity with other women (and perhaps with other oppressed peoples). This politics counters the solidarity of oppressors, who inscribe women's bodies as places of male control and who script women's assignments in ways that rehearse gender relations of inequality, with a collective effort to seek out and root up the core of transgressions on woman that goes by the name of patriarchy.

In the 1970s, radical solidarity with women took the form of gynocentric feminist (I. Young, 1985) or biological essentialism in a drive to explore what was unique, inspirational, and salvationist about inhabiting a female body in a patriarchal society. For some, mothering was the central activity of all women's lives. Whether we actually bore and raised children of our own, radical maternalists depicted women as carriers of a preservative love (Ruddick, 1983)[8] that translated into public peace-lovingness (Brock-Utne, 1985) and into positive values of nurturance and human connectedness to a true humanist consciousness (Reardon, 1985). Contemporary French feminists, who have spoken of *l'écriture féminine* have sometimes been placed in this category as well (see A. Jones, 1981; Plaza, 1980), even though we tend to think of them as postmodernists.

Drawing a line between men and women through a difference

feminism with a vengeance often shaded into lines drawn between feminists who believed in women's solidarity around any number of common points and "unrehabilitated" women who were considered "male-identified." There was considerable divisiveness in the western women's movement as a result, with lesbians, participants of color, and working-class feminists expressing the concern that the standard of womanhood elevated in all the essentialist texts was white, heterosexual, and middle class or gender stereotyped.

Feminist standpoint politics turned in a less biological direction and became more cultural in the 1980s, sociologically announcing, in effect, that "[t]here is always a woman's culture within every culture" (Moschkovich, 1981: 82). Under the mantle of women's special culture, the Plaza de Mayo group of Argentinian mothers took advantage of the moral superiority historically ascribed to women in Latin societies to press for information on "disappeared" male relatives. International peace organizations, such as Women Strike for Peace and the Seneca Women's Peace Camp, developed an alternative politics of demilitarization based on their view of how women characteristically do things. In each case, radical feminists reconceived old values – not bodies – for new societies (Jaggar, 1983: 253) and contributed, thereby, to feminist standpoint theorizing.

Although the term "radical" tends to suggest a sharp rejection of liberal approaches, the seemingly opposed projects of liberal and radical-standpoint feminisms share some common ground. Both can homogenize a welter of potentially diverse identities into one master "bad" identity – biased scientist or patriarch – and one "good" identity – citizen or woman. Both can, in their various permutations, assume that men and women have a transhistorical existence prior to politics and are not constituted and reconstituted by intersections of political, economic, and social trends. Fundamentally, both can assume that abiding realities exist (woman, equality) that can be discovered and/or valorized. At the same time, both provide opportunities to project the viewpoints of the marginalized onto a world guided by dominant and oppressive standpoints and actions: radical feminists would reverse the reputations of the current rulers and liberal feminists would have our causes embraced by the gatekeepers of his causes.

From feminist standpoint thinking of all kinds come particularistic lessons on how to tap the "potentiality available in the actuality" (Hartsock, 1983: 246) of different tasks. There are valuable lessons here on theorizing more generally from the lives of a variety of outsiders within, whether or not the touchstone is women's lives only and whether or not those lives are consistent with one another (which,

51

given class, race, and imperialism in the world seems very unlikely). Put differently, feminist standpoint enables us to move beyond asking the feminist empiricist question of what IR would look like if individuals called women were included in the enterprise of theory building and in the roles that men are assigned in diplomacy, to ask what IR would look like if feminism as an achieved standpoint became the basis of theorizing and job assignments. The latter research posture would require all of us to rethink what we have come to understand as the components of power and interdependence, rationality and cooperation, domestic and international, great powers and their balances of power and so on. "Ours" could be the starting point, in other words, for more carefully crafted and variegated understandings of "relations" and of "international."

Postmodern Skepticism and Socialist Feminist Practice: The Difference Among "Women" Feminisms

Feminist postmodernism is the name given to an epistemology that reflects the postmodern turn in western philosophy and its posture of radical skepticism about "the self, gender, knowledge, social relations, and culture [understood by] linear, teleological, hierarchical, holistic, or binary ways of thinking and being" (Flax, 1987: 622). It overlaps but is not to be confused with something else, a postmodern feminism that combines elements of skepticism, particularly about the social formation of subjects, with elements of a standpoint feminism that have us acknowledging and interpreting what subjects say.

Both feminisms of the postmodern turn deconstruct gender. Feminist postmodernism is by no means a monolithic approach, but it can encourage us to question the stories and the lines that contribute to other feminist epistemologies, on the grounds that any projection of Truth "can have 'a' structure only from the falsely universalizing perspective of a dominant group" (Flax, 1987: 633–4), be that group elite white "men" or western feminists. Postmodern feminism is skeptical about lines of thinking that unproblematically accept the meaningful existence of women, but does not run roughshod over people who find meaning in these subject statuses.

Both feminisms of the postmodern turn would portray the feminist empiricist project as naively wedded to the idea, captured in a remark by Elshtain (1987: 90–1), that "women and the sphere with which they have been historically linked remains an absence that helps to make possible the much cherished 'parsimony' of the preferred model, or framework, or simulation, or analysis in the first place." One should ask whether women and men exist in a way that is conducive to doing scientific research. Postmodern feminism, however, can use the gender-distorted and the corrected data of science to consider the ways our scientific understanding of "women," though reflective of the "bizarre beliefs and practices of the indigenous peoples who rule the modern West" (Harding, 1991: 16), nonetheless provide an authoritative home space for many people. Those data help us to see identity manipulations and also to appreciate that the embrace of politicized gender identity may be a strategy to find meaning in a dizzy postmodern world. If gender is a home for some "women," then it makes no sense to refuse them that identity because, technically, it is not real.

Yet one does not simply wish to reverse the order of social dominance by putting women's lives first and foremost as a foundation for knowledge. On this point the two postmodern epistemologies would overlap, because such an extreme standpoint strategy would threaten to change the terms of dominance without breaking the pattern of certainty and oppressive bifurcation that marks modern knowledge. It is preferable "to recognize the ambivalences and contradictions within both feminist and androcentric thinking and learn how to cherish beneficial tendencies while struggling against the social conditions that make possible regressive tendencies in both" (Harding, 1986a: 164). The subtle point of difference between a feminist postmodern and postmodern feminist position would be that the latter would tolerate the politics of self-assertion on the way to a politics of empathetic cooperation.

An initial valorization of exaggerated Self asserts, against all evidence presented by the dominant side, that someone of your group really exists. Only when ontology is affirmed can the politicized Self relax into many hyphenated identities. Thus we remember the Afro hairstyle of the 1960s, worn defiantly in the face of social caricatures of African hair quality as kinky and unaesthetic. We remember times in the early western women's movement when "women" took pleasure in thinking about menstruation as a source of a special power denied men. We remember national liberation struggles proclaiming the pride of anticolonial difference, the solidarity of a people denied identity. In each case, once the point was made and the discredited ways of knowing and being asserted, the statements of Self became more multifaceted. From studying national liberation efforts, in particular, we know that an initial assertion of difference from colonialism rarely erases all remnants of that otherizing experience. In part, "[t]o be oppressed means to be disenabled not only from grasping an 'identity,' but also from reclaiming it" (Alarcon, 1990: 364). In part, the escape from some oppressions can change the nature of one's usual experience and multiply subjectivities in ways that crowd "the" agenda of liberation politics (Sylvester, 1991a; 1989). Such multiplications and hyphenations are not signs that the subject has disappeared, but that one's self-reference – and perhaps one's subject status – is diffuse.[9]

Feminist postmodernism must often defend against the charge that it reduces all conventions and subjects to rubble and fragmentation in a cynical and final separatism from Self-assertion. Harding (1986a: 246) points out, however, that the "feminism" in postmodernism is an articulation of solidarity in "fidelity to (parameters of) dissonance within and between assumptions of patriarchal discourses." But what are those parameters? A feminist wedded to certain postmodernist "intellectual styles" is hard pressed to defend feminist solidarity when "meaning is never truly present, but is only constructed through the potentially endless process of referring to other, absent signifiers" (Moi, 1985: 106). On whose behalf do we work when "liberation becomes impossible [because t]here is no one who persists, who remembers, whose experience and suffering counts; there is no one to emancipate" (Tress, 1988: 197)?

Yet both feminisms of the postmodern turn usefully question the tendency of modern social theory to paint over the diversity of lived experiences in the world with broad universalizing brush strokes, thereby creating coherent and totalizing images (supposedly) identifiable to anyone living anywhere – the white madonna in the third world church, "the" feminist. They question feminist empiricist practices of toting survey research instruments to the third world, say, and seeking to discipline (albeit sensitively) the responses of nonwestern women to fit Likert scales. We certainly do not want to project western white womanhood, motherhood, heterosexuality onto all "sisters," thereby rendering "hers" "ours." Both feminist responses to postmodernity, therefore, equivocate on issues of truth and "the good" for all. In this there is an avoidance of parodying modern theory by writing yet another story with supposedly universal salience in the postmodern era.

Whereas postmodernism can problematize "the" modern answers as too arrogant and intolerant of ambivalences and incommensurabilities for an age of uncertainty about where we have been, in theory and practice, and where we are going in the twenty-first century, postmodern feminism can problematize postmodernism's unproblematized penchant for arrogance and intolerance and its naivety about the process of giving voice. It takes to heart the critique of postmodernism

54

that asks how, at the moment when third-worlders are able to assert themselves, postmodernism can relay the message that the voice of national liberation is a subterfuge for sovereignty. Can we say, on the one hand, that we need to hear from the voices of exiles and dissidents, and then lament the fact that some are speaking too loudly or wrongly? If we consider ways of hearing others differently, thereby avoiding the loud mistakes of the past, we can concentrate on fleshing out the process by which socialities, relations, and connections can alter the contours of a homeless voice from a sad moan or bellow in a cold modern world to a hopeful conversation responding to the complexities of postmodernity.

These two feminist reflections of postmodernity are appropriately seeking the excluded voices and in-betweens structured out of Enlightenment-based efforts to theorize from "a God's eye view" (Nicholson, 1990: 2) of science, the bourgeoisie, the proletariat, or any other authority. We may indeed wonder whether there is truth or falsity, religion or superstition, war or peace, men or women, reason or irrationality – posed in those bifurcated ways – except in the epistemological position of modernity; outside that tradition and the people who inhabit it, these modes of thought and understanding can sound alien. Thus, to say that women are a sex class, that women are childbearers – in body or spirit – that women are oppressed, indeed even that women exist, may be to wear western hand-me-down gender stories as though they were natural. But, says this postmodern feminist, to denaturalize gender must not be tantamount to erasing the gendered (among other things) person standing before you who has one foot in modernity and another in postmodernity.

Jean Elshtain stands at the concentric points of feminist postmodernism and postmodern feminism in *Women and War* (1987). In that work, she considers war a narrative that fixes notions of gender solidarity around accustomed roles. There is paradox, however, in the narrative. The (male) Warrior/(female) Beautiful Soul imagery that usually operates to suppress alternative gender images and war stories cannot destroy countervailing, indeed seemingly incommensurable, possibilities around which new notions of civic identity can be forged. Elshtain demonstrates this by hosting a conversation among knowledges of men's and women's places inside and outside war respectively, that reveals an intriguing conflation at the intersection of two identities that are not usually conjoined into one: mothers and soldiers. She says the good soldier is like the good mother in war and peace stories. Both try to do their duties and yet feel considerable guilt about jobs that could have been done better: "One might have acted

55

differently and a buddy been saved. One might have lived up to this ideal and a child spared that trauma or this distress" (ibid.: 222). Both "are similarly immersed in worlds revolving around stomachs, bodily harm or well-being, the search for protection" (ibid.: 223), and yet "[w]omen are excluded from war talk; men from baby talk" (ibid.: 225). A just warrior goes on a killing binge and we say he has "lost it"; a "mother who batters her child has lost it, having gone from protector to attacker" (ibid.: 224).

The point is that there are shadowy places at the borderlands of seemingly incommensurable narrated stories that supposedly specify who we definitively are and what we must definitively do, but which nearly always contain the opposite messages as well in a textual doubleness that subverts fixed meanings, knowledge claims, and usual solidarities. What we must do to avoid doing what we are supposed to do (which is, find exclusive meaning in proper homeplaces), is move away from the "ahistorical abstractions, unreflective celebrations ... moralizing and dogmatizing" (ibid.: 240) and "quicken rather than blunt civic democratic impulses" (ibid.: 244). We must revitalize politics and relieve it of its inherited identity assignments and power turfs. In this case, we must render homeless the masculine soldiers and feminine mothers and expose this commonplace nostalgia for gender place as overdrawn, lacking foundation, and rife with nondemocratic impulses.

There are echoes in *Women and War* of a postmodernist quest to deconstruct "meaning claims in order to look for the modes of power they carry and to force open a space for the emergence of counter-meanings" (K. Ferguson, 1991: 324). There are also reverberations of postmodern feminism in a methodology that reveals and encourages identity slippages so that, like chastened patriots, we can reject "counsels of cynicism" (Elshtain, 1987: 252) and change inherited scripts and identities. Elshtain: "The chastened patriot is committed *and* detached: enough apart so that she and he can be reflective about patriotic ties and loyalties, cherishing many loyalties rather than valorizing one alone" (ibid.: 253). This purposiveness is one mark of postmodern feminism and the notion of changing or hyphenating identity is another.

One sees in Elshtain's book a combination of standpoint and postmodernist approaches to epistemology. Postmodernist concern with textual deconstruction mixes with a standpoint concern for the public enhancement of women's mediated experiences. "Pure" standpoint thinking might retain unmodified "women's experiences, feelings, and voices as sources and certifications of postfoundational political truth" (W. Brown, 1991: 71), using a method that privileges "[t]he material excavated there, like the material uncovered in psychoanalysis or delivered in confession ... as the hidden truth of women's existence – true because it is hidden, and hidden because women are oppressed, silenced and privatized" (ibid.: 72). The "pure" postmodernist might find the notion of a "chastened patriot" altogether too beholden to inherited categories of being, preferring to abandon the searches, openly or covertly, for the proper moral stance, for justice finally defined and activated, and for good moralities (standpoints, forms of science) to juxtapose against bad moralities. The postmodern feminist maintains what Kathy Ferguson (1991: 324) refers to as the "contrasting themes running through the fabric of feminist theory," the theme of women's voice and the theme of deconstructed gender tyranny. This is what Elshtain does in *Women and War*, and the result is that we are able to confront the usual nostalgias of gender place as overdrawn and lacking foundation. The public/private divide is unhinged and this means that masculine soldiers and feminine mothers are rendered homeless vis-à-vis the places designated for them in the usual gender stories. This does not mean, however, that they now suffer a lack, a violent evacuation from their respective homesteads. Rather, each now has mobile subjectivities to homestead "the" inherited identities without destroying them altogether.

Harding (1991: 49) tells us that feminist standpoint and feminist postmodernism can indeed be joined by following "the logic of standpoint approaches into postmodernist terrains while trying, *en route*, to refashion familiar but incompetent conceptual utensils into useful ones for everyday work in the sciences, philosophy, and democratic struggles of the present moment."[10] Hirschmann (1992) speaks of "postmodern feminism" to remind us that one can have, indeed must retain, feminist standpoints – multiple rather than singular but based in lives – in this era of postmodernity or the very issues around which feminism first emerged will get lost before they have been adequately addressed and rectified (also Sylvester, 1989; Parpart, 1991). Nancy Fraser and Linda Nicholson (1990: 35) admonish us to move toward a postmodern feminist theory that "would look more like a tapestry composed of threads of many different hues than one woven in a single color."

We return to the point, therefore, that postmodern feminism is postmodernist enough to recognize that gender is achieved with mirrors: "women" is the inferior absence of "men," but men rely on the women for manly identity. It is feminist enough to refuse to write women out of existence before people who walk around in particular bodies, and who experience certain things as the result of being at the inferior side of the men/women dichotomy, tell "our" stories, and reveal "our" subjectifications, and examine "our" unheralded perspectives. In this hybrid feminism, postmodern feminism out-blasphemes the postmodernist blasphemers by recognizing that *feminist* postmodernism must be standpointed or else "we" would not exist (Di Stefano, 1990).

One way "we" would not exist shows up in the postmodernist lament about the marginalization of the feminine from philosophy and the (sudden) virtues of "becoming woman." Jacques Derrida (1973: 299) says: "I would love to write like (a) woman. I am trying ... " He is trying because woman is the important absence in phallocentric philosophy that can be discovered to rehabilitate an unfashionably man-as-sovereign field. Derrida (1979: 54–5) tells us that "[t]hat which will not be pinned down by truth is, in truth – *feminine*." According to feminist philosopher Rosi Braidotti (1991: 101–2), this unpin-downable feminine is:

> the creative void at the heart of the will-to-know, the drive to theorize. Non-truth of the truth, woman is sign, and therefore text, space of writing (*écriture*); she is the mark of an excess, of a surplus-value through which the truth of the split subject can be heard. This is why when philosophy undertakes a genealogical deconstruction of its own premises, it cannot avoid the question of the feminine.

Lest feminists become excited about our new entry into philosophy, Braidotti points to the Derridean postmodernist "metaphorization of the feminine with a view better to assimilate it to a falsely neutral mode of thinking" (Braidotti, 1991: 98). That this is so can be read in Derrida's (1987) expressed disdain for feminism (because it is not a neutral mode of thinking) as another phallic-type discourse that normatizes and normalizes in its search for law. The true sign of the feminine, apparently, is that it has no name or subject voice. It is "the sign of silence, the non-said, absence" (Braidotti, 1991: 105). When it speaks, it is damned as "a man *manqué*" (ibid.), another castrating force.[11]

David Harvey (1989: 117) thinks postmodernism is rife with moves of that type:

> while it opens up a radical prospect by acknowledging the authenticity of other voices, postmodernist thinking immediately shuts off those other voices from access to more universal sources of power by ghettoizing them within an opaque otherness, the specificity of this or that language game. It thereby disempowers those voices (of

women, ethnic and racial minorities, colonized peoples, the unemployed, youth, etc.) in a world of lop-sided power relations.

Postmodern feminism will not have this. It wraps its very apparent skepticisms about our assigned identities, therefore, in and around a feminism that articulates women's voices on the road to achieving a certain "chastened" homelessness within the usual understandings of "women." Under this mantle one finds a combination of the feminist standpoint effort to interpret the subject women, and the postmodernist effort to examine how specific subjects came to be (or not) and what they have to say. It combines interest in continuities of "women" over time and in the discontinuities that mark moments of resistance to dominant discourse. It looks for differences in voices and standpoints and marks the connections that may exist across the differences. It looks for new forms and mobilities of subjectivity that can replace single-subject categories, inherited homes, without denying, nonrecognizing, the currently existing subject.

Whereas standpointers admonish us to theorize from the lives of those we have designated as "others" (Mohanty, 1991), or "reinvent ourselves as others" (Harding, 1991: ch. 11), a postmodern feminist may wonder whether it is preferable within feminist method to unlearn (deny) ourselves or to hyphenate with others empathetically in ways that avoid "progressive" replications of past erasures and reborn nostalgias for unity. Hence the emphasis on multiple standpoints, on being (ontologically) several things at once in a prismatic postmodern world – rural-black-mother-agriculturalist-socialist-cooperator – and, therefore, being homeless as a single-identity knowing Self. Norma Alarcon (1990: 365, 366) speaks of "multiple registers of existence" as "discourses that transverse consciousness" and that are relational "between one's selves and those of others as an ongoing process of struggle, effort and tension ... lived in resistance to competing notions of one's allegiance or self-identification." A "multiple-voiced subjectivity," as Alarcon puts it (ibid.: 366), makes us less amenable to arguments about "experiential foundationalism" and more open to the possibility that any one experience can hide the other realities of our lives (Harding, 1991: 311). If we hope to theorize "women," we must realize that there is no necessary "life" that any one of us inhabits. "Women" is shred to bits (Riley, 1988: 114) and this cancels out "the" subject, but not necessarily subjects with multiple and mobile (transversing) subjectivities.

Is it not possible, however, that while postmodern feminism seeks out our homelessness in and around the modern self, into the void in certainty will march those less cautious and moderate in their assessments, like "woman"-controlling fundamentalist religions (Falk, 1988)? Harvey (1989: 350) links this type of dreaded outcome to the philosophy of deconstruction:

> in challenging all consensual standards of truth and justice, of ethics, and meaning, and in pursuing the dissolution of all narratives and meta-theories into a diffuse universe of language games, deconstructionism end[s] up, in spite of the best intentions of its more radical practitioners, by reducing knowledge and meaning to a rubble of signifiers ... prepar[ing] the ground for the re-emergence of a charismatic politics and even more simplistic propositions than those which were deconstructed.

Yet why is it, asks Wendy Brown (1991: 73), by way of an indirect retort to Harvey's sentiment, that we fear "the replacement of truth with politics, philosophy with struggle, privileged knowledge with a cacophony of unequal voices clamoring for position?" Why, I would add, do we fear the relations that make the clamoring voices possible to hear?

Donna Haraway (1988: 586) suggests an answer to these questions when she argues that "[s]plitting, not being, is the privileged image for feminist epistemologies of scientific knowledge." To "split" into heterogeneous multiplicities is ostensibly to lose oneself and one's usual way. When one imagines a way that once existed has been lost, one courts the lies of nostalgia – the comment to me in 1992 from an Indian South African that life had been better, less chaotic under Prime Minister Botha; the periodic eastern German lament for the days when the Berlin Wall brought order, jobs, and general security; the remark sometimes tossed off by African businessmen that the colonists should not have left. Such nostalgias refuse the postmodern moment when "no particular doctrine of representation or decoding or discovery guarantees anything" (ibid.: 593).

In this moment people are called upon to be politically active as a social and intellectual response to diffusion and splitting; else the spoils could indeed go to those who fancy themselves at home in the turmoil. But after years of being modern subjects subjected to techniques of scientific thought and action, we often do not know how to act. Harvey is on to something when he suggests that postmodern*ist* responses to the postmodern era have not helped to ease the fears. We have overemphasized deconstruction and underemphasized the importance of conceptualizing methods that revision "the world as coding trickster *with whom we must learn to converse*" (ibid.: 596 [emphasis added]). Deconstruction alone leaves us stuck in the rubble of old meanings of "comprehensive homelessness, the lack of a common

60

place, and the devastation of public culture" (Haraway, 1992: 68). Uma Narayan (1989) suggests that people in this situation feel alienated and are not able to appreciate their supposed epistemic advantage. But, she says, "[t]his sense of alienation may be minimized if the critical straddling of two contexts is part of an ongoing critical politics, due to the support of others and a deeper understanding of what is going on" (ibid.: 266–7).

This postmodern feminist recognizes the practical and personal difficulties that can arise from critiques of reason and morality and foundational truth – critiques of some people's homesteads. Nor is it possible to delude oneself about the difficult work required "to eliminate the fascism in our heads ... build upon the open qualities of human discourse, and thereby intervene in the way knowledge is produced and constituted at the particular sites where a localized power-discourse prevails" (Harvey, 1989: 45–6). One must "have something to deconstruct" (K. Ferguson, 1991: 335), some sense of fascism to reject. But one can also encourage conversations about fear and about methods that help us to avoid both rerooting our identity at "home," in a fit of nostalgia for place, and sinking into the very real and painful condition of bag-lady homelessness, so common in the world's urban centers. The latter is the result of refused recognition of homelessness, refusals of difficult conversations, escapes into the "secure" knowledge that it is impossible to craft a theory or methodology or condition that erases all doubts, all inconsistencies, all potential tyrannies, and all bag-ladies.[12]

We are capable of more than this. We can rehabilitate a sociality of mutual recognition that goes back to our earliest social ties in life. Our identities can expand, shift, hyphenate, and become collectively homeless. And we can gravitate even more when that happens toward "the support of others" in social relationships that bring out the homesteading possibilities in the situation. Ruby's paintings render those who listen and read them somewhat homeless in the usual job-description of "elephant-keepers"; but in that homelessness, other possibilities for knowing open up, particularly if the erstwhile elephant-keepers communicate, as they have done, in order to publicize this difference. That process is what I have in mind when I speak of postmodern feminism.

Let me put it differently. Postmodern feminism amalgamates ontology and epistemology in the face of longstanding rationalist and empiricist philosophical moves to keep being and knowing separate.[13] The knower and known join and objective knowledge and identity, thereby, become disabled. This means that one is suddenly homeless in the pseudo-parented "secure" (non)places that modern philosophy and civic practice have created for us. As security slips, other identities and selves come "out" that we can hear and recognize in others. Rather than being existentially lonely in our homelessness, we can enter the "participatory politics of mutual recognition" (Hirschmann, 1992: 333), where we can finally "construct and join rational conversations and fantastic imaginings that change history" (Haraway, 1988: 586).

Having said all this, I cannot refuse to recognize that fear and angst cannot be made to disappear with the arrival of feminist method for a postmodern era. They cannot be erased by any good intentions, only nudged into view, faced, and discussed. After all, joining the knower and the known may disable the positivist practice of attaining "objectivity" by putting a methodological mask over one's face. But we do not want to fall into triumphalist thinking about some new method that issues rules and regulations for achieving true knowledge. The postmodern feminist method of empathetic cooperation revolves around continuous conversations and negotiations about knowledge. (One imagines a concept like "anarchy" or "balance of power" discussed with an eye to including perspectives on anarchies, balances, and powers that have not been considered relevant before.) It discovers and justifies locally and in conversations that move across and conjoin locales.

Postmodern feminism can usefully raise "strange" questions about stories we have accepted about "his" world that deny "us" agency in IR. Who indeed is ontologically "him" and how does "he" connect with "our" notion of IR? How do "we" write IR without encrusting an artificial "our"-selves within theory and practice? If "we" are indeed hyphenated, then do not the voices of "we" comprise a cacophonous anarchy against which to judge the ordered anarchy of the "anarchic" international system?

Keohane (1989b: 249) tells us that postmodernism ruins the possibility of explanation and that "it would be disastrous for feminist international relations theory to pursue this path." His understanding of the nihilistic dangers of postmodernism is not entirely applicable to postmodern feminism. His concern to uncover universals that can allow us to explain in grand terms is not a postmodern feminist cause either. Postmodern feminism assumes a (probably ongoing) process of identity slippage that leads to simultaneous and changing homesteading strategies. Moreover, although postmodern feminism recognizes that positivism is not necessarily "the" enemy of feminists (Harding, 1991; Narayan, 1989), it is not content with feminist empiricist methods. Nor, by the same token, is it enamored with the common-place deconstructive task of leveling subject statuses on principle. It is postmodernism with a standpoint bent.

Keohane wants standpoint thinking to blend into empiricism, not with anything postmodern, it seems, on the grounds that "agreement on epistemological essentials constitutes a valuable scientific asset" (Keohane, 1989b: 249). His "essentials" are what blend feminist ontol-ogical-epistemological positions into his ontological-epistemological position to form our usual basis for explanation in IR. This *faux* tolerance for ways of knowing that defy one's proclaimed method smokescreens a strategic orientation aimed at controlling the other.

As postmodern feminism reveals the metaphors of gender in the texts and inter-texts of "our" disciplining discipline, we are wary both of "agreement on epistemological essentials" and on relying on meta-phors and ironies to do all the feminist work for us. A metaphor can parody the possibilities. Irony can reveal a commonplace as strange and amusingly double-sided. Neither can necessarily unmake a prac-tice. That takes a variety of actions. Knowing something about gender trouble (Butler, 1990), we look at the material as well as the textual contexts of power to see "the tensions we long to repress, to hide" (Harding, 1986a: 243) in order to avoid modern forms of homeless-ness.[14] We combine, hyphenate, and consider the stories, places, meanings, and splits that others relate.

For some, socialist feminism will seem the appropriate politics of postmodern feminism. A combination of radical and Marxist femin-isms, western and third world strategies, it expresses skepticism about claims of patriarchy and capitalism and, as an activist and theoretical stream, views women (and men) as agents of social change. This practical feminism helps us appreciate one important tension that exists within current feminist theory; namely the tension "between articulating women's voices and deconstructing gender" (K. Ferguson, 1991: 322).

Socialist Feminism

Socialist feminism can seem an unlikely candidate to team with post-modern currents of thought. Like many second-wave feminist the-ories, it seeks to find an answer to the oppression of real women, in this case at the fulcrum of two intersecting institutions – capitalism and patriarchy. Patriarchy, which is assumed to be constituted at different times in different locations, seems to some to indicate the alienation of men from the processes of fetal growth and childbirth that women

63

alone experience (O'Brien, 1981); it finds its best nesting ground, therefore, in the power relations of the household. Capitalism, by contrast, lodges in the economy of most modern societies and is the latest economic arm of patriarchy. Together, the two systems of power institutionalize a multilayered division of labor with three nodal points: at procreation, where men control the reproductive choices and emotional labor of women; in the production of commodities for exchange in markets, with men defining production as more historically important than reproduction; and at commodity production, such that women perform different jobs in the economy than do men and are compensated at systematically lower rates (Jaggar, 1983). The socialist feminist goal is to eliminate sexual divisions of labor at each of the nodal points and "liberate everybody else who is also oppressed ... Socialist feminism is a radical, disciplined, and all-encompassing solution to the problems of race, sex, sexuality, and class struggle" (Wong, 1991: 290).

Clearly this sounds the notes of a feminist standpoint project, particularly in the emphasis on struggling to achieve a comprehensive guideline for social action. But socialist feminism also lines up with postmodern feminism by suggesting that women are socially produced and socially capable of producing a life-politics of struggle against complex systems of oppression. It holds out the possibility of drastically altering one's subjectivity in the process of recognizing a spacious homelessness in the gender identities that patriarchy and capitalism impose.

Socialist feminism offers the "women's groups strategy" as an initial way of conversing empathetically about the structural distortions that dictate the meanings of "women." One then reenters patriarchal-capitalist society to work-converse with other groups (for example, trade unions, national liberation movements, antivivisection groups) for change. There is a participatory politics of mutual recognition operating at both moments of strategy that resonates with the empathetic cooperation of postmodern feminist method. This aspect appeals to many third world feminists and first world women of color as a way of working with "men" and with sympathetic international groups to torch assigned ontological homes in colonialism.

Socialist feminism can also help us to identify cases of western feminist participation in "foreign" oppression. Western feminists who vacation in the Caribbean may be liberated by their sojourn to places that were once considered off-limits to the unescorted woman. Yet they contribute to the gender-linked oppression of local Caribbean women when their rooms are made up each day by a "chambermaid"

(Enloe, 1989). Says Angela Gilliam (1991: 229), "[i]t is not enough to romanticize about the Guatemalan Indians' concept of Mother Earth and how that affects the way they view the world. Equally important is to realize that the Indian peoples in that country are being exterminated in this twentieth-century version of the 'Indian Wars.'" In socialist feminism as in international relations, the western-situated feminist recognizes the homey comforts of her privilege and multiplies her subjectivities by engaging empathetically with those she once denied, ignored, and pushed off the terrain of significance. She also turns those subjectivities loose on her own context as tools of self-evaluation:

> [w]hereas we set out by believing that various forms of machismo and patriarchy which we encountered in Asia and Latin America were characteristics of underdevelopment, we soon came to realize that our own situation was not entirely different. And it was while undertaking a more detailed study of the historical roots of male dominance that we made our most important discovery, namely that far from being signs of backwardness, sexism and patriarchy are central ideological and institutional props of the industrial system and its model of accumulation. (Mies, 1988: 2)

With cross-cultural self–other recognition in one's backpack, an anti-passive revolution against the women-cooptative – women-denying forces of IR becomes possible.[15] Indeed:

> armed with further information on the use of Depo Provera and forced sterilization in Namibia, [European women] may be able to expand this area of solidarity work ... and [thereby] expand understanding among British women of the context in which these issues arise for Namibians and to reassert the reality of Namibian women's particular struggle in this sphere. (SWAPO, 1986: 72–3)

In the never final analysis, socialist feminism is about expressing deep skepticisms, forging new alliances, and searching identity. It has us talking to "women" who step out of the shadows of darkened geographical spaces to speak in contexts where listeners listen closely, and, in the process of doing so, find less ability to take refuge in ethnocentric feminist solutions that revolve around univocal cultural senses of patriarchy and capitalism. It also embodies a certain post-modernist ambivalence: "So far it consists more in a critique of prevailing conceptual models of women's contemporary situation than in the presentation of a systematic alternative framework" (Jaggar, 1983: 162).

For those of us who are interested in IR, socialist feminism leads us to ask what "we" in this field do to create and continually reinstate humanist patriarchy and capitalism, and in what ways people struggle against institutionalized power relations – how many logics and struggles are there in how many different systems? What are the salient divisions of labor within professionalized and practical international relations and where are coalitions forming to resist these rule-governing practices?

Cacophonous Feminisms

As of the late 1980s, it is no longer fashionable to speak of universal woman fighting or suffering universal man and his unified patriarchal power relations. One cannot intimidate with the charge that certain practices indicate a sell-out to monolithic patriarchy, capitalism, or heterosexuality. No longer is it kosher to spin feminist theory in a western vacuum or even to speak of women and the goal of equality with men as givens. Many feminists, however, have not heard all this destabilizing news because their material conditions are such that the challenge of countering coercive power relations presses on them more than the urgency of letting a hundred voices speak. A variety of feminist politics continues to exist, to assert correctness, and to tumble together with academic feminist theory.

Postmodern feminism sets in motion a process of identity destabilization that is a far cry from an evacuation of ontology from epistemology or "women" from IR theories. Slipped identities are brought to bear on fields that always seem to be ploughed the same way, disturbing them like so many elephants who take up brush and canvas in defiance of those who know for certain that animals do not have a sense of aesthetics.

As the feminisms of yesterday and today comingle, it is important to bear in mind that each makes a contribution to knowledge in a postmodern era (Flax, 1987). Feminist empiricist epistemology is a reminder that we need the workaday efforts of feminist scientists to uncover all the stories (if not all the truth) about men and women that biases in science keep from view. Standpoint epistemology grows increasingly sophisticated. Out the window with essentialism has flown the notion of single standpointed womanhood. Now multiple realities tied to the varieties of possible lived experiences claim "our" attention and blur the lines between standpoint and postmodernist thinking. Standpoint theorists tell us it is not just that most social theorists fail to ask how gender experiences and expectations may impinge on the claims of scientific accuracy, universality, coherence, and completeness. Rather, they fail to ask how the world really is from the vantage point of any outside group. Feminist postmodernists may prefer to ask whether IR exists in a monolithic way and by whose lights "it" establishes various regimes of truth that conflate "us" with us and with a host of "thems."

Postmodern feminism builds "an appropriate humility concerning theory and an ability to sustain the contrary pull of continuing to want what cannot be fully had" (K. Ferguson, 1991: 339). I call what cannot be fully had, a home. Postmodern feminism is an angle that cannot erase all our troubles, but that is not the point. People calling themselves feminists have often disagreed on the doubts and homes and troubles and nostalgias that plague us. Surely we will disagree on the merits for "women" of postmodern feminism, while at the same time gaining insights from it that help us to develop feminist knowledge and practice further. Few will disagree, however, with the proposition that there are many relations masked within official international relations. How those relations can be revealed by feminist readings – how so many invested terrains can be brush-cleared for iconoclastic el(l)e-phant homesteadings – is the subject of subsequent chapters.

2 THE EARLY FIELD OF IR – MUSINGS, ASSERTIONS, DEBATES, AND (NOW) FEMINIST INTERRUPTIONS

The stories of international relations theory are no more straight-forward to those who review them than are the stories of feminist theory. Read from the texts of IR "worthies," the epoch sagas have three acts organized around contemporary debates about the nature and appropriate methodology of the field, each claiming some grounding in tales of politics spun by philosophers of the past. This chapter focuses on the first discipline-defining debate in contemporary IR and on the antecedents to it as filtered through the lenses of conventional and unconventional interpreters.[1]

Pretheoretical "musings"

Across a span of nearly two millennia, Thucydides, Machiavelli, Dante, Hobbes, Rousseau, Kant, Grotius, Bentham and others who would become the foundational authorities of IR, wrote about wars between Athens and Sparta, counselled princes of Italian city-states on foreign affairs, considered the consequences of creating international organi-zations and law, introduced distinctions between an anarchic state of nature and properly governed states, and waxed prophetic about power balances. Their very different writings had points of conjunc-ture around what K. J. Holsti (1985: 7–8) enumerates as:

> a common set of questions or problems that, implicitly or explicitly, establish the boundaries as well as the core of the field ... 1) the causes of war and the conditions of peace/security/order; an essential sub-sidiary problem is the nature of power; 2) the essential actors and/or units of analysis; 3) images of the world/system/society of states.

It is the first concern, say most mainstream reviewers of the field today (e.g. Bull, 1977), that really fired up the origins. The second established the locus of international relations in abstract–tangible entities called states, and the third concern established constraints on states through the anarchy of decentralized sovereignties and the order of expanding capitalism.

The foundational philosophers and practitioners of IR often studied these elements systematically. Yet the post-World War II theorist Hans J. Morgenthau (quoted in K. Thompson, 1960: 17) claimed that "[m]en have generally dealt with international relations on one of three levels, all alien to theory: history, reform, or pragmatic manipulation." Kenneth Thompson (1960: 18) took this point further:

> History differs from theory in its resort to a chronological recital of events to demonstrate its oftentimes unavowed theoretical propositions. By comparison, the theorist turns from chronology to modes of analysis that can use the events of widely separated periods despite the fact that their only bond is their relationship to a principle and not proximity in time ... Reformers, in contrast to historians, make their theories explicit ... [but] focus, however, on international relations not as they are but as they ought to be ... Practitioners ... are inhibited ... in their concern with the theoretical by the imperatives of practice and policy and only rarely when these immediate demands recede into the background can they afford to make their theories explicit.

Thus, one reads Hobbes's story about the state of nature preceding the rise of Leviathans merely as a metaphor for contemporary states in anarchy. One finds in Thucydides' accounts of the Peloponnesian wars, and in Machiavelli's counsels, the echoes of transhistorical realist power concerns; and in Jean Jacques Rousseau's story of the stag hunt, there is resonance with contemporary game theory.

The fixation on theory developed in the United States when the social sciences sought to emulate natural sciences in writing theories that postulated general or narrow laws about recurring phenomena from which hypotheses could be derived and tested using empirical data collected with research detachment. Those concerned with virtue and justice, with foundational myths of society, and with extracting lessons from historical events, often from a base of personal involvement, could not bring us scientific explanation. And so, say contemporary chroniclers of the field, the early contributors to IR were unable to awaken from a Rip Van Winkle sleep that took them through the early Westphalia era, when the precept of sovereignty came to replace dynastic relations, through the golden age of diplomacy by foreign ministries and gallant state leaders, and into the twentieth century. "[N]owhere, whether in universities or in wider intellectual circles, was there organised study of current international affairs" (Carr, 1962: 1). Indeed, one of the early field's key analysts told us that "international theory, or what there is of it, is scattered, unsystematic ... largely repellent and intractable in form" (Wight, 1966: 20).

IR: born in war and debate

With the advent of World War I, IR commenced in earnest, both as an academic and a popular field of study. In E. H. Carr's (1962: 2) words, "[t]he war of 1914–18 made an end of the view that war is a matter which affects only professional soldiers and, in so doing, dissipated the corresponding impression that international politics could safely be left in the hands of professional diplomats." The people, at least those in the US where the debate originated (see Olson and Onuf, 1985), demanded IR in the sense that they no longer tolerated world events brought home to them through foreign wars. Academics scrambled to invent IR as a discipline and, in doing so, they fell into a great controversy that would occupy the field until the 1950s.

This first discipline-defining debate of contemporary IR was about the purposes and scope of the new field. William Olson and Nicholas Onuf (1985: 12) tell us that "[w]hat must never be forgotten in assessing the emergence of International Relations is that it grew out of a fervent desire to understand and therefore to find ways to control world politics in order to prevent future wars." But how best to understand and control such phenomena was not self-evident. Were there inescapable and inevitable facts about international relations that could not be manipulated, or was all a terrain for social engineering? Was the goal to hold sovereign rights to power and war constant and to study the intricacies of balance-of-power maneuvers, or was the field more properly dedicated to constraining sovereign power through League of Nations-type institutions of collective security? Were we talking about progress through elaborate social alchemies wrought of mass education combined with legal and constitutional constraints on states, or were we stuck working with unflappable drives for power and overdeveloped state mechanisms of war? Underneath these questions lay fundamental disagreements about human nature, about the nature of good government, and about what we now think of as issues of agency versus structure. Realists thought human agency unleashed a series of Cain and Abel scenarios played out at the level of international structures. Idealists assumed that "man, or at least the majority of men, is basically 'good,' 'considerate,' 'peaceful,' or that he is at least morally colorless so that education, right environment, or the right structure of society can render him [and his states] good" (Herz, 1951: 33). In neither tradition was there a discussion of gender and human agency or of "women."

70

Benevolent Modernity

Through the interwar years, we know that idealism was in the forefront of the fledgling field, and this meant that the emphasis was on certainties of "progress, common humanity, universal law, political freedom, democracy, general well-being, and peace" (Rothwell, 1973: 25). The first British professorship of international relations, established at the University College of Wales, Aberystwyth, was bestowed on idealist Alfred Zimmern, known for his writings on the League of Nations. In the US, Raymond Fosdick, Nicholas Murray Butler, and James T. Shotwell endeavored to install the very modern "twin convictions that a continuing progress – given the right ideas, correctly pursued – was well within human capacities and that an underlying harmony of interests existed among all the nations of the world" (M. Smith, 1986: 58). World War I, these theorists argued, had been caused by oligopolistic balances of power and by complicated treaties and tariffs that gave vent to "passions and atavistic appeals" (ibid.: 56). A universal international organization was necessary to open foreign policy to public scrutiny and thereby, it was hoped, nurture the good habit of gentlemanly negotiation. The time was finally right for an international shift away from anarchy because the advances of modern understanding were conspiring against strategies of self-help:

> A new attitude is forcing its way in international politics, – as it also is revealing itself in the world of business and international economics, – one which seeks to substitute for ruthless competition some measure of cooperation, so that each member of the community of nations may have a larger share in an increasing common good. This change in attitude is itself a fact of history. (Shotwell, 1929: v)

One often thinks today of those idealists as seeking to harness the presumably benevolent inclinations of modern populations through philosophical appeals to peace and international social engineering. Hans Morgenthau (1946) offers a different slant by telling us that the nineteenth century had been a time when a "science of peace" was established "as a separate branch of scientific knowledge" (ibid.: 92), and that branch of knowledge hit its stride in the Post-World I idealist era, when, "[p]receded by the Hague Conferences and hundreds of private peace congresses, the governments themselves embarked on a program of feverish activity, whose extent was unprecedented in all recorded history, with the purpose of solving all international problems through scientific methods" (ibid.: 94).

Scientific idealism culminated in the Pact of Paris signed August 27, 1928. Fifteen states (later there were more) agreed to renounce war

71

both as a solution to international conflict and as an instrument of national policy in international relations. There was some concern that only states enlightened by scientific understanding could fathom the new forces of history. Said Shotwell (1929: 5–6), "[w]here a people is in a semi-barbarous state, force, either applied or held in reserve, is the very condition of peace itself. International peace is applicable only to responsible governments that are able to comply with the conditions of the new regime." Nonetheless, the Pact signified that science was winning the war against international "barbarism":

> War, like slavery, was accepted as inevitable until the growth of modern science so changed human relationships as to make new conditions for both the day's work and the policies of nations. Moreover, just as practical science brought substitutes for labor, so its destructive inventions brought substitutes for the ancient ways of waging war. We are therefore at a point in human development in which science, having given the world a substitute for slavery, is challenging society to find the substitute for war. (Shotwell, 1929: 21)

In light of such certainty, Morgenthau (1946: 94) could reasonably claim that the scientific approach to IR was born with liberal idealism, and not, as others would later assume, with post-World War II behavioral realism.

The crowning idealist Pact of Paris was not only a manifestation of faith in science as " the magic formula, which, mechanically applied, will produce the desired result and thus substitute for the uncertainties and risks of political action the certitude of rational calculation" (Morthenthau, 1946: 95). It was also, and ironically, a manifestation of fledgling *realist* politics, that is, of the tendency for "no great power ... to deny the ideals of an orderly and peaceful world, even when behaving contrary to them" (Rothwell, 1973: 25). Three years after the Pact, Japan invaded Manchuria and would not be brought to book through the collective security mechanisms of the League of Nations. In 1934 Japan and Germany withdrew from the League and Italy invaded Abyssinia. Liberal idealism was then assaulted by the efforts of some states to harness modern methods to very particularistic national goals. Where there had been faith in peace as the quintessence of modern progress, there was now a replacement politics of international social Darwinism – the dark side of modernity. A measure of idealism's shallow base of support into the 1930s is contained in a 1935 survey the British League of Nations Union conducted to ascertain popular sentiments on war and peace. That survey of British public opinion (one does not know how many "women" were included in it) found that while "more than 11.5 million expressed overwhelming support for disarmament and collective security, in particular for all sanctions short of war against an aggressor, 6.8 million (versus 2 million against and 2 million abstentions) supported war as the final sanction" (M. Smith, 1986: 64, quoting A. J. P. Taylor, 1965: 381). Later that year, Abyssinia was "given" to Mussolini in the hope of forestalling war and Hitler occupied the Rhineland.

Malevolent Modernity

As preparations for war unfolded, the constancy of malevolence reemerged as "an inescapable fact ... [to which] the theory and practice of international relations must adjust..." (Maghoori, 1982: 11). It became acceptable to argue that the outbreak of World War II was the consequence of misplaced faith in the benevolence of modern populations and in Lockean international liberalism's free-floating vision of the Self with rationally conceived obligations (Elshtain, 1981: 116–17). The truth was that the international system was home to suspicious states and to populations prone to "atavistic appeals."

Carr (1962: 53) put the matter this way:

> The utopian assumption that there is a world interest in peace which is identifiable with the interest of each individual nation helped politicians and political writers everywhere to evade the unpalatable fact of a fundamental divergence of interest between nations desirous of maintaining the *status quo* and nations desirous of changing it.

To John Herz (1951: 42), the turn from idealism epitomized a more general principle about cyclical trends in politics: "Political Idealism has its time of greatness when it is in opposition to decadent political systems and the 'tide of the times' swells it toward victory. It degenerates as soon as it attains its final goal; and in victory it dies." To Morgenthau (1946: 101), idealism "produced as its inevitable result the substitution of scientific standards for political evaluations and, ultimately, the destruction of the ability to make intelligent political decisions at all."

In the ensuing years the question of good and of right in international relations came together in much of IR writing around the principle that power always motivates and national interest compels. Morgenthau became the sweetheart of political realism. Believing, at least in the early years of his career, that "there is no escape from the evil of power, regardless of what one does," and that "political ethics is indeed the ethics of doing evil," Morgenthau (1946: 201, 202) imbued his writings with a sense of certainty that politics was incapable of the

73

relational characteristics of idealism. At the same time, however, he insisted that "[i]n the international sphere the reduction of political problems to scientific propositions is never possible" (ibid.: 103). Essentially selfish man possessed the quality of self-recognition, Morgenthau said, and this enabled him to make choices, to be variable in his judgments, to escape "scientific propositions." Realist human nature was thus bifurcated – fundamentally corrupt, it also had rational and moral resources at its service (Donnelly, 1992: 93).

The essentially evil power-drives that Morgenthau stipulated merged with the variable qualities of judgment in the person of the statesman. He was the one who could not "fail to recognize the reality of international disputes for the solution of which no scientific formula is available" (Morgenthau, 1946: 105), and the one who could seek the least evil path down which to take the state in pursuit of its power interests. Pivotal to state diplomacy, the statesman could recognize that "[w]e are able to judge other nations as we judge our own and, having judged them in this fashion, we are then capable of pursuing policies that respect the interests of other nations, while protecting and promoting those of our own" (Morgenthau, 1965: 11; see also Wolfers, 1960).

The conditions of world politics that statesmen could see in relative terms, however, never cast doubt on "[t]he test to which political decisions in the international sphere must be subject ... to the measure in which those decisions affect the distribution of power in the international sphere ... the supreme value ... is power [not] truth" (Morgenthau, 1946: 101). Power had to do with establishing and maintaining the control of man over man, a condition that "degrades man to a means for other men" (ibid.: 195). Degradation made violence a constant threat and, in international relations, national interest was the shield to ward it off. Morgenthau believed that in an age of nationalism, each definition of national interest would be different and, accordingly, there could be no "lighthearted equation between a particular nationalism and the counsels of Providence" (Morgenthau, 1965: 11). No one view would be universal. No single standpoint on interest could prevail. The statesman, therefore, was confined to exerting moral judgment and pursuing power within the framework of his particular national-interest politics.

In hindsight, one can see Morgenthau operating to establish the validity of a standpoint epistemology as against the empiricism of scientific idealism. The critical measure of a good political outcome could not be its proximity to empirically testable truth – this was an impossibility given the many sites of vision that existed in the world –

but its consistency with a particular set of lived experiences having to do with a states*man*'s national identity. He was always the power broker, the one with privileged ability to negotiate national-interest politics at the borderlines of power constancies in politics without succumbing to the tricks and appeals aimed at the common man. His was certainly not a social position of subjugation; that is, his vision did not derive from deciphering the invisible codes of power that kept people like himself outside the realms of official influence. Quite to the contrary, this situated knower developed standpoint precisely because he could see, from a position of privilege, the damage done both to popular judgment and to the judgment of leaders by the pressures of life in a power-driven world system.

This ability to see through and around machinations was a characteristic that united all statesmen, wherever they were located in the system. All had the same functional task of safeguarding their nation-states through the exercise of good judgment, and all circulated rather easily throughout the states system in order to perform their duties. Richard Ashley (1981) suggests that the good judgment exerted by any particular statesman would thereby reflect a practical statesmanly interest in developing common understandings with others of one's kind. In other words, despite the existence of distinctive national interests, statesmen would inhabit a special community of shared meanings.

The good statesman had to honor and occasionally maneuver around a second key community of meaning in international relations – the community of the unitary nation-state. Morgenthau argues (as does Wolfers, 1960) that no line of morality demarcates the private realms of national civil societies from their public components. That is, there is not a dual morality that marks out "the private sphere [as] good and wholesome and the public sphere [as] sinister and evil and in need of being elevated to the ethical level of individual action" (Morgenthau, 1946: 187). Moreover, unlike Rousseau, Morgenthau apparently did not believe, or at least he did not state, that the private realm was the site of womanly passions that had to be isolated from the true realm of public national interest. Rather, he said that "[t]he evil that corrupts political action is the same evil that corrupts all action" (ibid.: 195), and "[t]he most that can be said concerning the moral character of a private, as over against a political, action is that an individual acting in one capacity may be more or less moral than when acting in the other" (ibid.: 187).

Notwithstanding his constant reference to "man," it is possible on the strength of Morgenthau's view to contemplate erasing the

75

commonplace divide between private and public. With all spheres tainted by evil, a certain commonality of condition would run through human actions, no matter how diverse the goals of different national populations or of "individuals" within them. Morgenthau (ibid.: 199) maintained that people did try to control themselves, and, in the modern era, they came to "believe that there is less evil in the aspiration for state power than there is in the lust for individual dominance" (ibid.). Thus the lust that was human, rather than attaching to a typical "man's" or "woman's" sphere, was displaced onto states lusting for power in international relations.

It was with these two sets of unities in mind – the reasoning community of statesmen and the community of "lust" – that one can evaluate the particular disunity that Morgenthau poses through the realist principle of autonomy of standards. He says pointedly that:

> Intellectually, the political realist maintains the autonomy of the political sphere, as the economist, the lawyer, the moralist maintain theirs ... [t]he political realist is not unaware of the existence and relevance of standards of thought other than political ones. As a political realist, he cannot but subordinate these other standards to those of politics. And he parts company with other schools when they impose standards of thought appropriate to other spheres upon the political sphere. (Morgenthau, 1965: 11–12)

Autonomy created a third community of realist theorists free to think "of interest defined as power, as in the economist thinks in terms of interest defined as wealth; the lawyer of the conformity of action with legal principles" (ibid.: 11). This community would share internal standards of interest and seal itself off from the idiosyncratic standards of groups whose knowledge bases might suggest the wisdom of moving into all geopolitical spaces, as the "the illusion of international law as a standard for political action, the illusion of a naturally harmonious social world ... of a social science imitating a model of the natural sciences ..." (Morgenthau, 1946: 121). The best way to guard against imperialist displays of knowledge-power would be to maintain measured distance from situated knowers whose standards might not accord with the realist's reluctance to generalize.

There is tension, however, in this line of reasoning. If the realist maintains knowledge-preserving autonomy from other standards, he risks developing an insular arrogance that can eventuate in campaigns to tame rather than coexist with those standards (including standards assigned to "women"). One thinks of the hegemonic stability school of realism asserting the benefits of attaching many national differences to "the" national interest of one heavily resourced state. This sense glimmers in Herz's (1951: 27) image of the political realist defensively finding himself autonomous from alien reigning standards and waiting his turn to be "the" momentary standard-bearer of universal political ethics. Herz says that political realism:

> arises inevitably whenever people become fully aware of the failure of repeated attempts to "reform" political life, to create a "better world," or to oust the "wicked" or "inefficient" group or class currently in power, and to replace it with one better qualified, wiser, more courageous, or activated by more elevated principles. History, which is the burial ground of such attempted changes, is also the birthplace of realist disillusionment. And disillusionment, in turn, gives rise to realism.

Interestingly, there is a certain postmodern sentiment lurking at the margins of this tension: the realist retains autonomy in part so that he is not entrapped by the project of another. In the past, say some realists, entrapment was not such an important concern. The nineteenth century had been a period of harmony of interest based on increased economic prosperity and recourse to existing colonies as outlets for economic and military competition (Carr, 1962). The Treaty of Versailles of 1815 demonstrated that an expanding system had room for everyone and could reabsorb enemies into workable political relationships rather than eliminate them or turn them into devils. The nasty competition for remaining geographical territories, which was waged from the 1860s, together with the creation of new states eager to make their mark, and new industrial centers in Asia, gave rise to economic nationalism. With World War II the inner meaning of the modern international crisis finally became clear: "the collapse of the whole structure of utopianism based on the concept of the harmony of interests" (Carr, 1962: 62).

"Autonomy" became a key strategy of survival after World War II. It is in the highly technological period of late modernity that the world shrinks and the possibilities of mass conquerings become possible. To keep knowledge and power sufficiently decentralized and anarchic is to rest safe from the risk of unwanted political mergers. To look backward to a golden time of harmony would be foolishly to think that the world had not changed in its capacity both to impose nonconsensual orders and to resist such activities. In good postmodern fashion, Carr (ibid.: 79) tells us that "[t]heories of social morality are always the product of a dominant group which identifies itself with the community as a whole, and which possesses facilities denied to subordinate groups or individuals for imposing its view of life on the community." Whereas it was once relatively safe to wrap oneself in a dominant modern interest, to do so again in a diverse, geopolitically broadened state system would be to multiply the possibilities for carnage and tyranny.

Morgenthau (1965: 22) also believed that World War II split "the moral unity of the political world, which has distinguished Western civilization during most of its history." The ethical system "that in the past imposed its restraints upon the day-to-day operations of foreign policy ... does so no longer [owing, in part, to] the substitution of nationalistic standards for universal ones" (ibid.: 244–5). He believed that the heartbeat of the old system had been lodged in the states-manly "sense of a highly personal moral obligation ... with regard to their colleagues in other countries" (ibid.: 248). In the past:

> writers of the seventeenth and eighteenth centuries counselled the monarch to safeguard his "honor" and his "reputation" as his most precious possessions ... A violation of his moral obligations, as they were recognized by his fellow monarchs for themselves, would set in motion not only his conscience but also the spontaneous reactions of the supranational aristocratic society, which would make him pay for the violation of its mores with a loss of prestige; that is, a loss of power. (ibid.: 248)

Now, in the age of competing nationalisms, moral, social, and political conditions prevented the configuring of "a" plan for good counsel. All was decentralized and statesmen were now guarding their knowledge jealously. The best the academic realist could do under those circum-stances was to "adopt the historian's pose in peering over the states-man's shoulder, listening in on his conversations, anticipating his thoughts" (Ashley, 1981: 209–10).

The fateful events of 1989 and beyond show us how closely we are still tied to the tensions articulated in that first debate and yet how inadequate those frameworks have been in a context of rapid change. Academic realists are, perhaps, too autonomous now, too far removed from the statesman's shoulder to listen in on his thoughts. Accord-ingly, the devolutions of power to mass publics and their statesmen in Eastern Europe and the Soviet Union were neither anticipated nor readily explainable within the classical realist framework. Pundits of academic idealism applauded the resurgence of territorial democracy and people's politics, only to watch a series of excesses unfold, not the least being the war that ended Yugoslavia.[2] In the confused responses are ghosts of what William Connolly (1991: 463) calls "nostalgic realism and idealism." There is a yearning to reestablish the basics of idealism: contiguous territory as the basis of internal politics; national unity as the foundation of a common moral life of place (notwithstanding a plurality of lifestyles therein); institutions of electoral accountability and constitutional restraint; and economic self-control. There is also a yearning to return to the realist practice of externally ratifying internal legitimacies of rule "by recognition of the sovereignty of each state by others" (ibid.: 463). If global turbulence (Rosenau, 1990) is yielding to "anarchy" at last, it is certainly a condition that troubles realists no less than idealists.

Feminists and "women" break in on pretheory and the first debate

This rendering of the first debate is already more than a bit off the usual track. To think of classical realists as framing a standpoint argument against science-minded idealists and then suffering the postmodern implications of shifting trends is certainly not the way the story is usually told. But there is more decentering to do. Before moving to a discussion of how scientific realism tames statesmen once and for all in the second great debate, before further sacralizing linear history and reciting yet another litany of famous male theorists' names, it is useful to plunge into greater iconoclasm. For despite introducing elements of unorthodoxy to the rerendered tale, one can still read the first foundational debate as an official bifurcation featuring a set of recognized idealists and realists and no one else. One can still accept the stature and duties of states*men* as establishing the line of judgment in realist IR, and the untapped generosity of reeducated mass publics as the idealist key to changing the world.

If one takes all of this in with the sunset, one begins to conceive of the actors of IR in relation to tropes and myths. The contemporary feminist does not wish to perpetuate certain elements of the story; nor can she wait her turn in the second and third debates before pointing this out. By then much damage is done and much has been assumed to be normal. By then the feminist voice sounds out of place, mawkish, whining interest-groupish. So we jump the queue to tell of other tensions in and around realist–idealist IR. We point to gender absences and subjugated presences in the stories of IR and to heroes, musings, and story lines that conventional (and sometimes even unconventional) renderings do not reveal.

We notice right away that the realist/idealist debate does not attend to the historical activities of two gender groups in forming the daily events of international relations and, thereby, in forming the contexts for theory. Through feminist scholarship we know that some "women" helped to shape the sovereign state and to safeguard

79

contiguous territory through judicious royal marriages. Some engaged in acts of territorial defense when ruling lords were away: Isabella D'Este is known for doing this on behalf of Francesco Gonzaga and many royal wives did likewise in courts all over Europe (Anderson and Zinsser, 1988: 45; Power, 1975). In a different role, and with a different class background to contemplate, we remember Joan of Arc's heroics in the service of a besieged monarch and her subsequent consignment to the peep-house of odd and curious happenings in the course of European state formation. Such "women" lose out in historical recountings of foundational deeds in international relations because their bodies do not fit the mold of realist statesmen or soldiers; nor, of course, do they carry rights of citizenship that would later give publics authorial signatures as idealists. "Women" have a problem that has only recently been named: heroics configure the state and such actions have been associated with "men."

Eliminated from centers constituting the first debate yet subjected to those centers, "women" – as people and as ensembles of traits – lurk in the silences of a controversy that established the organized study of international relations in only partial ways. We loiter in the shadows of realist/idealist declarations that history is on one's respective side, even as both sides fail to address the common gender dimension that historically binds them. We ask how the exclusions started and, although there has been no full-fledged feminist effort to deconstruct the realist/idealist debate, we begin to fill in the pieces by returning to those "pretheoretical musings" the field ostensibly consigned to metaphors, echoes, and resonances.

A Gender Ode to IR's Pretheoretical Musings

Machiavelli is one of the precursors of classical realist thinking, trotted out time and again to illustrate the statesman-advisor who grasped the necessities of national interest politics and who helped to replace the theme of political legitimacy with the issue of political power. Machiavelli devoted a chapter in *The Discourses* to "How States are Ruined on Account of Women." Realists do not draw direct attention to this chapter; it is an absence warranted by the habit of thinking that there are no lessons here to immortalize. And yet Machiavelli's concern hangs heavily in the realist air. In that chapter, Machiavelli presented a sphere of private morality – a place for women – that he felt should be kept separate from the sphere of politics at all costs. A leader (statesman) was not to be judged by his conduct there – at home, in private. A woman, on the other hand, was to be judged *only*

80

by the standards of private morality (Elshtain, 1981: 92–9). This simple view helped establish the tedious public/private division of labor that has bedeviled many a feminist since then. But that divided sociality did not march its way into realism and idealism in a direct way. Morgenthau initially denied separate spheres of morality as did the idealists more implicitly when they cavalierly put their faith in the wisdom of indivisible democratic publics. In the image of realists autonomous from other standards, however, the public/private split was reborn. Moreover, in the effort to keep the vote away from US "women" during the idealist era, public/private was an idea toasted in many a peaceable setting.

A second realist hero, Hobbes, claimed that men and women were equal in the mythical state of nature: both were cunning and strong. However, Hobbes gave people called women, understood as biological females, an assignment he gave no one else – mother-rights to children. There is some power for "women" in this assignment; but there is also a doubleness to the story, and the other side is that certain people then had to defend themselves and children against others who were not given involuntary obligations to weaker parties. Accordingly, says Carole Pateman (1988), women were conquered more frequently than men, although some men were conquered and made into servants and confederates – into entire colonies of vanquished men.

Women and other conquered peoples were unable to negotiate the mythical social contract because they were not free-standing individuals. They were brought into that contract, therefore, in an ambiguous relationship to citizenship and rights. Conquered men were periodically released from servitude through amendments to their contracts: We can think of the fourteenth and fifteenth amendments to the US Constitution in this light, as well as the myriad independence arrangements that have released third world men from servitude to conquerors. Conquered women, by contrast, could not be released from their servitude to enter the nation-state's politics because they had ongoing tasks in this heterosexual story that centered on family support services for the conquerors. "Women" were (always) in the master's homes, in those private places that were shuttled into the social contract as a civil sphere that would stand apart from the public civil society where "men" would have politics.

One might say that Morgenthau brought the Hobbesian state of nature to life once again in his early work, collapsing private and public activities into one selfish struggle for power. But some in that social unity must have been defeated or eclipsed. Else why did one sociality become so statesman-identified and so "standards"-conscious?

81

Arguably, statecraft became mancraft (Ashley, 1989) as classical realism configured an environment in which "man" was the interpreter and keeper of various interrelated contracts of importance to other "men" and their creations of nation-states and theories. Sovereignty was theirs. It was the preserve of judging and reasoning "men" and not, *contra* Kenneth Waltz's conclusion in *Man, the State and War* (1959), the preserve of a war-inducing but abstract system or, we must now add, of nonstatesmen.[3]

Idealist knowledge also resonates with the "wisdom" of the not-so-ancients.[4] A new attitude of peace-lovingness and cooperation was supposedly forcing its way into international politics. But it was an attitude laden with gender meanings. In the US, the attitude of peace occupied space in time with last-ditch efforts to maintain a franchise that echoed Machiavelli's concerns about women ruining the state, and that reinforced the Hobbesian social contract as an affair for conquering men only. Woodrow Wilson, the former president of elite Princeton University, campaigned for the US presidency on a platform advocating peace and disfavoring women's suffrage, ostensibly because the people – the voice of idealist reason – opposed this extension of the franchise. "The people" opposing "women's" vote while favoring peace, however, had voice only through the socially contracted citizen "men" of the country. The positing of a common human interest in peace, therefore, was a mock essentializing move in that it did not equate "the people" and "humanity" with people called "women." One might say that the common peace was on the side of idealist "men" who were no less descendants of the conquerors of Hobbesian nature than realist "men."

In the United Kingdom, the gender conditions surrounding the issue of peace were only a little different. Idealists may have argued that some ideas become unthinkable over time and war was about to join slavery as a once accepted and then abandoned idea, overthrown as we learned more about ourselves and our needs through the growth of modern science. The Foreign Service of the UK, however, could not bring itself to take newly enfranchised "women" into its employ (Miller, 1991), as though some ideas simply could not be countenanced as other ideas were changing.[5] Diplomat-scholar Harold Nicholson (1966: 376) echoed Machiavelli's fears by saying: "I expect that the historians of our decline and fall will say we were done the moment we gave the women the vote" because women are prone to qualities of zeal, sympathy and intuition which "unless kept under the firmest control, are dangerous qualities in international affairs" (Nicholson, 1942). As late as 1962, a full sixteen years after "women"

82

were admitted to the Foreign Service of the UK, there was still controversy there over "whether or not a woman ambassador, appointed to the Court of St. James from Costa Rica, should be requested to leave the dinner table when the port was served" (Miller, 1991: 77).

The final victory of equivalence for "men" and statesmanly entitlement could be traced through many sources – Rousseau is an especially rich read on the public/private minuet of normal liberal life. But, the point made, let us move on to the victory found in Morgenthau's eery silence about activities he should have investigated at the borderlands of collapsed private and public spheres, where common evil lurked. Even in his moments of public–private amalgamations, Morgenthau did not explore the Boschian netherworld of seamless national–international evil. He did not go private-side to discuss how evil in homebound activities could manifest itself in state building; nor public-side to enumerate the ways that evil in statecraft can affect homebound "women" and other nonstatesmen.[6] And yet, his initial suggestion of one indivisible sociality suggests, in feminist resonating style, that the realm of the personal is political.

Morgenthau's failure to explore the nooks, crannies, and counterfactuals of his own basic premise about power drives suggests that he is part of a fledgling community of IR theorists who will come to accept unquestioningly the stories pretheorists told about the separability in space and in morality of public and private spheres. He will accept the relevance of the former to IR and help to establish that the political is autonomous from the personal. And yet, as Enloe (1989: 196) argues, it is clear that practical daily international relations always relies on "certain kinds of allegedly private relationships – Governments need more than secrecy and intelligence agencies; they need wives who are willing to provide their diplomatic husbands [statesmen] with unpaid services so those men can develop trusting relationships with other diplomatic husbands." Insisting axiomatically that realism is an autonomous sphere of thinking, Morgenthau ignores any evidence that both the statesman and the realist theorist might be in a relationship of heteronomy with "women." With this in mind, we remember realist Arnold Wolfers's (1960: 283) claim that "[w]here men wield as much power as they do in international politics there is room for an infinite variety of abuses for which 'the necessity of state' can serve as a convenient cloak."

While idealizing domestic democracies for their potential to promote legitimacy *cum* diversity, the foundations of peaceful global society, idealism is gender-distinguished from realism only in its unblushing appropriation of certain traits often, but not exclusively,

83

assigned to "women" (for example, peace-lovingness). Idealists reverse the reputation of realist human nature to craft images of democratic publics acting more like gossamer-draped Beautiful Souls than the loin-girded Just Warriors of the realist state system (see Elshtain, 1987). But they do not provide a citation for their power move. They do not admit that a common understanding of "women" is the basis of this new "public" virtue. Instead, idealists plagiarize the social script and thereby avoid appearing gender confused, which is to say that they avoid undercutting masculine sovereignty.

Following Mary Daly (1978), Beverly Thiele (1986: 42) calls this type of plagiarism the appropriation/reversal mode of causing women to disappear from discourses. It features "[i]mages/symbols/descriptions which are stolen from women-centered processes and reversed for male scholarship," as in Marx's suggestion that men make history and women make babies (thereby appropriating and reversing the power of birth). When wielded by the idealists, appropriation/reversal keeps many of us in the dark and far from learning about "women" in the peace-striving politics of the day. We are prevented from imagining realist women by a slightly different realist methodological twist, also identified by Thiele (1986), that combines universalism – generic politics as the struggle for power, or the generic statesman – with a naturalism that requires of investigators no gender-aware contextual analysis to substantiate their points. Both methodologies embody, in different ways, a strategic nostalgia in which "men" are the voice of the species and "women" have exaggerated private traits that are either grotesque versions of masculine virtue (realism) or are different and valued versions of humanity only if they are represented by "men" as human traits (idealism).

Not all feminist theorists would agree that "women" are the model for idealism or that "women" are really part of realist "men." There could be postmodernist objections to the notion that idealism has plagiarized "women" on the grounds that this point merely perpetuates commonplace gender differences. And yet the conclusion about idealist cross-dressing comes from deconstructing the men/women dichotomy to see the ways in which the first category relies on the second for meaning. In this regard we remember the old feminist adage that if "men" really became women, as "women" has been socially constructed in many societies, housekeeping or having babies would be the prestige careers. Plagiarism forestalls this cross-over by appropriating "women" to the dominant side of the dichotomy. Similarly, there could be maternalist standpoint objections to the argument that realism and women could possibly go together. But then one

84

would have to erase offending realist women from the historical record or try to explain their enthusiasms away as special indications of caretaking. Neither possibility is sound or helpful.

One could argue genealogically that the social memories of "women" that skirt realism and idealism reflect a combination of pretheoretical musings about gender and specific polarized images of "women" that occupied the nineteenth-century imagination. According to Joyce Berkman (1990), one nineteenth-century metaphor for "women" was the fabled Amazons of antiquity. These women lived in an all-female society at the border of the known world and skillfully battled Greek warriors (Heracles and Theseus among them) when the Amazon kingdom was invaded and their queen abducted. The Amazons "did not marry, they controlled their own offspring, they were warriors, and they lived 'outside'" (Kirk, 1988: 30). They were, in effect, autonomous from spheres other than their own. Their relationships with "men" were strictly of a controlling type and they were prone to military conflict with those who threatened their sovereignty. Amazons were realists in drag. Remembering them, Morgenthau would have no reason to think of gender as a location of differences in political realism: Amazon women and realist men were one in type.

The model of "women" with socially valued but uncited characteristics of idealism harbors the distorted nineteenth-century memory of a good Athenian mother. She was the woman who did marry, who did not control her own offspring, and who lived "inside," preferably without warring against men but who, in the event of doing so, could expect social criticism of this sort: a chief officer of the Paris Commune, visited by a "deputation of women protesting the dissolution of their clubs in October 1793, reprimanded them for renouncing their sex and abandoning 'the pious duties of their households, their children's cradles'" (Pierson, 1988: 211, quoting Abray, 1975: 57). The Victorians honed the Athenian mother image and carried it around the world through colonial activities and with the assurance of science that something called male biological cells were more active and aggressive than the quiescent cells of women (Geddes and Thomson, 1890).

Of course, neither image corresponded to reality. The Athenian state had negative consequences for women, the main one being that it scripted "women" as private, motherly, and family-oriented out of a history of "women" that was more multifacetedly embedded in complex relationships and social rules (Peterson, 1922b). Also, in the first debate of IR, neither the Amazonian nor the Athenian image of "women" really triumphed because "women" had already been tamed by the pretheorists into a condition of nonexistence for this sphere of politics. And yet the realist emphasis on autonomy, defense, and human evil does not eliminate the Amazon memory so much as it appropriates/reverses it for the "men" of international relations. Likewise, the idealist emphasis on peace cannot be sharply separated from the memory of Athenian "women," even though every effort was made to effect a cross-over of this memory to "men."

When we ask, as some standpoint feminists would, what real women were actually doing during the realist/idealist debate, we find that their actions place them on both sides and somewhere in-between the nostalgias of identity and place. Many feminists publicly pursued the cause of women's suffrage alongside the cause of international peace and the cause of national interest alongside feminism. Peace activists, for instance, scored a major point in the politics of the post-World War I period when the Women's Peace Union persuaded Republican Senator Lynn Joseph Frazier of North Dakota to introduce in 1926 a constitutional amendment outlawing war (Alonso, 1989; 1993). We do not remember this as part of the idealist effort. Wilson and Shotwell loom large as idealist heroes, but the usual accounts fail to note that the first woman in the US Congress, Jeanette Rankin, was a staunch pacifist and the only member of Congress to vote against US participation in both World Wars I and II. Also hidden from official view are the Women's Peace Party in the US, the Conference of International Socialist Women, and the International Women's Congress. All called for an end to war.[7]

Variegating the story somewhat, we also note that certain "women for peace" argued that women held the virtues required to bring peace into the public arena, thereby themselves collapsing the public and the private into an essentialized benevolence as far removed from the image of Amazon warriors as possible. Many were blind to class differences in the construction of feminist-idealist virtue. Working-class "women" did not share softened hearths with their middle-class "sisters." Indeed, "women" of color in the West were often softeners of the hearths for middle-class "women," their names unlisted and their deeds unrecorded. Yet there was little spreading of middle-class mantles to nether-spaces of privacy kept by "our" domestic workers, or to geopolitical territories outside the western fold. In the feminist complicities with racism and naturalism, we find the echoes of the general idealist complicity with sexism.

Realist women were Amazons only of a sort because they were in league with realist men. They gathered most obviously in the Women's Section of the Navy League to support war preparations in the years preceding the Second World War. Some kept alive the

Daughters of the American Revolution to emphasize "that only through a sufficient national defense" would America be "insured for peace and able to bear her part in the council of nations" (Steinson, 1982: 179–80). Between the end of World War II and the beginning of the contemporary women's movement, some feminist struggles borrowed from the McCarthyite tactics that helped fuel a hideously crude realist international relations, "even though the movement for the most part did not support McCarthy and his followers" (Taylor and Rupp, 1991: 129).

We do not get to appreciate these stories because, although realists and idealists strove to be different from each other, they shared the tendency to exile "women" at the intersection of "barbarism," where reason does not quite prevail, and an innocent "primitivism" in which some are quiet and enable others to steal, mark, and write IR for all of us (categories from Rosow, 1990). Together, the two "isms" comprised one moral regime, such that whoever won the first debate, the losers would be counted among people called women. Those who argue that there is no single tradition of realism or idealism, but rather "a knot of historically constituted tensions and contradictions" (R. Walker, 1987: 65; see also Donnelly, 1992), need to articulate this particular point of convergence.

The first part of the story of IR, then, tells us little about the gendering of an incipient field through foundational "musings" and memories that embed as IR the activities of interlocking communities of states, statesmen, and theorists. Thus, we remember the realist/idealist debate as a conflict even though it emerges on closer examination as a schism within one gender-unified church.

Feminists Debate the First Debate

What to do about the many gender absences and distorted presences that constitute "our" first debate, the point of reference for the field? Casting our eyes about the multivectored field of feminist theory, we find no single answer.

Liberal feminism, particularly in its incarnation as feminist empiricism, reveals the isolation of women from texts of realism and idealism simply by revealing women's unheralded activities in international relations (Enloe, 1989; Stiehm, 1989; Schwartz-Shea and Burrington, 1990); presumably I am contributing to these efforts by recuperating lost voices of women in idealism and realism and by tracing the patterns of their exclusion. There is also a body of liberal-resonating literature that publicizes the absence of women in the category of

87

development subject (e.g., Boserup, 1970) and that argues that women can and should be integrated into realism/idealism/modernization, into the very processes that are seen as inequitable (Goetz, 1991: 135). These analyses are useful for revealing the boundaries of seemingly all-encompassing knowledges. But they can give liberal feminism a reputation for "buying into" frameworks that were not intended to and are, for reasons of epistemology and in-built sense of ontology, unable to accommodate "women."

Mona Harrington (1992: 65) seeks to revive liberal feminism for IR by arguing that "the liberal state [at least] is a suitable, even elegant, agent to advance a feminist agenda in both domestic and international relations." She maintains that the centralization of political power through the liberal state usefully foils the workings of traditional patriarchy, class, and race hierarchies. She bolsters her point by reminding us that the state moved against the industrial giants of the late nineteenth century and the welfare systems of the post-depression years. For these reasons, and notwithstanding the warlike character of the international state system, she argues that feminists should resist the idealist argument that international organization is a more promising locus of political power in a world made both more democratic by the liberal state and terrifyingly war-mongering. She says that "[t]o move from national to international regulatory arenas is to shift policymaking further than it has already gone from legislative to executive bases – that is, from potentially democratic and constituent-based to definitively bureaucratic and elite-based authority." The example of the international foray into collective security over the Persian Gulf crisis proves the point: "Who instructs the delegations to the United Nations? National executives do ... International rulemaking enthrones the outlook and interests of professional foreign policy elites" (ibid.: 67).

Harrington wants us to contemplate a reformed liberal state, rather than the state that oversees the social contract, as a sanctuary for the relatively powerless. Marginalized people are the ones who are otherwise homeless in an international system of elite power. "Why," asks Harrington (ibid.: 73), "*not* talk about the social liberal tradition?" Social liberalism is premised on the idea that "the individual must have social support for self-definition, a resistance against socially imposed identities, stereotypes, limitations to the range of mind, imagination, movement, work, or role" (ibid.: 74). The emphasis on allowing the individual to be left alone does not necessarily entail wary detachment from others as would-be tramplers on terrains of identity. Rather, "[s]ocial liberals insist ... that one element of human

88

personality is a capacity and need for relation to others, that relatedness is part of individuality, not its opposite" (ibid.: 74).

Harrington's otherwise sage analysis, however, does not address the
historical trends that tend to conflate male citizens with the liberal
state, thereby skewing the standards of rule-governed relatedness in
one direction. This means that she also underestimates the extent to
which the national and international are interrelated zones of gendered relationships. These zones operate by similar rules of exclusion
that make it seem normal for "women" to be undertheorized in liberal
contexts. Is it not a circular endeavor for "women" to use liberalism for
a sustained assault on liberal cooperative autonomies from "women"?
"Good intentions and liberal commitments are not in themselves
sufficient" (Peterson, 1990: 306). Needed is a reconstitution of national
and international norms from "women's" perspectives or from perspectives combining a variety of subjectivities that are mobile, empathetic, and politically difficult but negotiable.

Harrington blames feminist psychoanalytic thinking, which
emphasizes "men's" struggles to individuate against "women"
carried into politics, for blinding feminists to liberalism's positive
social capacity (although she concedes that Pateman (1988) has a
point in arguing that liberal social contract theory has placed restrictions on women's lives). I want to argue that the troubled relationship between "women" and "individuals" and "women" and the
first debate in IR cannot be disentangled from a psychoanalytic
explanation of gendering in tandem with a review of liberal social
contract thinking.

Recall that the psychoanalytic explanation grounds masculine
self-preserving theory in gendering experiences that make it difficult
for adult males to valorize connectedness as the main principle of
sociality. Gender is an exclusive category of identity that must be
learned. Becoming a man entails an exaggerated emphasis on separation: "a boy defines himself against the mother, as 'not-mother'
(Hirschmann, 1989: 1230). She becomes an object of difference, an
"other," and he carries the lessons of hard-won autonomy into an
adult sense of agency that operates best when the agent is protected
from other identity-threatening social relationships. In liberal political
theory, the cast of this "separateness and independence that is a reaction against others" (ibid.: 1230–1) appears in stories of abstract social
contracts entered into, seemingly, by "orphans who have reared
themselves, whose desires are situated within and reflect nothing but
independently generated movement" (Di Stefano, 1983: 639). Realist
IR theory follows in this mold, even as it focuses on those anarchic

spaces that elude social contract. It depicts states as "individuals" separated from history and others by lone rights of sovereignty that are backed up, for good measure, by military hardware and by involvements in international conventions and institutions only on a voluntary basis.[8]

How do adult "men" come to dominate "women" politically, at "home" and in international relations, after escaping psychic femaleness? Feminist psychoanalytic thinking implies that patriarchal right derives from women's position as mothers. As long as primary caretaking falls to women, identity differentiation occurs first against her and then against others. Pateman (1988: 34), however, argues that "[t]he meaning and value accorded to motherhood in civil society is ... a consequence of the patriarchal construction of sexual difference as political difference." This construction, we recall, has origins in a symbolic sexual contract that subordinated women before the social contract came into effect. Women were conquered in the state of nature when we had to defend ourselves and children from men who were free from such obligations. As conquered "servants," we joined other vanquished people in being partly left behind in nature, through various nativizing moves to proclaim our traits as natural as opposed to civilized, and partly brought into social control in family institutions governed by citizen individuals; thus our ambiguous relationship to citizenship and rights.

This feminist reinterpretation of the social contract explains why "men" are dominant forces inside those families that are ostensibly outside the important realms of civil society, and why "men" excluded "women" from participation in the original social contract and there-after from public spaces of "significance." Conquered peoples are sketched in our minds for years to come as physically and/or intellectually and culturally subordinate to the conquerors. One way of looking at the psychoanalytic gendering process is that it roots out of boys any sense of having ever been among the conquered and under-scores their identity as a privileged offspring of conquerors. Thus, adult "men" tend to denigrate and dominate "women" in liberal societies, even at this point in history when, as Harrington points out, we are far from the originary moments of social contract.

Taking this argument in a slightly different direction, it follows that "women" would have considerable difficulty throwing off their troubled beginnings with Leviathans. During the Westphalia century, independent "women" who had escaped the sexual contract and the subordinating lessons of gendering to be women, were broken through state-sponsored witch hunts:

90

> Historians once believed that there were two major outbreaks of witchcraft in Europe, the mass executions in fourteenth-century France and Italy and those in the early modern era. But recent research has shown conclusively that this picture was based on forgeries; in fact, there were comparatively few trials in the fourteenth century ... Events reached fever pitch during the decade of the 1620s; the trials continued throughout the century ... [and were] directed and organized by governmental elites. (Boxer and Quataert, 1987: 32–3)

Servants-natives-witches then had to struggle for the vote in liberal societies and now remain other in many public policy debates – to be protected, denied, denounced, and rejected, notwithstanding their considerable history of resistance to marginalization.

Harrington underestimates this history of setbacks in liberal societies. She invests popular struggles and state responses to them with a bit too much efficacy. The liberal nation-state has been a tenuous home for some of us: "we" could not freely negotiate it for ourselves and our parameters of being within it are not as wide, therefore, as those enjoyed by unconquered liberal "individuals." Moreover, our conquerings recur through the daily repetition of commonplace gendering practices that teach "women's" place as being properly outside the public realm of politics.

Let us turn to the household, "women's" explicitly assigned institution in liberal society. Might it be that we are less homeless in homes tucked away inside the nation-state, come what may in IR? Apparently not. Following Pateman's logic, the household is the site of that sexual contract that predates the social contract and disallows "women" the same contract-making rights as "men." Household is a place of women's labor without the type of recompense that other laborers receive in the public sphere of liberal states. It is the place where women are eternal volunteers, eternal caretakers, whose work of feeding, nurturing, and growing food is controlled by citizen men who place these activities outside Gross National Product. Recall Aida Hurtado's (1989) argument that women of color in the US cannot even take solace in some of the genuinely warm spaces of the private household because their "private" childbearing decisions are publicly scrutinized and their shopping lists queried for signs of squandered public assistance money. These women are placed outside "household" as it has been constituted in European–US canons. For them, household is a minefield of a home for women. For European–American "women," the household is both a welcome home – the place one belongs – and a restricted space. Harrington's defense of the liberal state does not fully explore the privatizing practices of that state and social liberalism's scrutiny of private women who are poor. Both are "otherizing" practices that psychoanalytic feminism would expect of male-dominated states.

In the first debate of IR, therefore, it is not surprising that we find international relations constructed as a zone of domestic gender politics. Realism offered anarchy as a controlled community of national statesmen, among whom any serious talk of or admission of not-women to the club was out of place. Idealism told us that these realist statesmen could do the bidding of peace-loving publics because, in effect, none of us had really succeeded in eradicating our memory of early connected relationships with "women"; thus, one could evoke "woman" (although not speak it) in idealist political practices.

The troubled liberal relationship between "women" and "individuals" and "IR" can also be viewed apart from a psychoanalytic understanding of social contract liberalism. The social contract established national governance by and for some in the name of all. Certain elite members of the conquering class of contractors then declared themselves sovereigns of their territories. Louis XIV's audacious statement that *l'etat c'est moi* stands as a touchstone for many such practical conflations of liberal "individuals" and "states." Notwithstanding years of warfare over the status of certain sovereigns and territories, some tacit cooperation can be detected among the sovereigns as they jointly recreated beyond their respective borderlands the imaginary wild state of nature they had left at home via their respective social contracts. They agreed, it seems, that there would be a place "out there" where statesmen could jockey for power and bask in moments of egoistic cooperation (for example, the Concert of Europe) as they safeguarded sovereign existence.

With this move to reinvent the state of nature in international relations, "women" momentarily came close to being inside official politics. "Women" were partly in nature by virtue of being evacuated from the social contract. In recreating nature as international relations, some IR theorists suddenly, albeit implicitly, gave "women" a place in the politics of ungoverned space. Of course, this home did not resonate with nostalgias for "Athenian women" and so the unexpected entry of "women" into politics was ultimately denied. IR's first debaters proceeded to write theory as though the question of who should be where in politics was long solved. They did not theorize gender at all, all the while, however, projecting certain characteristics of assigned genders into their schemas – the realists by emphasizing the wary separateness of states concerned with their own relative

gains, and the idealists by evoking for "men" the relational autonomies that are nurtured in little girls and rehearsed into "women's"
adulthood. This simultaneous denial of gender and insertion of "men"
in a fledgling field helped constitute the now commonplace, but
always unacknowledged, principle of the cooperative autonomy of
international relations from "women" (see discussion in Sylvester,
1993a; 1993b).

Thus the historical record for IR bears the mark of liberal contract
theory backed up by the social-psychological expectations that are
encrusted in gendering processes. This means that any attempt to
reconcile feminism and international relations presupposes working
with liberalism (Sarah Brown, 1988) and, therefore, presupposes cooptation into the contract and conditioning process. Hirschmann (1992:
25), herself an advocate of transforming liberalism's basic premises so
as to bring a new notion of social democracy to fruition, argues that:

> If the entrenchment in liberal theory of the public/private dichotomy
> guarantees the obliteration of women's experience from our
> ordinary-language understanding of political obligation, and if
> gender bias relates to the very epistemological framework that
> defines the conceptual terminology in which theories operate, then
> any analysis of "the problem of women" within the boundaries of
> existing theories of obligation will only be able to go so far.

An alternative postmodern feminist epistemology is her way to
recuperate a liberal-based field for "women."

J. Ann Tickner (1988), by contrast, leans on feminist standpoint
thinking to expose the liberal gender marks that inform Morgenthau's
principles of political realism. She argues that the mature Morgenthau
operates, contrary to his disclaimers in early work, within the rubric of
science. First of all, he leads us to believe that "it is possible to develop
a rational (and unemotional) theory of international politics based on
objective laws that have their roots in human nature" (Tickner
1988: 431). Tickner says that objectivity of this sort is the product of "a
network of interactions between gender development, a belief system
that equates objectivity with masculinity, and a set of cultural values
that simultaneously (and cojointly) elevates what is defined as scientific and what is defined as masculine" (quoting Keller, 1985: 89: 432).
Second, Morgenthau posits an abstract political man who is more
reminiscent of a control-oriented, conflictual, and amoral human than
of political humans of other possible orientations. We ask ourselves
who among us is likely to say that "[t]o know with despair that the
political act is inevitably evil, and to act nevertheless, is moral courage"
(Morgenthau, 1946: 203)? To the feminist standpointer, this type of

voice sounds the notes of some alien community at a distance from less harsh communities of thought and action. It is this voice, Tickner (1988: 433) suggests, that diminishes the capacity of IR "to tolerate cultural differences and to seek potential for building community in spite of these differences," understood as community beyond states-men, nation-states, and masculine IR theorists.

Elshtain (1981: 100–1), who is only partly a feminist standpointer, points out that "women's" views from the kitchen, courtyard, nursery, and inner chamber were once actively part of international relations. This means that there is knowledge and power for IR to recover, valorize, and learn from. She maintains that "women" had particular legitimacy in the Christian era, before the steady build-up of unitary images of the world began and before the state system came fully into being. Then entreaties to obedience and duty to God the King gave way to armed civic humanism and to the forbidding doctrine of *raison d'etat*. And then there was the *raison de puissance* of realism and we were lost. By contrast, radical feminist Mary Daly argues that when God became cast as a man, all men became Gods. The Christian era could allow non-Gods legitimacy only if they followed a God-given script and became "robotized tokens" (Daly, 1978: xv). To her, the recovery of women begins in taking back from patriarchy the positive and power-laden activities of women that common words for us, like shrew, nag, and bitch, evoke.

Standpoint feminism has yet to venture into critiques of idealism in IR, where, as Harrington suggests, there is much work to do.[9] I have argued that idealism's sovereign voice of reasoning man-publics fails to acknowledge a gender base from which concerns with peace seep out into wider society, that base being the usual assignment of peace to "women." Far from freeing the mind and politics from repetitions of malevolent modernity, liberal idealism shackles it through sacralizing "a" peace morality and "a" peaceful subject as everywhere – every-where, but nowhere gendered. By not theorizing gender, there can be a failure to recognize that the "humanity" of peace that idealists posit is not the essence of "publics" exercising good judgment. Rather, it evokes invented Athenian "women" who go about their usual (private) activities in life without hinting at any Amazonian remnant in their midst.

But then some who are comfortable with feminist standpoint theori-zing could argue that women *are* the Athenian memory, that we are peaceably inclined and concerned to avoid activities of statecraft in which "we" are in a competitive death struggle with "them" (Ruddick, 1983; Brock-Utne, 1985; Reardon, 1985). This defining characteristic would not be the result, necessarily, of the gendering process. Rather, it could be the consequence of developing, through repetition of assigned daily tasks, a distinctive orientation toward obligations and care, such that all of us could have the potential to enable "[m]oral problems [to] be expressed in terms of accommodating the needs of the self and of others, of balancing competition and cooperation, and of maintaining the social web of relations in which one finds oneself" (Tronto, 1987: 659).

The diversity of women's daily experience and feminist interpretations of that experience complicates the effort to define a feminist standpoint in the context of the first debate of IR. We do not want to recommit the first-debate error, aptly recalled by Carr (1962: 11), of ignoring "what was and what is in contemplation of what should be, and the inclination to deduce what should be from what was and what is," We must look at the historical evidence showing "women" arrayed for and against wars and warriorism, for and against realism, and differentially positioned vis-à-vis idealism. And we must look outside the European–US arena to find other historical "women" in IR, such as African "women" who were involved in international relations through slavery and through a capacity to produce commodified slave labor. These "women" were part and parcel of state building in international relations, only the states they helped to build were far from home.

Postmodern feminism occupies the borderlands of realism and idealism, and other identities and locations, asking who and why is "woman" and what do "we" want to contribute to this IR? What standpoints bear IR and what pieces of standard-bearing IR knowledge are not "we"? We know that in the interstices of the realist/idealist debate are many standards refusing totalization and many fears of suffocation by "alien" standards. Amid these refusals and fears, though, there are urgent reminders that "[a]s long as we continue seeing ourselves as the center of all the balancing projects ... we can rest assured that the world is not coming apart at the seams" (Corlett, 1989: 47). IR must preserve the seamless seams. The community of statesmen is the preserver of realist and idealist seamlessness. Its metaphysics rests on a gender "balance of dominance, interpreted as the foundation of cooperation ... the former is a precondition of the latter – on physiological grounds" (Haraway, 1978: 33). In other words, there is a body politics in the first debate of IR that replicates a pretheoretical sense that "[i]n the beginning, there are man's biological impulses which see full expression. And then there is the social order" (Merton, 1949: 131).

95

But there is more too. Postmodern feminism can imagine, along with some postmodernism, that embodied social orders were more negotiable, less real and fixed, than they seemed. And, indeed, there is evidence that activists with decidedly hyphenated standpoints defied the either/or premises of IR's first debate and attempted to negotiate the social order of the day as somewhere between the approved points of war and peace. Warrior-peacemaker Clara Zetkin linked peace to the eventual triumph of socialism through militant worker struggles. As head of the American Union Against Militarism, Crystal Eastman developed a militant pacifist position toward world war. Even the Women's Section of the Navy League combined realist means with the general feminist sense "that the war provided unique opportunities for service and, through service, recognition and respect" (Steinson, 1982: 163).

These homesteadings resonate with what Gloria Anzaldua (1987: 78–9) refers to as "mestiza consciousness," the ability "to be on both shores at once, and at once see through the serpent and the eagle eyes." That consciousness helped to mark points of tangency on concentric circles of experience where variously located "women" could homestead on "men's" assigned shores without reaching for another pact of cooperative autonomy from difference. In the post-modern era we need additional homesteading spots that can accommodate el(l)e-phants and "artists" alike in their painterly – and other – (some yet to come) identities. Put differently, to move beyond the particular historical hyphenations of the first debate era we need to bring in new standpoints and create reciprocal relationships of being and knowing through processes of empathetic cooperation.

Beyond dialogue and debate

Empathy rests on the ability and willingness to enter into the feeling or spirit of something and appreciate it fully. It is to hear what the nativized say and to be transformed in part by our appreciation of their stories. Applied to IR, it is an ability and willingness to investigate questions of gender in ways that open us up to the stories, identities, and places that have been by-passed in "our" debates. It is to become mobile in our subjectivities rather than fixed to one place of seeing and aping sovereign man. We cooperate when we "negotiate respectfully with contentious others" (K. Ferguson, 1993: 154) rather than chant old standards like a mantra. We cooperate when we look for sites where assigned places are being renegotiated in violation of usual standards. Cooperation also entails joint probings of meaning and action in the face of that empathetic breakdown in cherished and despised identities that leaves us creatively homeless in old IR. Empathetic cooperation enables "different worlds and ourselves within them" as we become world-wise in our devotion to unmaskings (Lugones, 1990: 396). *Feminist* knowledges deinvisibilize "women" and mestiza consciousnesses and, therefore, provide a good launching point to move from IR established by and on the basis of the knowledge of some to a realm of deciding IR locally, contextually, in an atmosphere of creative homelessness where participants are chastened by shifting understandings at the borderlands of many stories.

Trinh Minh-ha (1989: 1) offers us an example of respectful negotiations in a hypothetical village meeting held in an unnamed third world setting. She describes it this way:

> On the day and at the time agreed, each member eats, washes her/himself, and arrives only when s/he is ready. Things proceed smoothly as usual, and the discussion does not have to begin at a precise time, since it does not break in on daily village life but slips naturally into it. A mother continues to bathe her child amidst the group; two men go on playing a game they have started; a woman finishes braiding another woman's hair. These activities do not prevent their listening or intervening when necessary.

As the villagers reach for a decision:

> Never does one open the discussion by coming right to the heart of the matter. For the heart of the matter is always somewhere else than where it is supposed to be. To allow it to emerge, people approach it indirectly by postponing until it matures, by letting it come when it is ready to come. There is no catching, no pushing, no directing, no breaking through, no need for a linear progression which gives the comforting illusion that one knows where one goes ... The chief of the village does not "have the floor" for himself, nor does he talk more than anyone else. He is there to listen, to absorb, and to ascertain at the close what everybody has already felt or grown to feel during the session. (Ibid.: 1–2)

This seemingly far-off politics echoes in Tickner's standpoint concern to disable classical realism with a dynamic objectivity that shifts, sorts, and gradually moves us toward a more equitable, fluid, and less warring sense of community. It resonates in Elshtain's (1990a) call to construct communities that separate patriotism from nationalism on the basis of knowing limits and not trying to expand into all spaces to conquer homestead after homestead. Following up on themes she introduced in *Women and War*, Elshtain (1987: 175–6) later says:

> The chastened patriot – chastened in the sense of stripped of the excesses of nationalism – has learned the past. Rejecting a counsel of cynicism, she modulates the rhetoric of high patriotic purpose by keeping alive the distancing voice of ironic remembrance and rueful recognition of the way patriotism can shade into rapacious nationalism ... Chastened patriots cherish many loyalties and speak in many voices: a reclaimed patriotic choir is polyphonic.

A reclaimed patriotic choir in IR would be polyphonic precisely because its tones would emanate from many villages and from many homesteading experiences.

Empathetic conditions must hold for identities to slide and shift. Why else should women give up exclusive assignments as hair braiders and men give up chairing all meetings? Joyce Nielsen (1991: 29) argues that:

> If the context or setting is free enough – if the two people respect and trust each other and are roughly equal in materialistic terms – then both are free to engage in unlimited dialogue, and the resulting conversation is potentially very constructive, creative, and somewhat indeterminant (that is, not very predictable) ... Because verbal interaction is so dynamic, the discussants' ideas, thoughts, beliefs, and statements get developed, modified, and expanded in the course of being juxtaposed with other ideas, thoughts, theories, and so on.

This condition of equality seems to be the basis for the third world village meeting, a somewhat stateless setting, perhaps. What of dialogues between those who are not equal? How, Trinh (1989: 28) asks, to "inscribe difference without bursting into a series of euphoric narcissistic accounts of yourself and your own kind? ... Woman (with a capital W) may ... kill women if She loses the contact and speaks of Herself only according to what She wants to hear about Herself."

To empathize is to communicate across equal (commensurable) and unequal (incommensurable) subject positions until there is a general mobility of subjectivities, a general sense of some homelessness within the fixed positions one might have brought to the "village meeting," that inspires cooperative relations of theory building. This homelessness is not homesick for nostalgic realism and idealism. It is not a home port homelessness that leads established autonomous states to cooperate so as to avoid suboptimal outcomes. It is not the homey homelessness that comes from being the woman one is assigned to be. It is a politically achieved standpoint that keeps an eye on the serpent, who will not join the exercise, and the eagle who soars above it, while steadfastly keeping a third eye on the important process of rescripting ourselves as a way to begin rescripting IR.

The postmodern feminist approach to theorizing IR suggests the importance of re-viewing the body politics and re-doing our homework so that we consider, for the first time, that invested home spaces have a lot to do with what IR theory discusses and omits. To borrow a thought from Biddy Martin and Chandra Mohanty (1986: 192), what we have here is a process for a postmodern era that "unsettles not only any notion of feminism as an all-encompassing home but also the assumption that there are discrete, coherent, and absolutely separate identities – homes within feminism, so to speak [and within IR] – based on absolute divisions between various sexual, racial, or ethnic [and national] identities." The many dimensions of an empathetically cooperative postmodern feminist IR will surface as we continue into the second and third debates of a field.

Seekers of full-blown revisions, alternative models, and immediate replacement politics will be disappointed with this evaluation of the first debate in IR. We must be "we," however, and remember the many texts of complicity with and resistance to evacuations. We must recuperate stories and rewrite-homestead ourselves, in doing so, basing rewrites of IR on empathetic cooperation with difference. This can happen only if subalterns, the exiles from privacy and public action in-out of IR, get to contribute to homesteading projects without overrepresentation by those more fluent in the languages of IR (see Spivak, 1988). This is not the politics of liberalism, the hope of reconciling feminism and the first debate legacies of IR. It is the politics of liminality.

Remembering

The feminist break-in is a reminder that politics occurs in the recounting of realms of theory, in the crafting of a debate through point–counterpoint logic, in the building of a field of knowledge. It occurs in the power to draft "a defense against ... evocations of female power" (Elshtain, 1981: 16) and a defense against deconstructed subjects. This break-in is also a reminder that the first ones mentioned are usually the first ones remembered. The conventional placing of certain founding fathers before founding mothers often marks the originators indelibly and naturally as first and as foremost. The appropriation of a gendered script to the project of one group helps us remember all the appropriators (including some privileged women). The move toward a politics of empathetic cooperation, by contrast, teaches us the important lesson that we all have authority and yet "[n]one of us can pride ourselves on being sure-footed" (Trinh, 1989: 28).

3 THE SECOND DEBATE IN IR REVISITED BY FEMINISTS

Yale Ferguson and Richard Mansbach (1988: 80) maintain that "most societies have been characterized by the presence of several normative strains simultaneously competing with one another [and f]or this reason, theories of international relations which reflect one or another extreme have rarely monopolized scholarly discourse." IR's second debate corresponds, particularly in its later years, to the period in feminist theory known as the second wave – a time when feminist liberals, Marxists, socialists, and radicals systematically theorized and debated the forces of women's subjugation to or inequality with men, a time when they worked politically for public policy changes. IR's second debate also overlaps with feminist theory's third wave, particularly in as much as one can detect a convergence of IR fascination with science with feminist empiricist discussions of scientific ways of knowing.

Each wave of feminist theorizing borrowed from other social theories and included ideas explored in IR, such as the role of the state in structuring and restructuring gender relations. IR, by contrast, had a debate about methods and theory in isolation from feminist currents, as though the field had nothing to learn about gender, or as though IR's limited debate partners and issues refused challenges to authority and control that movements like feminism represented.

In the pages that follow, I rehearse aspects of the second debate in IR as a reminder of how the contemporary field emerged and as a prelude to comparisons between IR's debated methods – science versus tradition – and second-wave feminist insights. Where reasonable to do so, I also jump ahead in linear time, out of the queue again, to moments in feminism's third wave when developments in feminist empiricist and standpoint epistemologies help us mark the trail of IR's contemporary gender troubles, its "locus of intractability" that "presuppose[s] and preempts[s] the possibilities of imaginable and realizable gender configurations within culture" (Butler, 1990: 9).

100

IR's traditionalists and scientists lock horns

In the 1960s Hedley Bull offered his case for the classical method of IR analysis. He told us, in one of IR's more famous run-on sentences, what he meant by "classical":

> the approach to theorizing that derives from philosophy, history, and law, and that is characterized above all by explicit reliance upon the exercise of judgment and by the assumptions that if we confine ourselves to strict standards of verification and proof there is very little of significance that can be said about international relations, that general propositions about this subject must therefore derive from a scientifically imperfect process of perception or intuition, and that these general propositions cannot be accorded anything more than the tentative and inconclusive status appropriate to their doubtful origins. (Bull, 1969: 20)

Bull accused science-minded colleagues of intellectual puritanism in their insistence on building "a theory of international relations whose propositions are based either upon logical or mathematical proof, or upon strict, empirical procedures of verification" (ibid.: 21). He said: "they are committing themselves to a course ... that keeps them (or would keep them if they really adhered to it) as remote from the substance of international politics as the inmates of a Victorian nunnery were from the study of sex" (ibid.: 26). He pursued the metaphor of scientists as sequestered, implicitly priggish women further, by saying that when confronted with questions of theoretical weight, such as "does the collectivity of sovereign states constitute a political society or system, or does it not" (ibid.: 27), science-minded colleagues tended to:

> shy away and devote themselves to peripheral subjects – methodologies for dealing with the subject ... or they break free of their own code and resort suddenly and without acknowledging that this is what they are doing to the methods of the classical approach – methods that in some cases they employ very badly, their preoccupations and training having left them still strangers to the substance of the subject. (ibid.: 27–8)

Bull then reviewed the research of leading scientists and judged the quality as "sometimes high" (ibid.: 23) but likely "to contribute very little to the theory of international relations" (ibid.: 26), in part because the subject of IR "slip[s] between our fingers even as we try to categorize it" (ibid.: 30) and partly because the scientific approach "slips easily into a dogmatism ... attributing to the model a connection with reality it does not have" (ibid.: 31). In addition, Bull claimed that

101

the scientific approach suffered a "fetish for measurement ... [that] leads us to ignore relevant differences between the phenomena that are being counted" (ibid.: 33–4). Finally, he charged that:

> the practitioners of the scientific approach, by cutting themselves off from history and philosophy, have deprived themselves of the means of self-criticism, and in consequence have a view of their subject and its possibilities that is callow and brash ... their thinking is certainly characterized by a lack of any sense of inquiry into international politics as a continuing tradition to which they are the latest recruits; by an insensitivity to the conditions of recent history that have produced them, provided them with the preoccupations and perspectives they have, and colored these in ways of which they might not be aware ... by an uncritical attitude ... toward the moral and political attitudes that have a central but unacknowledged position in much of what they say. (ibid.: 37)

Advocates of science as a replacement for traditional analyses of IR, when they could agree on what science meant, offered two major critiques of traditionalism. First, they deemed it intolerable to continue cloaking IR in what they saw as a tradition of subjective interpretation lodged in the classicist's belief "that his training and experience have enabled him to glean from the data all the relevant meanings they contain" (Knorr and Rosenau, 1969: 15). Where the traditionalist has "confused the relationship between intuition and scientific knowledge" (M. Kaplan, 1969: 42), the scientist is compelled to view his own judgments as only a beginning; he must "render his findings as independent of himself as possible" (Knorr and Rosenau, 1969: 15). Second, there was the intolerable matter of single-variable analyses in classical IR – "the" drive for power, for instance – that had not been subjected to rigorous testing. The traditionalist rested too content with "statements about empirical regularities in various classes of phenomena" (O. Young, 1969: 132–3), ignoring the concerns of those "who wish to verify or extend his findings ... [s]atisfied that he has exercised the best judgment of which he is capable, [he] is not concerned about whether his findings can be replicated or refined under varying conditions" (Knorr and Rosenau, 1969: 16). The scientist, by contrast, claimed that one could not build theory in the absence of "a set of generalized propositions containing variables, hopefully with deductive interdependencies among the members of the set" (Levy, 1969: 92).

The arguments flew and civility was often lost as the scientists ganged up on the traditionalists. Morton Kaplan (1969: 59) pointedly claimed that traditionalists had no special grasp on philosophical analysis – "few of them ... have demonstrated any disciplined know-ledge of philosophy" – and offered the nationalist riposte that tradi-tionalism was lodged in the "somewhat less distinguished" English branch of political science. Marion Levy (1969: 87) described Bull as anti-intellectual when it came to science: "He thinks Those Others cannot deliver the goods called for in their heavenly pronounce-ments." Oran Young (1969: 134) charged that traditionalist Raymond Aron's (1966) work was "studded with statements that are nominally in the form of empirical generalizations [that] ... degenerate very quickly into an informed search for insights."

If the debate tended at times to juxtapose tyrannical philistinisms against one another, it did occasionally avoid the worst sinking recri-minations. J. David Singer (1969) attempted to illustrate that the turn to science represented more continuity than discontinuity with prescien-tific approaches. David Vital (1969: 151) thought there was some dis-continuity of an unexpected type in the scientific approach: "while one can sense and sympathize with the urgency of the desire of the 'scientists' to introduce new techniques and new topics into the field, one remains unconvinced that the preferred combinations of topics and techniques are all of such weight as to contribute even indirectly to a substantially improved understanding of the matter in hand"; in the end he also came down against the classical tradition (for obscur-ing the facts of international life) and pronounced a middle, discipline-integrating ground as the study of governments in their foreign rela-tions. Michael Haas (1969) pleaded for bridge-building exercises; Robert Jervis (1969), foreshadowing the third discipline-defining debate in IR, argued for plural approaches; and Klaus Knorr and James Rosenau (1969: 18) asked simply: "why could not the adherents of each approach exploit each other's work?"

Certain accommodations, however, were not made, and in the absence of a feminist intervention at this point one might not notice them. From the unveiling of de Beauvoir's *Second Sex* in the late 1940s into the radical years of the 1960s and early 1970s, feminists looked for ways "to situate themselves in reality so as to redesign their 'feminine' condition" (Braidotti, 1991: 147). They were nothing if not energetic in devising projects to recover and valorize "women's intellectual facul-ties, creativity, imagination, and intelligence, as well as ... their civil and political rights, and ... places of production and the transmission of knowledge" (ibid.: 148). Their innovative reformulations of theory and practice then entered the university through women's studies programs.

IR, struggling to make its independent mark on knowledge and practice, did not explore the feminist places inside and around their texts. It was not necessary to do so any more than it was necessary to take into account literary theory, geology, or art history, although it was apparently crucial, some second-debaters argued, to take on board aspects of physics, psychology, sociology, mathematics, and history. Perhaps feminism was too fantastical to take seriously because of its "soft" attention to matters of language use, biology, spirituality, and social critique. There was also the spectacle of "women" writing theory to ponder:

> how could women elaborate a true theory? A theory which would be rigorous, systematic, linear? Women, the eternal dark continent of man-kind, the blindspot of all processes of theorization, beggars at the philosophical banquet, seem unable to come into their own theoretically. A women's truth, expressed by women, seems endlessly fragmented, scattered, divided within itself – and always devalued. (ibid.: 149–50)

Feminist theorizing also paid attention to norms and to a range of ideals encompassing equality, emancipation, separatism, and political struggle. In the climate of IR's second debate, "the language of power and interests rather than ideals or norms" was *de rigueur* (Keohane, 1986: 9). Thus, Bull could blithely and without guile call IR scientists "women" as a way of discrediting them. Levy could paint Bull as a high and mighty authority vis-à-vis "Those Others" who "cannot deliver the goods," an accusation laden with emasculative meaning owing to the usual association of the other with "woman." The scientists in general supposed they could step outside themselves so completely that they could, ideally, discover "construction[s] that cannot assume a human constructor prior to the construction" (Butler, 1990: 8). What the second-debaters did not see was that their disparaging labels for each other, as "women" or as Those Others, brought the fantastical ones into the texts of IR. "Women" were necessary to help define what the field was not.

Occasionally, "women" entered IR texts in other ways. Consider this passage from scientists in the science/tradition debate:

> The relationship between a scholar and his subject matter is inevitably an intimate and delicate one. His materials make demands on his talent, challenge his beliefs, tax his patience, resist his advances. His data can test his tolerance, provoke his curiosity, sustain his confidence. His findings can humiliate or exhilarate, perplex or enlighten, dismay or encourage. (Knorr and Rosenau, 1969: 6–7)

At first glance, here is the tiresome grammar of men owning the identity of "scholar" and approaching their "otherized" subject matter like some of them advance on "women" (when they are being polite) – with curiosity, patience and hope of avoiding a humiliating rejection for the exhilaration of a relationship. Knorr and Rosenau also speak, however, of an intimacy in the scholar–subject relationship that some maternalist feminist standpointers might associate with a mother and the person who is of her and yet simultaneously apart – her child. Children make demands, challenge, tax, and resist their mothers. The mother finds the experience provoking and sustaining, humiliating or exhilarating (male parents can also identify with this scripting). This piece of text has a standpoint to it that absents "women" (and tasks historically assigned to them, irrespective of whether some "men" may perform parenting) by appropriating their usual travails. It should be read against the language of the despised "women" inserted in the texts when needed to foil Those Others who encroach on proper IR.

As for the traditionalists in the debate, Bull had said that scientists were ignorant of the historical sources of their perspectives. He had suggested that they take a critical posture toward the moral and political attitudes encrusted in what they said. Both admonitions could have opened the door to new explorations of the history, culture, and politics of gender and race in international relations. Indeed, Bull's charges intimated that there was more to the stories of international relations than met the eye. He brought the other stories to the brink of voice, however, and, along with his colleagues, went no further.

IR as a science: Waltzian neorealism

As the rhetoric of this abstract moment in the debate ebbed, the scientists won the political science departments of land grant universities in the US and the traditionalists ensconced themselves in British universities and in some US Ivy League institutions. On both sides of the Atlantic and both sides of the methods debate, the fight continued over "professional and institutional well-being in the face of theoretical disarray and disciplinary adversity" (Ferguson and Mansbach, 1988: 22).

Although the scientists were stern about the technical requirements of the field, by the late 1970s one among them, Kenneth Waltz (1979), was speaking disparagingly about the state of scientific knowledge. "Students of international politics," he told us, "use the term 'theory' freely, often to cover any work that departs from mere description and seldom to refer only to work that meets philosophy-of-science standards" (ibid.: 1). Moreover, they habitually prefer to work inductively rather than deductively, examining "numerous cases with the hope

105

that connections and patterns will emerge and that those connections and patterns will represent the frequently mentioned 'reality that is out there'" (ibid.: 4).

These comments took aim both at "historically minded traditionalists and scientifically oriented modernists ... [on the grounds that] the difference in the methods they use obscures the similarity of their methodology" (ibid.: 61). Waltz swung his axe at the cast of science buffs who had skewered Bull, accusing many of them of turning the results they observed in their analyses into causes they then assigned to actors. He decapitated the traditionalists for similarly grounding their studies in "the attitudes and characteristics of states" (ibid.: 62). Both groups were closet behavioralists, he claimed, who endeavored to keep the realist state at the center of their correlational analyses at the expense of higher-order configurations that could explain what states are in the international system and what they can do. They did not seem to appreciate that "theory is not the occurrences seen and the associations recorded, but is instead the explanation of them" (ibid.: 9).

To be sure, one could and should, Waltz said (ibid.: 12), emulate the analytical method of classical physics and apply statistics when the number of variables becomes large. But "[m]any modern students spend much of their time calculating Pearsonian coefficients of correlation ... attaching numbers to the kinds of impressionistic associations between internal conditions and international outcomes that traditionalists so frequently offer" (ibid.: 64). Theory was languishing and so was the authority of the theorist, for whom "[t]he urge to explain is not born of idle curiosity alone [but] is produced also by the desire to control, or at least to know if control is possible, rather than merely to predict" (ibid.: 6).

Indeed, the field of IR had an impressive amount of scientific work in print; but even within the ranks, there were fissures around the question of what, specifically, the researcher should study – foreign policy, leadership qualities, war – and at what level the important puzzles of IR should be addressed. The field was dogged by "temperamental differences among individual scholars" (Olson and Onuf, 1985: 8) as well as by methodological pluralism. Realism was an echo in everyone's head at the time; some say it was a paradigm (Holsti, 1985). But from Waltz's perspective, there was no grand theory, no movement from realist echoes to a theory of IR with precise specifications.

Waltz (1979) responded by metamorphosing realism into scientific realism, kneading his understanding of theory with scientific method into a stiff and icy beast meant to overwhelm all vicissitudes and unorthodoxies. In his scheme of things, a theory of international

106

politics would tell us how "outcomes are affected not only by the properties and interconnections of variables but also by the way in which they are organized" (ibid.: 39). His theory would be properly systemic because "[i]n international politics, system-level forces seem to be at work" (ibid.) (and because, one might add, it was *au courant* in the natural sciences to speak of General Systems Theory, and political science was desperate to attain the legitimacy of those sciences). While "still talking about the same old things" (Ferguson and Mansbach, 1988: 195), Waltz invented the international state system in the following neorealist terms.

Anarchy, the lack of formal governance, stood as the main ordering principle of system structure. The units of the system – states – were scripted as functionally undifferentiated entities that always struggle for security and survival through the accumulation and use of capabilities. Anarchy inclined states to be egoistic self-helpers who "determine their interests and strategies on the basis of calculations about their own positions in the system" (Keohane, 1989a: 41). Each one had to spend "a portion of its efforts, not in forwarding its own good, but in providing the means of protecting itself against others" (Waltz, 1979: 105). And, "as in any self-help system, the units of greatest capability set the scene of action for others as well as for themselves" (ibid.: 72). This system structure removed as an incentive for cooperation the prospect of absolute gains for all involved, owing to a ubiquitous concern with each other's prospects for relative gains in capabilities. "Fear of such unwanted consequences stimulates states to behave in ways that tend toward the creation of balances of power" (ibid.: 118).

Waltz believed that the enduring anarchy of the state system could "not be wished away, although many fail to understand this" (ibid.: 109). Moreover, he saw virtue in the lower maintenance costs of anarchic structure and in the moderating tendencies such a system has on the use of force: "[t]he possibility that conflicts among nations may lead to long and costly wars has ... sobering effects" (ibid.: 114). One sobering effect that Waltz especially celebrated was the bipolar balance of power. In his view, this balance was keeping the peace in a cold war era by decreasing interdependence in the system and, by Waltz's economic reasoning, reducing dangerous vulnerabilities. Moreover, "[w]ith only two great powers, both can be expected to act to maintain the system" (ibid.: 204). Thus, "[t]he inequality of states, though it provides no guarantee, at least makes peace and stability possible" (ibid.: 132), just as an oligopolistic arrangement of firms increases economic stability (ibid.: 134–5).

Neorealism as strategic reasoning dressed up and at home

There have been many critiques of neorealism from within the field of international relations (see e.g., Keohane, 1986; Ashley, 1984; Wendt, 1987; Ferguson and Mansbach, 1988). Virtually none of these, however, has focused on the gender implications of the Waltzian picture.[1] Starting with Waltz's views on theory, third-wave feminist empiricists and second-wave critics of women-denying societies turn the tables around each subsequent feature of his edifice.

Good science, Sandra Harding (1991: 16) maintains, exposes the "culturewide interests, values, and assumptions that end up functioning as evidence 'behind the back' of the natural and social sciences." Bad science reveals its makers as people "who do not worry about how being men may distort their intellectual work" (Flax, 1987: 629). What about "good" and "bad" theories? What would feminists say are their characteristics?

A good theory, like good science, say feminist empiricists, is embedded in a context that the theorist acknowledges. That context infuses the critical plane of researcher and subject just as much as it circulates "out there." In other words, the theorist is not someone apart, someone able to escape into deductive logic to gain a special gaze that is immune from the contaminations of daily inductions. The theorist should not, therefore, try to mask social location with appeals to culturewide, state, or system interests. The good theory should especially avoid the tasteless exhibit of masculine taxidermy in the Hall of Mankind (next to the gallery of large vertebrate (fixedly) non-humans, like elephants). Good theory simply cannot be the vision of one group furtively collapsed into the vision of all. It is not "man" infused into the constructs he creates, shaking his fist at the very idea that "men" could make such a reductionist mistake.

In the spirit of Waltz commenting on his colleagues' creations of good and bad theory in IR, we can turn in a parallel direction to consider lessons that emerge for IR from a feminist scientist's evaluations of theory building in the field of primatology. The evaluator in question is Donna Haraway (1989) and the research she contrasts is by Linda Marie Fedigan (1982; 1986), whose insights on evolution are upheld as good theory, and John Tooby and Irven DeVore (1987), who have not learned their feminist lessons and therefore attempt to imbue a social process with fixed and timeless qualities.

Physical anthropologist Fedigan explores the way gender plays out in the scientific effort to build models of human evolution. She argues that sex and gender are usually narrated at the boundary between the hominoid and the hominid and this constrains how we think about what it means to be a man or a woman. A little background is necessary to appreciate this argument.

The study of evolution, particularly from primates to humans, has tended to project onto primates and early humans the social institutions and mental processes (or lack thereof) that we commonly associate with contemporary human life. Humanness becomes marked by the appearance of the familiar, physically and socially. At the turn of the century, for example, Robert Yerkes (e.g., 1930) studied "scales of mental function as an indicator of increased organizational complexity (Haraway, 1989: 74) and presented the "family" as a key sign of evolution in consciousness, a move, Haraway points out, that contributes to a scientific construction of compulsory heterosexuality. He and others painted evolving beings as occupants of peaceful nuclear units that seemed to operate by a sexual division of labor, with the male always the head of the household. One can observe the fruits of this "scientific" interpretation in the dioramas of the American Museum of Natural History (New York). In one, a giant male primate stands as a double for man, beating his chest in alarm as he prepares to protect his family from danger. He is the Giant of Karisimbi "at the interface of the Age of Mammals and the Age of Man" (Haraway, 1989: 31). Then there is Lucy, the three-million-year-old grandmother skeleton. Lucy "was quickly made into a hominid mother and faithful wife, a more efficient producing machine than her apish sisters and a reliable, if poorly upholstered, sex doll" (ibid.: 281–2).

There are other projections of familiar familial mores in the supposedly scientific literature of primatology. Owen Lovejoy (1981; 1984) "explains" the sexual division of labor as a moment of humanizing change in primates, a moment when, in Haraway's (1989: 192–3) paraphrasing of his work:

> [f]emales had reached their maximum of ergonomic efficiency and just couldn't make babies fast enough in new conditions without some help. Always imagined to be in excess of mere functional requirements, male energy, this time, at least, directed toward helping out at home, propelled the species over the line between nature and culture and into that marvelous adaptation called ever after "the family."

This is utter masculinism, says Haraway, and shoddy science. Nothing a female could do could lead the species across the hominoid–hominid boundary. According to Lovejoy, she was already doing the best nature allowed: "Maternity is inherently conservative and requires

109

husbanding to become truly fruitful, to move from animal to human" (Haraway, 1989: 282). Lovejoy crowned his "scientific" study with a strategic explanation: "[m]ales arose to stand upright so that ... provisioning [of a sedentary maternal mate] would be rewarded by making them into Man, a father, desiring subject, and author" (ibid.: 282). This type of explanation assumes, of course, that "the female must remain constantly attractive to the male" (ibid.: 282).

Switching now to Fedigan, Haraway says that her explicit interest in studying gender in evolution marks a departure from the usual research. It is a focus that is wholly appropriate to theory building because Fedigan endeavors to construct "accounts *of* and *for* specific kinds of life" (ibid.: 8), rather than trying to comment without acknowledged political intent on the truth of something. Fedigan's method is also exemplary. It:

> draws from literatures and debates marked as both scientific and feminist. [Fedigan] highlights the immersion of evolutionary science in western cultural history, and she uses recent literary scholarship to analyze the structure of narrative in evolutionary modeling. None of this destroys the authority of her scientific discourse; it constructs a different model of authority with a strong premium on explicit discussion of deeply constitutive cultural mediation, including mediations of her own writing. Several kinds of reasoning are given historical location, to show how they might make sense to constituencies inside certain discursive traditions. She does not reduce models of legitimate reason and explanation to agonistic strategic reasoning. Her histories do not lump together all feminist interventions into evolutionary arguments, but differentiate among contending feminist accounts and lineages of arguments. (ibid.: 325)

What results is an account of "laws" about gender and the construction of evolutionary narratives that explains where the seeming fixity of gender has been embedded in models of evolution and how those "laws" are really just narratives that unfold over time. Fedigan shatters notions of female primates as passive, family-bound reproducers and shows individual females engaged in recreation, and ageing, communicating and otherwise being agents of their own daily experience. She throws water on the usual strategic understanding of all primate behavior as bearing signs of adaptation; reproductive modes, for instance, emerge for her as possibilities rather than as laws. Going further, she traces the transition of sex to gender as a topic in relation to some understandings of human evolution and warns that "if people become what they think they are, *what* they think they are is exceedingly important" (Fedigan, 1982: 7).

Fedigan's and Haraway's approaches to theory building seem

greatly at odds with, and more resonant with critical theoretical approaches than, Waltz's project. Haraway maintains, however, that there is little difference between feminist science and the goals of science in general. Both are "critical projects built in order to destabilize and reimagine their methods and objects of knowledge in complex power fields. Addressed to each other, western feminist and scientific discourses "warp each other's story fields and redraw possible positions for claiming to know something about the world ..." (Haraway, 1989: 324).

You would not know that from reading the study of evolutionary models that is presented by Tooby and DeVore (1987). To Haraway, their work can sound scientific precisely because it does not explore the "cultural and intellectual history of nineteenth and twentieth century discourses on evolution [as] *problems of narration and representation*" (Haraway, 1989: 326 [emphasis added]). Rather:

> Tooby and DeVore appeal to the potent mythic history of great physical science and its grand models of heaven and earth ... [a]dvocating what they call "conceptual models" that privilege "strong deductive principles" claimed to be available now to biology ... Tooby and DeVore affiliate their own form of argument to Maxwell, Newton, and Einstein. (ibid.: 326)

Their theory also advances the notion of "strategic reasoning" as the sign of early human behavior, as the *modus vivendi* of human activity. Says Haraway (1989: 327), not only the hunting activities that anthropologists have usually assigned to men, but "[a]ll the important actors, from gene to organism are recast in [the Tooby and DeVore and other] evolutionary narratives as strategists in a vast game whose stakes are reproductive fitness, i.e., staying in the game as long as possible." Haraway's analysis suggests that Tooby and DeVore reach, as an explicator of evolution's logic, for the strategic reasoning that ensures "reproductive fitness," without problematizing "reproductive fitness" or strategic reasoning as sites "of discourse about the limits and promises of the self as individual" (ibid.: 352). In fact, one could say that reproductive fitness is something of a bogus concern, since individuals cannot really reproduce themselves – with fitness and elan or with anything else – because the gene "issue from the self is always (an)other" (ibid.: 352). That is, as de Beauvoir (1952, ch. 1) pointed out decades ago, no one body can claim authorship of reproduction because genes are composite materials from two individuals. Says Haraway (1989: 352): "Short of cloning, that staple of science fiction, neither parent is continued in the child, who is a randomly reassembled genetic package." With strategic reasoning rather than human

111

interaction preserving the species, we are not surprised to learn that all of the papers Tooby and DeVore cite as providing the "theory" or "strong conceptual models" that feed their own research are by "men" (ibid.: 326).

To Haraway, these moves unify "[t]he world of theory and the world itself" around "exercises in military-like strategies" in the face of a timeless dilemma. She says the language of strategic reasoning "itself militarizes the field of biological interaction and the cognitive processes of human reasoning, including what will count as scientific theory" (ibid.: 327). The work of Tooby and DeVore is the lone entry in a conference volume under the subsection "Theoretical Issues": their piece has the imprimatur of science and "all the other papers ... become examples of this or that model, but not theory itself" (ibid.: 326). The military-like strategy plays out to the end.

The approach to theory that Haraway applauds stands upright, or is four-legged, if one prefers, on the cusp of seemingly incommensurable ways of knowing. One can see in her evaluation considerable feminist empiricist concern to promote a science that features the researcher doing his homework thoroughly and checking to see that the work of feminists makes it into the analyses. This simple measure is an exercise in bias-reduction; one cannot, after taking this step, then construct research questions in isolation from the often startlingly unorthodox conclusions that gender-sensitive research can generate. One cannot, for instance, continue to talk about human moral development in the male-biased ways that Kohlberg did once Gilligan's corrective work is taken into account (whether one happens to agree with all aspects of her approach or not), without raising alarm in some readers.

Haraway, however, is also a postmodernist thinker, particularly in her attention to the structure of narratives and concern with representation in primatology. Moreover, feminist standpoint thinking comes to play in her interest in the historical and cultural traditions that help shape our understanding of evolution in a masculine way. Her rich approach is fully consonant with Harding's (1991: 138) descriptions of a scientific process that is part of the critical social sciences in its acknowledgement of "the social-situatedness – the historicity – of the very best beliefs any culture has arrived at or could in principle 'discover.'" This is science with a stronger version of objectivity than the corner-cutting approach Haraway finds in Tooby and DeVore, where "conceptual models" and "strong deductive principles" are asserted as sources of authority.

Now think of Waltz on scientific theory. Waltz wants "to redraw possible positions for claiming to know something about the world";

112

but like Tooby and DeVore, he draws on a very narrow and limited understanding of "positions." His work, no less than theirs, proffers a litany of "men's" efforts, in this case to explain the reproduction of realist international relations. It foregrounds the repetitive propensity of modern societies to take as given the equation of culture with masculinity. Thus Waltz does not see that the state-in-anarchy is reminiscent of an adolescent male who is trying desperately to be correct as a "man" and who, therefore, black-boxes internal conflicts and embraces the order associated with an out(of)law gang. He does not explore the possibility that "anarchy" may key into the scientific aspiration to control disorderliness by balancing powers and reducing vulnerabilities. He criticizes men who do not share his standards of science and, indeed, black-boxes all men in his effort to locate system dynamics beyond statesmen. But he cannot relegate "men" to homelessness because they have a place in the public sphere of science and politics. It is their interpretations we hear. Relatedly, he does not fully explore the question of state capabilities by asking how "women" figure into state resources (see Sylvester, 1992a). He does not help the reader appreciate any potential interrelationship of gender and state and anarchy. Gender is irrelevant. Evolutionary in tone and tact – Waltz will finally move us to the pinnacle of theory and reduce other efforts to a laughable status – trends in feminist scholarship that challenge masculinist evolutions to gender-blind systems theory are not acknowledged. Waltz shifts the level of analysis to system dynamics, but the masculine is there too, in a gender reductionism that defies his critique of other behavioralist reductionisms in IR.

Consider a few feminist angles on Waltzian-type analysis. From a radical feminist perspective, anarchy may be a subterfuge that keeps women from discerning patterns of patriarchy in the whole. Mary Daly (1978: 19) contends, with characteristic irreverence and more than a shade of military-emulating strategizing herself, that in "'the Land of the Fathers,' the more blatant the lie the greater its credibility, for it is then most consistent with the general pattern of bizarre beliefs." Anarchy would be one of those great lies and bizarre beliefs that denies "the interconnectedness of things" (ibid.: 19–20), that prevents us from "seeing through The Whole Thing" (ibid.: 20). Its sign frightens and immobilizes us into thinking that an absence of male-led governance on the international level makes it imperative to accept the protections of men at "home," even though in doing so "women" are mocked in our cultures for being so vulnerable. Anarchy, in this understanding, would be part of a "protection racket," all the pieces of which work to obscure our locations and choices and the extent to which the protectors escape accountability by perpetuating the lie that the unitary state is comprised of equal parties to a contract (Peterson, 1992b).

From a liberal feminist perspective, women are "protected" as a substitute for having equal rights with men. Men can be eligible for better jobs and pay in liberal societies while the extension of these privileges to women always entails a struggle accompanied by talk of impending social anarchy and ruined families. One would think that local social order just crumbled whenever women were "allowed" to cross-dress in garb suit-able for public arenas. In this, one reads the doubleness of a move to contain national anarchic tendencies by entrusting women with the orderly transmission of masculine values from one generation to another, while implicitly placing "women" in a state of anarchic nature by assigning us to a fixed irrationality and unruliness (said a fellow passenger to me on a recent domestic flight: "My god! Is that a woman's voice up there in the cockpit? Is she going to try and fly this plane?").

Feminist socialists claim that the master balance of power that underlies all other relationships is capitalist-patriarchy. The anarchy of the capitalist market justifies discrimination against women in employment, and patriarchy determines that the public realm is "defined in opposition to dangerous, disorderly, and irrational forces ... consistently conceptualized as female" (Hartsock, 1982: 238). Waltz may have thought of anarchy as the absence of formal authority and not as the presence of chaos or disorder (Donnelly, 1992: 87). However, those who set themselves up as scientific authorities on the international system, all the while denying that official authority exists for that system, decide that anarchy means the absence of formal governance "out there." They do not recognize that the political realm of no government is actually a gender-ruled space that forecloses a potential site for (disorderly) "women" in politics.

Taking this point further, Waltz may also have demoted the state in systemic IR in a manner analogous to the way social contract theorists smothered "women" in the nation-state. At "home," "women" were controlled through the sexual contract that kept them marginal to the socially contracted public realm. Analogously, neorealism ratified a realist anarchy contract that would keep states in the system while constraining what they could do there. However, states were at least given rationality and capabilities by the neorealists (and realists before them), whereas "women" inside states were outside the public sphere of rationality. Functionally similar rational states could go about their self-regarding neorealist business of survival in their own ways: "we do not ask whether states are revolutionary or legitimate, authoritarian or democratic, ideological or pragmatic. We abstract from every attribute of states except their capabilities" (Waltz, 1979: 99). "Women" could not go about any important public business. Groups of "women" could attempt to challenge the routes of survival that their states followed, but neorealist theorists would not-see their efforts, owing to "women's" long evacuation from politics and to the invention of the state as a nonsocial place. Placed outside politics in the private civil sphere of the nation, "women's" actions would surely be incapable of affecting the capabilities of socially isolated neorealist states. These functionally similar states would be given no language in which to formulate the idea that "women" might become public resources – say in combat military roles – in ways that could translate into relative gains (Sylvester, 1992a).

Profiled against feminist activities of the 1970s, the timing of neorealism's rise is revealing. At a moment when there was militancy in "1968" Europe and in the US (in part attributable to the Vietnam war), Waltz was endeavoring to black-box every feature of states except their capabilities "to stay in the game as long as possible."[2] He made a system that was transhistorically stable and whose tenets legitimated the ideological superstructure of the capitalist world-system better than realism alone could (thus Waltz's analogies with firms and markets). That superstructure existed "for its cadres who [a]re, along with the thin stratum of large-scale accumulators of capital, its principal beneficiaries" (Wallerstein, 1991: 117). While the women's movement challenged the preserves of gender and class privilege within the societies that neorealists black-boxed, and within the theories that provided the pillars of western knowledge, the neorealist project in strategic reasoning bolstered "the potent mythic history" of "men's" authority in science, the key symbol of modern humanist control. It put "men" on top of the evolutionary chain.

Neorealism thus was free from the distractions of race, class, national, and gender differences: if the South was less effectual in international relations than the North, it had to be because the states of that region had low capabilities and were constrained by the system. Through the levels-of-analysis convention that was adopted during the second debate (see Singer, 1961), neorealism was also preserved from "strangely" located investigations that would reveal the underpinnings of gender within it.

Overall, neorealism emerged as "theory" policing social boundaries in the name of scientific explanation. By contrast, the type of theory that Haraway discusses exposes the privileges and biases built into boundary drawings and explains them as a means of explaining the issue at hand. Some feminist theorizing of the second and third waves replicated boundary exercises in ways that resonated with the neorealist effort (that is, radical feminism and essentialist streams in feminist standpoint). The ensemble of feminist theorizing, however, unlike second-debate theorizing in IR, "warped each other's stories" as it redrew possible positions for "claiming to know something about the world."

Other projects in scientific IR – with feminist responses

Waltz's emphasis on a systemically savvy scientific IR spawned new, and justified existing, neorealist-resonating projects. Security studies, for example, gathered impetus before the Second World War and took off after it as a study, in part, of deterrence strategies and systems (this will be discussed in chapter 5). Various large data-gathering projects analyzed international transactions (Rummel, 1969; McClelland and Hoggard, 1969). A plethora of neorealist-resonating research emerged on balance-of-power politics and war (e.g., Mandelbaum, 1981; Bueno de Mesquita, 1981; Singer, 1979), on hegemonic stability and world-systems (Gilpin, 1981; Wallerstein, 1974; 1980);[3] on long cycles (Modelski, 1987; Goldstein, 1988); and on power transitions (Organski and Kugler, 1980). There is now an extensive neorealist literature on international political economy (e.g. Krasner, 1985; Gilpin, 1987; Grieco, 1990).

The turn to science in US-based IR also egged on a variety of scientific critiques of realist assumptions and spawned efforts to refine Waltz's systemic theory. Aspects of two challenging literatures – on decision making and on cooperation under anarchy – are highlighted next to show that the IR many of us inherited from the second debate is in a world of gender trouble over, beyond, through, and around its many scientific projects.[4]

Issues of bounded rationality

The realist assumption that states rationally pursue national interest, which is reiterated in neorealist assumptions of rational unitary states, was never fully consensual. It coexisted with efforts to show that the state (effectively the US state), conducted foreign policy in a field of bounded rather than full rationality (Verba, 1961). Graham Allison (1969; 1971), for instance, proffered three decision-making models, one based on rationality and the others grounded in less rational organizational and bureaucratic processes. Alexander George published *Presidential Decisionmaking in Foreign Policy* in 1980 in an effort to help policymakers minimize the irrationalities in decision making to which Allison alerted us. Both works are now part of a large literature that addresses the psychological (individual personality characteristics, cognitive codes, perceptual lenses, attitudes, and belief systems) and the operational milieux (bureaucracies, group dynamics, elite characteristics) of policymaking. This literature operates, ostensibly, at a different level of analysis than the one Waltz sought to elevate as "the" level for IR theorizing. It shows that there is considerable gender continuity across all the spaces and hierarchies that mark contemporary IR (see R. Walker, 1993).

As we all know, the quintessential individual in decision making is a government official or member of the elite whose career path has placed him in proximity to official foreign policymaking. He brings to the process a particular history and corresponding world view comprised of beliefs about how the world works and values about how it should work (see overview in Little and Smith, 1988) that resist changes in information, tolerance for ambiguity being especially weak in crisis situations (A. George, 1974; Lebow, 1981; O. Holsti, 1969). These prisms guide goal formation at the same time that they "distort what is seen" (Holsti, 1969: 544) and reduce the possibility of reaching a rational decision strategically by ranking values and goals, weighing alternative courses of action, and calculating the costs and benefits of each action.

In *Presidential Decisionmaking in Foreign Policy*, Alexander George (1980: 4) asks us to consider "impediments that can lower the quality of information, analysis, and advice available for making important foreign-policy decisions and that can distort the president's judgment in making such choices." These impediments, he tells us, include "value-complexity" – multiple, competing values and interests embedded in a single issue that result in trade-off decisions or that "arouse a variety of motives and interests extraneous to values associated with even a broad conception of the 'national interest'" (ibid.: 26–7). There is also the impediment of uncertainty, owing to "the lack of adequate information about the situation at hand and/or the inadequacy of available general knowledge needed for assessing the expected outcomes of different courses of action" (ibid.: 27).

The decision maker must make a decision or foreign policy will be rudderless. All decision makers, however, must tame value complexity and reduce uncertainty in order to decide, and the way any individual

117

decision maker does so seems to depend on the tools he draws from a sack of packaged strategies. George discusses "devices" to reduce uncertainty and offers seven "rules" for success, among them satisficing to settle for a less than maximum payoff, aiming at a series of small decisions rather than one major decision, and sequencing decisions. A rule framework of this type must depend on objectified forms of knowledge that are independent of particular subjectivities and that appear in rationally standardized forms invariant as to time, place, and the particular perspectives, interests, and will of participants (D. Smith, 1990). George imposes a rational framework of rules on the problem of decision making even as he seeks to explain the impediments to rationality.

His "impediments," "devices," and "rules," however, are incomplete because he does not consider issues of rationality that feminists have pondered. He does not consider the second-wave feminist psychoanalytic insight, for instance, that the gendering process in western societies sets up the framework for irrationality by irrationally encouraging "men" to establish reactive autonomy – initially from "women" and then from other close attachments – as a central tendency in their lives. The flip side of that coin is that rationality assumptions may derive from unexamined cultural expectations that "men are supposed to be motivated by calculations of instrumental or other 'rational' considerations" (Harding, 1986a: 86; see Millman and Kanter, 1975). Indeed, George neglects to tell us that the decision maker is assumed unproblematically to be and, in fact, usually is a "man," which means that "non-decision-makers" are unproblematically "not-men." As long as "women" do not occupy more high decision making posts in foreign policy, emphases on rationality in the IR literature can bolster the commonplace view that international politics is a "man's" domain.

Thus, "women" appear in George's analysis only briefly but replete with typical mind-numbing traits:

> Taft's ambitious wife helped Roosevelt drag Taft into running as the Republican presidential candidate in 1908. Taft's eighty-year-old mother, on the other hand, knew her son well enough to write to him in 1907, trying to discourage him from agreeing to become Roosevelt's hand-appointed successor: she pointedly observed that "Roosevelt is a good fighter and enjoys it, but the malice of politics would make you miserable." This proved to be an accurate prediction! (George, 1980: 6, quoting Hargrove, 1966: 76)

Taft's wife and her mother-in-law are hereby naturalized as parenthetical representations of the knowing mother, from whom one

THE SECOND DEBATE IN IR

separates at some cost in self-knowledge, in competition with the ambitious siren whose tempting words alone can lead a good man to make a bad decision. If only Taft had listened to his mother. But can a western adult "man" listen to the one he has struggled to deny in himself through the long gendering process without getting into some gender trouble? Alternatively, are there not ways to render emotional aspects of decisions rational when "men" engage in them, as when they become positive or negative altruists in certain game-theoretic contexts (Gowa, 1986)?

Graham Allison's (1969) three scenarios of decision making during the Cuban missile crisis cut the rationality problem differently by featuring successive moves away from rational certainty. The rational policy scenario, Allison's "standard frame of reference" (ibid.: 693), presents decision making as a cool and calculated process that involves talking heads with no bodily needs, no prior histories, no social dysfunctions, and no distractions. Nothing mars the exercise of judgment, neither intrigue, distrust, neurosis, sabotage, alcoholism, parental demands, or physical discomfort. There is "one set of perceived options, and a single estimate of the consequences that follow from each alternative" (ibid.: 694). Cost-effective value maximization is the rational choice and the procedure for reaching it entails a fairly mechanical estimation of the net valuation of each set of consequences.

Allison points out that the rational decision-making model "is an analogue of the theory of the rational entrepreneur which has been developed extensively in economic theories of the firm and the consumer" (ibid.: 694, n27). It features a strategic form of rationality as an abstract calculus of means to ends over other possible types of rationality, including affective or more choice-oriented varieties. Implicitly, it also features the talking heads of otherwise male-bodied people, for there is not a she-body among the ExCom members deliberating about missiles in Cuba or among the leading organizational and bureaucratic figures that Allison factors into the Cuban missile crisis. One is meant to think that this does not matter, that decisional processes are not gendered. A feminist empiricist perspective, however, takes note of a scenario that is based on the experiences of one gender, and very elite members of that gender at that, and reminds us that it is not valid and reliable to build generalizable models of decision making on a partial base. The gender-neutrality of the models must be justified or one can argue that they are biased by the cultural construction of "men" as Every-body.

Against a sterile (but decidedly not apolitical) model of decision

119

making under assumptions of rationality, Allison juxtaposes messier scenarios displaying organizational and bureaucratic processes. The organizational scenario centers the decision process around loosely allied state agencies that are presided over by top government leaders. Each agency has a particularistic mission, set of priorities in advancing that mission, and an independent information base that reflects its own standard operating procedures. All this padding assists the agency in avoiding the prospect of nakedness on the main streets of opportunity. An organization is the backdrop against which men caught up in larger-than-life machinery lose their identities (rather than hyphenating them) to take on roles. But who exactly is caught up this way? Would we decenter this model by asking the feminist standpoint question of whether a secretary to the organizational man is similarly molded by her employment? Is it the case that she becomes intimate with the machinery of agency reproduction such that her identities merge with her organizational role, or is "role" in this context another term for male bonding, patriarchy, alienation from sites of "women"?

Allison's third scenario features knowers who are objectified as sports-metaphored "players[s] in a central, competitive game" (Allison, 1969: 707) with high stakes. Who runs with the ball, fumbling it, landing at the bottom of a pile-on, or pulling off a touchdown? In case the reader should not know, Allison (ibid.) tells us in the most straightforward of gender terms: "Men share power. Men differ concerning what must be done. The differences matter." Allison feels no need to explain his choice of words and the substantive characteristics they convey. This limits his work. It would be refreshing to see a recreation of the Cuban Missile Crisis from the situated standpoint of John McCone's wife. She experienced, and perhaps even influenced, the first round of the bureaucratic politics game, when her new husband bombarded the President with the famous honeymoon cables from their marriage suite in Paris. But this is beside Allison's point.

To Allison, politics is a question of man's personality and how he manages to "stand the heat in the kitchen" (ibid.: 709). This is an appropriation/reversal mix of gender metaphors. How many "men" stand in any kitchen long enough to feel heat? Only the chefs, presumably, who tend already to be appropriators of the usual food preparation narrative which has "women" in the everyday domiciles that are far from the "kitchen cabinets" of power. Still, there is doubleness in this appropriation: there must be power in the kitchen or researchers would not find this image sufficiently compelling to appropriate. It must be that "the problems for the players are both narrower and broader than *the* strategic problem" (ibid.: 710).

There are numerous discussions in the policy making literature of other narrower and broader influences on foreign policy, such as struggles between Congress and the President (Friedberg, 1992) and the role of public opinion (Ornstein and Schmitt, 1992). Much of the focus of this literature is the US and its peculiar moment of existence as both the sole remaining superpower and the hegemon in decline. There is in the rise and decline discussions, in particular, a sense of the superpower as, simultaneously, the feared mother of a boy's youth transposed into the global provider of milk, honey, and endless security, and the aging dowager who can still dress up for the ball but who – according to the stereotypes – can no longer project the charisma, and gather around her the friends and hangers-on, that she could when she possessed the resources of youth. Meanwhile, the discussions of public opinion keep painting a surreal picture of the public: John Reilly (1992) recently reviewed results of public opinion surveys conducted by the Chicago Council on Foreign Relations using a universalized language that reveals the present absence of gender differentiation within the public and among opinion leaders. Why, the feminist empiricist in all of us asks, report data for a gross aggregate called "Americans" and not also report the differences that enrich, defy, and give meaning to this identity group? Many foreign policy public opinion surveys seem unduly influenced by the neorealist image of the unified state and, perhaps, by the putative cultural equation of "men," with the active public and with politics.

As with neorealism, the decision-making literatures have been critiqued from a variety of mainstream IR positions. Ferguson and Mansbach (1988: 149) offer especially pointed criticisms, starting with the rational model as a tautological construction – "'rational' decisions were presumed to result from 'rational' decisionmaking even when they were as blatantly out of touch with the 'real world' as Lyndon Johnson's bombing campaign of North Vietnam." They go on to say that when analysts try to focus on the individual decision maker, they often fail to realize that one man is unable to let fly with his individuality because he is hemmed in by pluralist politics. When the shift is to the organizational or bureaucratic settings, there is a tendency to generalize the US case inappropriately: "The foreign-policy role of the U.S. president is hardly identical with, for example, that of the British prime minister, a charismatic leader like Castro, a military junta, or a Soviet premier/general secretary" (ibid.: 181). Jonathan Bender and Thomas Hammond (1992: 318) very pointedly criticize the internal logic of Allison's decision-making models, arguing that "a close examination of these models shows that they are much less rigorously

121

formulated than is generally recognized." Ferguson and Mansbach (1988: 163) even question the foreign/domestic dichotomy. But gender biases in the reconstruction of the Cuban Missile Crisis and in the construction of strategic models of decision making do not leap out at them. Gender does not compute in the second debate nor even in some of the more recent efforts to correct second-debate shortcomings.

The new institutionalists

The literature on cooperation under anarchy, under the security dilemma, among egoists, and after hegemony (Axelrod, 1984; Oye, 1986; Jervis 1978; Keohane, 1984) is at home with the science of IR, but whether it is at home with neorealism is a more difficult question. Ostensibly, this literature manifests a structuralism modified, and thus a neorealism modified, based on the idea that "*both* conflict *and* cooperation can be explained by a single logical apparatus" (Kratochwil and Ruggie, 1986: 762) having to do with situational and not just structural determinants of state action. This is not, however, a consensual view among those who wish to establish themselves as different from political realism and neorealism.

While decision-making analysts were dissecting the rationality assumption in neorealism, the precursors to neoliberal institutionalism were arguing, contra neorealism, that postwar patterns in state inter-actions had rendered cooperation through international regimes far more ubiquitous in the international system than those "particles of government" Waltz (1979: 114) saw. They shifted that argument in the 1980s, rendering cooperation less central to the system than it had been touted to be in the 1960s and 1970s, when international organi-zations-celebrating theories of functionalism, neofunctionalism, and regional integration held sway (e.g., E. Haas, 1964; Lindberg, 1963; Nye, 1971).

Why the shift? The post-war institutionalists saw prospects for regional and then global integration – for eventual system change – in circumstances of growing economic interdependence and in the revival of institutionalized international relations in the United Nations, in early treaties of the European Community, and in func-tionalist organizations attached to those two master organizations. (The realists, by contrast, applauded the rise of the US as the main manager of the bipolar system and downplayed the autonomy of international organizations). The new institutionalists of the 1980s witnessed the paralysis of the UN on many cold war issues and its metamorphosis into a third world organization after 1960. They were also sobered by the problems of political agreement dogging the European Community. And yet these organizations persisted. The new institutionalists explained that there was more cooperation in the system than the neorealists scripted and less than earlier institutionalists reported, owing to many situations in which states attempted to hold to independent decision making and egoistic interest only to find that the results of their actions yielded Pareto-deficient outcomes. Egoistic actors would then agree to accept obligations that precluded "making calculations about advantage in particular situations, if they believe that doing so will have better consequences in the long run than failure to accept any rules or acceptance of any other politically feasible set of rules" (Keohane, 1984: 13). New institutionalism has thus exposed problems with, but has not unraveled, the self-help incentives built into the structure of neorealism.

New institutionalism has also shifted attention in the study of international cooperation from formal organizations to less formal rules, principles, and norms in the system that constitute "regimes." When Robert Keohane (1989a: 4) uses the term regimes, he means "institutions with explicit rules, agreed upon by governments, that pertain to particular sets of issues in international relations."[5] Others mean "negotiated orders" (O. Young, 1982: 283), or circumstances in which "the interaction between the parties is constrained or is based on joint decision making" (Stein, 1990: 28). One problem with the regime focus is that it can be encompassingly broad, which means that delimiting the scope of regimes has been as problematic in this literature as ascertaining the relative importance of anarchy versus situational context.

The term "neoliberal" has been appended to some of the new institutionalists as a way of signifying that for them "[c]ooperation and liberalism are conceptually distinct" (Keohane, 1984: 34n). Whereas liberalism grants a superior position to the market as a regulator, neoliberals stress "the importance of international institutions, constructed by states, in facilitating mutually beneficial policy coordination among governments" (Keohane, 1989a: 10). Keohane (ibid.: 16n) claims that his neoliberalism (it is not, he says, a theory) also pays attention to strategic interaction, which means that "actors must be careful to assess the *indirect* effects of their actions on their future payoffs (effects that operate through the power and incentives of their partners)."

Neoliberal Keohane puts the story of regimes together this way. Using the discord evidenced by states in anarchy to stimulate mutual adjustment, states with mutual interests (strategically) plan and

123

negotiate regimes voluntarily. Once established, regimes can deepen the original contracts by offering participating decision makers high quality information and an environment in which norms of honesty and straightforwardness can emerge to counter realist values. Hence, when egoistic actors agree to accept initial obligations, a complex train of events can lead them to accept more obligations. This can move them from specific reciprocities to diffuse reciprocity, understood as working for the good of the group of which one is a member. Unanticipated in neorealism, such moves can change the system. Indeed, Keohane rejects neorealism because it fails to take into account unfolding institutional characteristics of the system and, therefore, provides no way for the system to change systemically except when the capabilities of states change.

Arthur Stein (1990) is not a follower of neoliberalism. He thinks that realist and institutionalist literatures share liberal assumptions about the absence of binding global laws, the state as a relevant actor in world politics (liberals think firms are also relevant), and the self-interested, purposive, and calculated behaviors of the relevant actors. These commonalities, he contends, lead in a convergent direction and intersect at the point where "realist assumptions are consistent with international cooperation and liberal assumptions with international conflict" (ibid.: 12). To study interactions around this convergence point, he advocates considering the common omission in both approaches, which he understands to be factors that influence the *decisions* nations make about whether to cooperate with one another at any given point in time. He claims that his difference with Keohane has to do, in part, with Keohane's assumption that "regimes presume a preexisting demand for agreements" (ibid.: 31n); this begs the issue of explaining the demand.

Strategic interaction constitutes for Stein a level of analysis that bridges the systemic assumption of anarchy with decision-making approaches that stress both self-interest and perceptions. He argues that "[a]ctors misperceive" (ibid.: 190). "They employ competitive and conjoint decision criteria as well as solely self-regarding ones. They differ in attitudes toward risk as a function of their status quo position and their expectations ... [There is a] proliferation of dilemmas." Indeed, in certain dilemmas, misperception can lead to cooperation, instead of presumed conflict, because "[n]either all cooperation nor all conflict is of a piece; there exists a diversity of each" (ibid.: 196).

The concern with strategic problems of cooperation jumps out of these particular cooperation texts and warrants comment. For Keohane, the main issue in strategic interaction is not just staying alive and in the game as long as possible. That is the neorealist problem. Rather, it is exploring the ways states stay in the game of cooperation longer than they probably intended to do given the inducements of anarchy. This is the jist of the specific-to-diffuse problematic of reciprocity. Keohane says a state keeps its eye on the shadow and promise of future relations and avoids sabotaging tomorrow's interactions through short-term calculations of gain today. This means that states must pay attention to a variety of effects that their actions of the moment will have on the welfare of their colleagues, for changes in *their* utilities will affect *your* calculation of utility. Thus, Keohane (1989b: 247) distinguishes specific from diffuse reciprocity in this way: "specific reciprocity is based on individualistic and egoistic premises ... it is a procedure for coexistence based on 'tit for tat' ... [whereas] diffuse reciprocity ... is based on social norms and a widespread pattern of obligation." States are assisted in keeping their eyes on the future by the effects of interaction within a regime context: assuming that a history of specific reciprocity is positive, the benefits of future cooperation are driven home and states begin to develop a broader identification with a regime-mediated community. Whether the "publics" of the states involved participate in this community is an out-of-place question.

This cooperation scenario suggests, in effect, that states can develop empathetic cooperation with the neorealist neighbors they once distrusted, shifting identity from potential defector to cooperator in concert with other similarly satisfied reciprocators. Keohane (1989b: 247) thinks the same dynamic works among people: "The norms on which diffuse reciprocity rests may reflect empathy of people toward one another, and could therefore be consistent with what Carol Gilligan refers to as 'an ethic of care' and what Joan Tronto discusses as a conception of identity describable as 'the connected self.'" He also says, however, that reciprocity assumes some equivalence of benefits, such that "good is returned for good, and bad for bad" (Keohane, 1989a: 136). That is the rub.

Keohane can see reasons to compare the prospects of individual empathy with the diffuse reciprocity he studies among states. And yet he foregoes a key test of his principle of strategic interaction at the point where states and people do, in fact, intersect in regimes. "Nearly 90 per cent of the secretaries and clerical personnel at the World Bank are women, but women occupy less than 3 per cent of its 'senior level' positions" (Enloe, 1989: 120). As well, in 1984 women at the United Nations "made up more than half of the Secretary General's staff, but held only 22.3 per cent of the professional international civil-service posts, as compared with 83 per cent of its clerical and secretarial jobs" (Enloe, 1989: 121). Today, the situation is possibly worse in some areas. Secretary General Boutros Boutros-Ghali has restructured the organization in a way that eliminates the only two senior women in the Secretariat (Kirshenbaum, 1992). A recent report by the UN steering committee for the Improvement of the Status of Women concludes that if traditional personnel policies persist at the professional level, "it will take 50 years to achieve overall equality in numbers among men and women" (Kirshenbaum, 1992: 18). "Women's" good will and support for the group they have joined by virtue of working for the regime is returned with bad will or with a lack of will to investigate the omission of "women" from ideas of international cooperation and reciprocity. The connectedness Keohane posits is there in these examples, but it is *strategic* in reflecting calculations of utility that ensure that the benefits of regime-participation flow from "women" to "men" and not ever the other way round.

This must mean that the male regimists have no worries about "women" regimists defecting in response to "men's" continual defection from diffuse reciprocity with "women." Indeed, "the U.N.'s immunity from national law means that charges of discrimination or harassment can only be brought to U.N. committees [comprised of men] – and the loss of a U.N. job can mean deportation" (ibid.: 17). As for "women" who accept low-paying positions in the organizations with the hope that their contributions will be reciprocated in due time, they get boxed in by a two-tier administrative structure (General Service and Professionals) and cannot easily move. "Yet men rise, even from GS" (ibid.: 18). As well, the "women" may operate on a different time dimension than the "men" or behave like Hobbes's "family women" under the social contract and consent to work with and for their conqueror because he is not an alien so much as he is a community member. Or, they may actually defect in subtle ways not yet explored. In any case, the assumptions underlying Keohane's use of strategic interaction need reviewing from a feminist standpoint perspective, because they do not seem to take into account all relevant calculations and calculators.[6]

For Stein, the issue is how a state decides to get into and to stay in a game of cooperation when the information available is marred by bounded rationality and by circumstance. He differentiates between reciprocators and opportunists. Reciprocators are "prepared to cooperate if others cooperate, and prepared to stand firm if others fail to bend" (Stein, 1990: 69). Opportunists are "prepared to stand firm if others cooperate, but are prepared to cooperate if they stand firm"

126

(ibid.: 69) (although it is possible that an actor might not have a dominant strategy). The beliefs that actors have about each other's strategies are crucial, because neither strategy, on its own, presupposes cooperation or conflict. Moreover, an actor may not have the information needed to decide which strategy is engaged at any time.

Thus, to continue with the example posed above, reciprocators can become diffuse reciprocators with "women" regimists for the good of the organization. But they need not turn in that direction unless others signal a willingness to cooperate with "women" on this issue, or reciprocators think others will do so. Opportunists can refuse to cooperate with cooperators. They are the ones, it seems, who can watch "women" regimists working at low-status jobs and refuse to act even when others are willing to do so. Neither of these dichotomously drawn strategic thinkers displays an ethics of care, a sense of connectedness, or a process of empathetic cooperation. Rather, each is nostalgically at home in a cultural context of abstract masculinity, where all is strategic. Context counts, as Stein claims, but only if it is constituted from the standpoints of people who view the world as he does. Thus, on top of the criticisms of regime analysis that have already surfaced in the literature – ethnocentricity, an emphasis on order (Strange, 1982), and a rehabilitated version of law (Ferguson and Mansbach, 1988) – we can add that this new institutionalism is a prisoner of gendered assumptions that torpedo its claims of difference from realism.

Traditional IR today

What about the contemporary traditionalists of IR? Can feminists find empathetic cooperation in their science-denying ranks? For some feminists, it might seem so. There is, after all, an echo of standpoint feminist concern in the traditionalist view that their very good and useful approaches have been denigrated by scientific IR as archaic and lacking in robust explanatory capacity. A traditionalist like Bull hangs his hat on the fine art of interpretation and suffers for his efforts the science-beholden epithet that he is engaged in bringing forth "heavenly pronouncements." In addition, think of Bull's critiques of science that give the traditionalist tacit permission to explore the cultural, political, and historical meanings of science and gender in IR. Through all of this, however, traditionalism remains a less than sympatico tradition of scholarship for feminists.

The traditional methods of analyzing international relations lean on history, philosophy, and law and on the crucial role of judgment in analysis. Feminist historians argue that "the writing of women into

127

history necessarily involves redefining and enlarging traditional notions of historical significance, to encompass personal, subjective experience as well as public and political activities ... such a methodology implies not only a new history of women, but also a new history" (Gordon, Buhle, and Dye, 1976: 89). This new history would alert us to the key question of "[h]ow does gender give meaning to the organization and perception of historical knowledge?" (Scott, 1989: 83). Indeed. How does it operate in the constitution of scientific IR, in the formulation of anarchy as the neorealist touchstone, in the determination of what stands for analytic judgment at any point in time? Importantly, how does gender signify the distribution of power in various realms of concern to the traditional IR scholar and how does it interact with the privileges of class and race in shaping the contours of international society? Questions of this type do not suggest themselves under unreconstituted traditionalism because, traditionally, "women have been invisible as historical subjects" (ibid.: 100), and "gender" sounds like "women."

Rosi Braidotti (1991: 174) subtitles a chapter in *Patterns of Dissonance: A Study of Women in Contemporary Philosophy*, "I Think Therefore He Is," after French feminist Luce Irigaray's chapter in *Speculum of the Other Woman* (1985a). Many feminists view philosophy as the most stolidly masculine of the academic disciplines, the most committed traditionally to "the setting up of the male subject as the measure of all things," a task that "requires the positing of the woman as other-than, that is to say less-than, and subordinate to the main point of reference" (Braidotti, 1991: 176–7). We remember, in this light, IR's pretheoretical roots in the philosophies of Hobbes, Machiavelli, Rousseau, et al., thinkers who "felt compelled to speak about the differences between the sexes," but who agreed that "women's activities and attributes made women incompetent to engage in political activities" (Jones and Jonasdottir, 1988: 1). This is hardly the type of tradition that, unmodified by feminist concerns, lends itself to questions of knowledge-authorship, to say nothing of the issue of whether people called "women" can claim any knowledge at all.

As for law as a source of traditional wisdom, we know some of the gender-encrustations associated with the liberal subject of law, the individual. We know that since international law grew out of rules developed by the sovereign states of Europe in the sixteenth and seventeenth centuries, its units, principles, and precedents can reveal particularistic values at best. Radical feminists argue that "[m]en founded and developed the discipline [of law], once monopolized it, continue to dominate it, identify its chief concerns in ways that come out of their experience and reflect their interests, and select and socialize its practitioners to carry on the male tradition" (Baer, 1991: 3). Not all feminists are as condemnatory and as radically wedded to feminist standpoint. Katharine Bartlett (1990: 832), for one, rejects "the sharp dichotomy between abstract, deductive ("male") reasoning, and concrete, contextualized ("female") reasoning because it misdescribes both conventional understandings of legal method and feminist methods themselves." Elshtain (1990b), taking a similar stand vis-à-vis just-war doctrine, argues that it is preferable to accept the possibility of conflict and sort out its justifications than assume that war equals absolute disorder and feminism equals pure peace and absolute order.

Still, international law traditionally mimics domestic practices by seeking predictable norms and principles, regimes and institutions, that order a sea of aloof and competitive sovereignties. This is most evident in the world peace through world law tradition (Clark and Sohn, 1966), but it also animates much of the European Community tradition and efforts of third-world states to craft a New International Economic Order that extends principles of domestic welfare to the international system. It scatters, as well, through some of the international regimes literature. International law is not a "woman"-friendly tradition of thinking. Recently, people called "women" have become international-rights bearers in their capacities as individuals. They do not, however, "exist as autonomous actors in world society at some Olympian level above the state, but receive their identity as members of a particular community corralled into the state" (Vincent, 1992: 261).

We recall that Bull wanted to preserve the realm of judgment in IR and yet he rehearsed only the male names of ideal passers of judgment on the field – "Alfred Zimmern, E. H. Carr, Hans Morgenthau, Georg Schwazenberger, Raymond Aron, and Martin Wight" (Bull, 1969: 20–1), only occasionally pulling back from his certainties to acknowledge that:

> we are largely ignorant of what the new literature contains and … our rejection of it stems much less from any reasoned critique than it does from feelings of aesthetic revulsion against its language and methods, irritation at its sometimes arrogant and preposterous claims, frustrations at our inability to grasp its meaning, or employ its tools, *a priori* confidence that as an intellectual enterprise it is bound to fail, and professional insecurity induced by the awful gnawing thought that it might perhaps succeed. (Ibid.: 23)

A more recent example of traditionalist scholarship, also from a scholar in the United Kingdom, is still "ignorant of what the new literature contains"; only this time the new literature is feminist. It makes its way

129

through and around the gender-implicated literatures on the "domestic analogy" in IR without giving a thought to the insights of feminist scholarship on issues of domesticity.

Hidemi Suganami (1989: 1) opens his study with this question: "How beneficial is it from the viewpoint of world order to transfer to the domain of international relations those legal and political principles which sustain order within states?" IR feminists of some persuasions would be prone to answer that question in the negative, pointing out, as we have already seen, that the few institutions of international governance that do exist can be far removed from accountability to domestic populations (Harrington, 1992). There is also the argument that the law of domestic states is not gender neutral (MacKinnon, 1989), that states are entities triumphant over women (Staudt, 1987), and so on. Suganami recognizes that the longstanding argument for the transfer of conditions of order within states to the international level assumes that there are already similarities between the two realms. In this feminists would concur. But he proceeds to evaluate the domestic analogy without reference to the particular similarities that make the international realm a zone of domestic gender politics in which "women" still have contracts to conquerors.

Suganami's authority sources are Hobbes, Kant, Morgenthau, Bull, and a host of male British and European thinkers with pedigrees established through the endorsements of other "men." His analysis of the range and types of domestic analogies extends from the equation of orderly social life among states with orderly life within them, to concerns to set up an apparatus of international order to solve a domestic problem, to confederalism, international welfarism, and new forms of universalism. He offers nineteenth-century examples of the domestic analogy and more recent proposals and doctrines. His is a virtuoso study – of the thinking of certain pedigreed "men" about what constitutes the "domestic" and how it should or should not be transferred to the "international." Without reference to recent feminist writings, the discussion seems old-fashioned, one-sided, shallow. It is insensitive to domestic institutions that engulf "women" and to international applications of domestic practice that could exacerbate sexism even while they reform other shortcomings in the system. For example, he talks about a form of welfare internationalism that can "promote the welfare of individuals located in separate states" (Suganami, 1989: 191). But, as we have discussed earlier, "individuals" do not necessarily include "women." If "those states who have a common set of problems are to create their own institutions specifically adjusted to their needs" (ibid.: 192), then what is to prevent those needs from

130

being defined in the usual gendered ways of state lexicon? Suganami is more concerned with the failure of welfare internationalists "to state clearly what form of institution is required and for which specific area of welfare needs" (ibid.: 196) than he is with this gender issue.

Because Suganami does not situate himself as a person called a "man" in a particular domestic setting commenting on other "men's" views of the domestic, because he does not study the history of "domestic" in various discourses on gender, he fails to anticipate some of the gender problems at the borderlands of domesticity and spaces international. He tells the reader that "[o]ne important feature of the debate about the domestic analogy is the extent to which writers' attitudes towards the analogy are influenced by the events and circumstances in the domestic and international spheres against the background of which their ideas about world order are formulated" (ibid: 197). He himself, however, does not speak about the background against which his own evaluations are spun and must be read. And, although he also tells the reader that "the knowledge of the ultimate structure matters far less than the awareness of the general direction in which international society must progress" (ibid.: 207), he does not query gender in the "international society."

Suganami's disinterest in the gender aspects of the domestic analogy is not completely typical of recent writings on what is alternately known as international, global, or world society. Whereas the realist understanding of such society, represented by Bull (1977), presents an ordered sociality of states within anarchy, and we have discussed the gendering of such entities, the contemporary alternatives are more gender savvy. The World Order Models Project, for instance, now emphasizes emergent global culture revealed by local groups struggling to realize anti-statist, life-affirming values (Mendlovitz and Walker, 1987); many of the local groups chronicled are peopled by "women." Immanuel Wallerstein's (1974, 1991) capitalist world-system is fueled by hierarchical economic zones and a decentralized state system prone to hegemonic cycles. It is a society of economic exchangers and differentially capable military guardians interlaced with several logics, including logics of sexism and racism, in which women figure both as anti-systemic agents and as victims of structure (Smith et al. 1988). There are various Marxist discussions of how the abolition of class conflict at the national level is or is not a prerequisite for the abolition of international conflict, and of how the idea of a community fits, or, as is more customary in the Marxist tradition, does not fit such analysis (C. Brown, 1992a: 237). These discussions struggle with the Woman Question. There is a multifaceted

131

liberal rights perspective that endeavors to establish "the level at which individuals are said to inhabit a great society or humankind ... the level at which states coexist in a society of states ... and the level at which groups other than states (such as multinational corporations and liberation organizations) jostle together in world society" (Vincent, 1992: 253). This is an approach in which it is increasingly noted that "individuals" and "women" do not necessarily equate.

These neotraditional world society approaches are advances over scholarship that has subsumed "women" in the category of mankind or assumed that "men" and "women" naturally exist in a single society rather than in separate societies based on gender divisions of status and labor. We must note, however, that the mere mention of *women* as members and victims of global society is not the same as engaging in depth explorations of *gender* in global society. There is still an unsubstantiated tendency to assume and accept "women" as coterminous with the bodies they inhabit rather than attempting to theorize gender as a socially constituted and politics-relevant identity that may or may not be body-linked or even constant cross-nationally. In other words, this somewhat "traditionalist" literature tends to count and comment on women in an empiricist way, observing bodies as the measure of gender. It does not evidence more than cursory familiarity with the debates in feminist theory on "women" and, therefore, it implicitly derives identities from socially acceptable but biased categorizations. This is the type of oversight that connects the more "woman"-aware neotraditionalist literature in IR with Suganami's unseeing eye on the gender dimensions of the domestic analogy.

I applaud the efforts of some latter-day traditionalists to alter our sense of what constitute "preposterous claims" by bringing the standpoints of "women" into their work. At the same time, the fact that so little traditional research picks up the feminist challenge – to methods and substance – has us remembering Bull's (1969: 38) parting shot to IR's scientists in his argument for a classical approach: "If we are to be hospitable to every approach (because 'something may come of it one day') and extend equal rights to every cliché (because 'there is, after all, a grain of truth in what he says'), there will be no end to the absurdities thrust upon us."

Debating anew

The absurdities. Even as second-wave feminist theory-practice unfolded before our eyes, some of us coming along at the cusp of feminism and IR needed time to feel and then wriggle free of the single loyalties that bound us to various IR heroes, heroic scripts, and methodological alchemies. "Women" in my generation entered university just as the feminist responses to masculine radical movements were percolating. That university was still a "man"-centered place, "a breeding ground not of humanism, but of masculine privilege" (Rich, 1979: 127).[7] We were then trained at the graduate level to build on and add to the knowledge established by numerous forefathers. We contributed to theories that, at best, sought to "link" women-occluded phenomena across levels of analysis instead of questioning why the occlusions and the levels were there. We were party to a professional contract – lucky to be among the chosen for IR – and saw no gender in our studies; rarely did anyone else, except only sometimes in the study of elite attitudes on foreign policy (Holsti and Rosenau, 1981). We controlled for the sex of respondents in certain studies, thinking of "women" as "females" and "men" as "males," as though biological and social identities were the same thing. Not knowing much feminist theory, we asked whether there was a difference when we controlled for sex that could be explained *post hoc* in terms of the IR theory we were testing. Usually we missed our feminist cues altogether; for instance, there were no females-women in the deliberations constituting the Cuban missile crisis and we did not query the meaning of that glaring social skew for the outcome of the crisis. We trained to be empiricists, not feminist empiricists; or we became traditionalists, not feminist reformulators of tradition.

IR's second debate, I submit, also suffered from the absence of feminist-informed input and, perhaps for that reason, among others, the second debate has been seen by some IR insiders as offering no "genuinely new theoretical visions" (Ferguson and Mansbach, 1988: 107). But our moment is not over. We can write science and tradition in ways that are more gender aware and perhaps more empathetically cooperative in approach to a whole range of el(l)ephants evacuated from the preserves of modern IR knowledge.

Consider one rewrite that Keohane (1989b) would like to see. He invites feminist empiricism to join hands with feminist standpoint in interfacing with neoliberal institutionalism; he calls it forming an alliance. He tells us that the feminist empiricist approach does the field a service by "investigating how gender (the institutionalisation of sex differences) affects the modern interstate system" (ibid.: 248). However, on its own,

> [t]o make a major impact on thinking about international relations . . .
> it will not be sufficient explicitly to point out that women have been
> marginalised in the state, and in interstate politics. This reality is

133

> well-known, even if conventional international relations theory has
> tended to ignore it. (Ibid.: 249)

Rather, one must travel into the realm of feminist standpoint to
emphasize:

> the role of purposeful human action and subjectivity in creating new
> conditions of life, and the need for what Evelyn Fox Keller calls
> "dynamic objectivity" in studying international relations – "a form of
> knowledge that grants to the world around us its independent
> integrity but does so in a way that remains cognizant of, indeed relies
> on, our connectivity with that world." (Ibid.: 247–8)

Together, feminist empiricism and standpoint could produce, in Keohane's eyes, "a" feminist theory of international relations that leads
inexorably into his camp with trumpets blaring an institutional version
of international relations. Feminism's unique contribution would be to
provide IR with "a network view, emphasizing how institutions could
promote lateral co-operation among organised entities, states or otherwise" (ibid.: 248).

Explicit in this analysis is yet another support assignment for
"women." We who are feminists in the academy are urged to come out
of our vague and homeless positions in IR in order to provide something that the mainsteam needs and cannot think through and
provide using its own powers of reflection. Moreover, what we
provide – a network view – can only be used if it conforms to mainstream scientific standards. In other words, our contributing dish must
be cooked to specifications and our paintings must display pregiven
standards. There is, in this admonition, little sense that feminists can
set an agenda for ourselves and for IR and really no sense that we may
want to interface differently and rewrite-repaint-recook the field
rather than join it. We are empathetically to reproduce the IR
delivered to us through rehearsals of strategic reasoning, because, as
noted in the last chapter, Keohane (and I doubt that he is alone on this)
believes that "agreement on epistemological essentials constitutes a
valuable scientific asset that should not be discarded lightly"
(ibid.: 249). With such agreement, "people with different substantive
views or intuitions can talk to each other in commensurable terms and
can perhaps come to an agreement with the aid of evidence" (ibid.).
This view cannot see the value of "needed incompatibles."

Now consider the possibilities in an analysis of how legal thinking
can be transformed by the infusion of feminist concerns. Bartlett
(1990: 832) tells us that traditional methods of legal analysis "over-
represent existing power structures" and undervalue "rule-flexibility

134

and the ability to identify missing points of view." Her preference, following Linda Alcoff (1988), is for a positionalist epistemology that "identifies experience as a foundation for knowledge and shapes an openness to points of view that otherwise would seem natural to exclude" (ibid.: 832).

Bartlett describes the assumptions (and methods) that inform positionality. First, one considers the gender implications of a social practice, rule, or judgment in the sense of considering whether and how the law may fail to reflect experiences that "seem more typical of women than of men ... or how existing legal standards and concepts might disadvantage women" (ibid.: 837). This is "asking the woman question." It is a useful contribution to IR's traditionalist methods and a good starting point to rescript scientific IR, because it demands that one ask whether a research question, selection of data, and method of analysis ignore and, therefore, disadvantage – at the level of assumptions or outcome – the experiences of "women."

Step two has us asking whether an emphasis on the exclusion of "women" from the analysis is not tantamount to emphasizing only the exclusion of people like oneself whose positions in society resonate with our position. This query introduces empathy into the proceedings and simultaneously decenters the asker's socially constituted privilege. Yet Bartlett acknowledges that there are limitations on the degree to which one situated person can represent others when "those who have not experienced [other oppressions] are likely to find them difficult to recognize" (ibid.: 849). This leads her to question whether adherence to broad principles, methodological rules, and legal precedents can ever guarantee objective truth and bring about an objective justice. Even when the researcher explains the chosen methods, reveals choices made, engages in responsible research, listens to people from different subject locations, one cannot be everywhere at once, cannot collect all the evidence and as many perspectives as are relevant. In IR, of course, other researchers are presumably free to enter the fray and reveal different slices of reality through their research. But the principles themselves stand in the way, ferreting out of the courtroom and the professional journals the situated knowledges of people who are not recognizable under the "law." Is this not, I ask, conducive to a bounded empathy?

Bartlett handles this problem by suggesting another. Is there not a problem with assuming that "women" is a critical point of exclusion? Do we not need to "reach forms of oppression made invisible not only by the dominant structures of power but also by the efforts to discover bias on behalf of women alone" (ibid.: 848)? Do we not need a method

135

"when one seeks something that does not correspond to one's own interests" (ibid.: 849)? Bartlett answers yes to all these questions. She wants to approach "problems as dilemmas with multiple perspectives, contradictions, and inconsistencies." She seeks rules that "check the inclination to be arbitrary" and that "represent accumulated past wisdom, which must be reconciled with the contingencies and practicalities presented by fresh facts" (ibid.: 852), while also leaving "room for new insights and perspectives generated by new contexts" (ibid.: 853). She wants to challenge "the legitimacy of the norms of those who claim to speak, through rules, for the community" because in fact, there are "many overlapping communities to which one might look for 'reason'" (ibid.: 855). One looks into all of this by, following Amelie Rorty (1988: 283), offering justifications for decisions in the actual reasons "that form [an] effective intentional description" (ibid.: 854), instead of offering some reasonable basis for a decision, as is common in the US legal system and as is embedded in probabilistic approaches to IR.

In an argument that echoes Haraway's defense of feminist science as science, Bartlett argues for a practical reasoning principle that is not the polar opposite of masculine method, of male reasoning, of deductive logic. This principle would open up "possibilities of new situations rather than limit them with prescribed categories of analysis" (ibid.: 857–8). To substantiate her point, she offers the New Jersey case of *State* v. *Smith*. There, the court rejected the defendant's claim that sex within marriage was not subject to charges of rape (the marital-exemption principle) after examining "the history of the exemption, the strength and evolution of the common law authority, the various justifications offered by the state for the exemption, the surrounding social and legal context in which the defendant asserted the defense, and the particular actions of the defendant in this case that gave rise to the prosecution" (ibid.: 858). That is, just as Haraway has us building theory on the basis of investigations of cultural and historical narratives that surround the issue at hand, Bartlett finds that in *State* v. *Smith*, the judge carefully reviewed the source of the marital exemption to rape and found it in a 300-year-old "bare, extra-judicial declaration" issued at a time when marriage was effectively a permanent state, "ending only by death or an act of Parliament." Since "attitudes towards the permanency of marriage have changed and divorce has become far easier to obtain," and since the initial proclamation was extra-judicial, the court determined that marital exemption "need not prevail when those conditions have changed." It then explored the justifications for New Jersey's retention of the principle and determined that none of them (marital unity, implied consent) fit the facts of the case. Bartlett concludes that instead of blindly following legal precedent, "the *Smith* court saw itself as an active participant in the formulation of legal authority" (ibid.: 860).

Without ignoring the importance to law of consistency and tradition, the court took an approach "sensitive to the human factors that a more mechanical application of precedent might ignore" (ibid.: 861). One might say that its formal legal method slipped in the face of an interpretative process that brought hidden legal issues and identities to the fore. If that court had also been following feminist practical reasoning, it would have identified "the perspective of the woman whose interest a marital rape exemption entirely subordinates to that of her estranged husband" (ibid.: 861). It would also have looked more closely at the interests of the *defendant* "who, when he acted, may have thought his actions were legal" (ibid.). Together, these additional considerations would "have given a fuller picture of the issues, as well as guidance for other courts to which these factors may seem more significant" (ibid.).

Far from scaring off the pundits of science or tradition in IR, Bartlett's approach suggests a way of improving research vision without factoring the knowledge and the "men" out of the field. Her method is especially useful for the traditionalists, pushing them to the margins of risk without depriving them of some of their cherished forms of argument. As well, with this method in hand, we might find that some of the distance between the Keohane and the Bartlett positions may not be great. Keohane, after all, wants feminists to respect the scientific precedents that prior recruits to IR established. He wants us to join an ongoing community and live by its rules while enlarging its interests, its sense of the facts, its methods, its objectivity. Implicitly, he wants us to lead sessions in IR consciousness-raising in order to help the neorealists escape their narrow visions of anarchy and appreciate the connectedness, the networks, that also characterize behavior. Overall, he wants IR to get it right, to improve, to push closer to truth by taking on board the feminist standpointers. Perhaps because IR's second debate had an adversarial quality to it that continues to mark the field, Keohane identifies only feminist standpoint with proper feminism; the scientists already own empiricism and postmodernism is an adversary.

Yet we cannot refuse the differences between Bartlett and Keohane. Bartlett too pulls the feminist challengers inside the community about which she writes. But she does not assume that the truth (facts) can be confined to any one community. Feminist standpoint epistemology, she suggests, is just one community of knowing. Its base of operations is "gender as a source of oppression" (ibid.: 873) and it has a strategic interest in pushing the notion of women's perspective, even though that position "duplicates the error of other legal theories that project the meaning speakers give to their own experiences onto the experiences of others" (ibid.: 874). Arguably, the feminist standpoint error (and not all subscribe to its existence) is similar to the one committed by IR's scientists and traditionalists alike, as they breezily go about *their* business and make it *our* business.

Somewhat dissatisfied with standpoint, Bartlett does not rule out the contributions of feminists who think in the postmodernist vein, and she offers several reasons for this. One is that they have shown the error in assuming that criteria for legal validity and legitimacy are universal givens. They have also helped bring attention to the notion that the law must be indeterminate, given the varieties of ways that facts can be construed, and have revealed hierarchies and distributions of power in notions of objectivity and neutrality. By contrast, we remember that Keohane (1989b: 249) writes off feminist postmodernism as "a dead-end in the study of international relations ... it would be disastrous for feminist international relations theory to pursue this path." Keohane thinks that postmodernists reject all reasons and end up with nothing.

This critique of postmodernism has become the encatchment of a vulgar analysis that is akin to the retorts of "reductionism" and "economism" that passed for depth criticisms of Marxism. Unaware of differences in the postmodern turn, it places silly carnival masks over complex arguments when, in fact, some of us have good reasons for employing a dynamic objectivity that can inter-face with people whom epistemological essentials have discarded lightly. Yet Bartlett also parts company with postmodernists over the issue of objectivity: "Without a notion of objectivity, feminists have difficulty claiming that their emergence from male hegemony is less artificial and constructed than that which they have cast off" (Bartlett, 1990: 879).

In the end, Bartlett uses the strengths of standpoint and postmodernism to move in a postmodern feminist direction, while Keohane seems unreflexively interested in applying standpoint to the ongoing project in IR of empiricism. We invite him into the conversation, though, because Bartlett specifically wants to make "a number of apparently inconsistent feminist 'truths' make sense" (ibid.: 880) and, presumably, (feminist) empiricism, feminist standpoint, and feminist postmodernism are examples of "inconsistent truths." Her view of positionality hums with the themes of empathetic cooperation as a method to rescript ourselves and a field of knowledge through a process that multiplies subjectivities and renders them mobile in the face of new knowledge about excluded experiences, so that we can recraft law, theory, science, tradition, IR. She says:

> Like standpoint epistemology, positionality retains a concept of knowledge based upon experience. Experience interacts with an individual's current perceptions to reveal new understandings and to help that individual, with others, make sense of those perceptions ... Like the postmodern position, however, positionality rejects the perfectibility, externality, or objectivity of truth. Instead, the positional knower conceives of truth as situated and partial. Truth is situated in that it emerges from particular involvements and relationships. Those relationships, not some essential or innate characteristics of the individual, define the individual's perspective and provide the location for meaning, identity, and political commitment. (Ibid.: 880)

To this, I would add, or perhaps emphasize, that positions *shift* as a result of involvements and relationships, and these shifts, shared within a community, enable us to rescript outselves and rescript a field in cycles of respectful negotiation.

As we contemplate rewriting IR methods, feminists remember that we cannot be banished for our sins. We are, after all, already among the homeless in the field. Our task is to seek out more positions of homelessness as well as to inter-face between the masks all of us wear, thrusting out to crack them (Anzaldua, 1990a: xv–xvi) with the unexpected flair that is denied those routinely culled from a herd.

4 THE THIRD DEBATE IN IR VISITED BY FEMINISTS

The third discipline-defining debate is a sizing up, mopping up, holding firm versus letting go affair. Instead of a general confrontation between (seemingly) two ways of proceeding, there are scattered jabs and ripostes, hand-wringings, dialogues, I-told-you-sos, efforts at strategic synthesis, intransigencies, refusals, and determined partings of the way. Those who insist on having a debate ask the practitioners of science and tradition to render an accounting of the field's knowledge and methods; they are concerned that IR has not amassed an impressive intellectual fortune in its seventy or so years of existence. Two problems, they say, reduce the potency of the field: one, theory building has been done badly or inappropriately; and, two, the crisis of late-modernity has not been acknowledged by a disciplinary turn to postmodern philosophy and methods. Advocates of science, meanwhile, chastened and less physics-envious than they were in the second debate, nonetheless continue to mine the possibilities of empirical data-based or deductive theory, swatting at the challengers as at so many mosquitos, taking on board some of the new currents in the air and not others, or behaving as though the third debate should not be happening. The traditionalists, meanwhile, carry on.

Some recriminations, refusals, and celebrations

To get a sense of the disappointments and refusals of disappointment that characterize a renewed period of controversy in academic IR, we need to consider a few markers of this moment in the field. We start with notes of concern from within the mainstream and then move into the more postpositivism-celebratory modes of critique.[1]

Disappointed but not despairing

Yale Ferguson and Richard Mansbach (1988: 3) open their *Elusive Quest* with an expression of a malaise:

140

> Many students of international relations, like the present authors,
> were once convinced that they were participants in a quest for theory
> which would, in time, unravel the arcane secrets of world politics.
> That quest would deepen our theoretical insights as we tested our
> ideas according to the canons of science. Knowledge and under-
> standing would be gradual and cumulative, but, in the end, they
> might even enable us to overcome age-old scourges like war. In
> subsequent decades, we have witnessed changes in discourse in the
> field, the development of intriguing and ingenious methodologies,
> the creation of new forms of data, and the diffusion of American
> social science techniques throughout the world. Yet, our understand-
> ing of key phenomena is expanding only very modestly, if at all.

The problem, in their view, is that IR's methods outran conceptual
advancements because the field bounced from pillar to post, partly
owing to the "needs and preferences of political practitioners and the
funding practices of government institutions, [t]he latter especially
account[ing] for the 'scientific' bent of American international relations
scholarship" (ibid.: 5). There was also the matter of the cold war, which
sanctified realism as something approaching scripture, even though a
close look at realism shows not so much a theory as a set of normative
emphases which shape theory; it is a self-contained syllogism that has
had the effect of closing off rather than of opening up possibilities for
analysis; it, in fact, has been most effective at sustaining a particular
ideology than at inspiring science (ibid.: 216). Faced with ideology
masking as theory, some analysts moved to define a different range of
puzzles (often simply reinventing idealism) or fell into a methodological field of poppies, regaining consciousness only in order to defend
square inches of turf in big and little skirmishes that made for a rigid
and ever less relevant IR.

At the current moment, Ferguson and Mansbach say, the field is
and should be abandoning its quest for a scientific revolution that it
could never rise above normative contexts to attain. How should it
proceed? In 1988 they tentatively suggested that IR try "to make sense
of the way in which humanists approach their materials," to understand "the shifting *Gestalten* of societies" (ibid.: 222). In 1991 they
expanded this argument and suggested that the field: emphasize
subjectivism in research and practice; avoid dichotomizing politics as
domestic versus international; be sensitive to context; recognize normative and ideological aspects of theory and practice; maintain a
skeptical posture toward the notion of finding permanent laws of
politics; and seek to bring individual human loyalties to various
politics into the range of IR analysis rather than focus too much on
structural constraints.

141

Refusing disheartenment

IR's scientists, however, do not want to abandon the second debate (con)quest and tend to react badly when told that they should consider literary theoretical techniques or emphasize subjectivism in their research. "Literary" and "subjective" signal to them the abandonment of science, the abandonment of theory building for a free-for-all of personal expression.

A recent issue of *International Studies Quarterly* – the journal of the International Studies Association – shows us that the scientists still dominate the mainstream texts. Joshua Goldstein (1991) provides an account of issues of reciprocity between the superpowers. Based on empirical theory, Goldstein approaches data in a way that he claims will avoid the biases, noise, and excessive aggregations of previous studies. His model of reciprocity is quasi-experimental. Terry Boswell and Mike Sweat (1991) sort out differing conceptions, measures, and units of analysis in studying hegemony. They specifically test a proposition associated with power transition theory using a time series regression analysis that corrects, they say, for previous failings in multivariate statistical rigor. Gregory Sanjian (1991: 173) takes us, in his own words, through an exercise in developing and testing "a fuzzy multi-criteria model of arms transfer decision-making ... [that] outperforms several naive models (including an autoregressive model) and an expected-utility model ... [n]inety strategies ... predicted, with an overall success rate of 87%." Timothy McKeown (1991) uses regression analysis to examine the relationship between the average openness of a trade system and variables representing political business cycles and hegemonic stability explanations of degree of openness of a trading system over time. The point is to explain the non-collapse of trading activity during a period of US hegemonic decline.

International Studies Quarterly is currently edited at Ohio State University, one of the US land grant universities where science hunkered down after the second debate. One expects a certain refusal of unorthodoxy from that corner of the field. And yet, when one looks closely at the aforementioned articles representing scientific IR, it is clear that the second-debate triumph has been affected by the times, metamorphosing, in most cases, into self-reflexive practice.

First, one can discern in these articles some concern to test competing theories rather than test hypotheses generated by one theory alone. Boswell and Sweat seek to compare systemic and realist theories of hegemony. Goldstein points out that differing predictions about reciprocity-based relations (leading to more cooperation versus more

142

hostility) pepper the literature and need to be sorted out to avoid what Ferguson and Mansbach (1991) would undoubtedly tell us is an example of IR's conceptual anarchy. Second, there is a bit more soul-searching and defensiveness in some of these scientific pieces. A review article on the state of security studies (Walt, 1991) happily announces that this area of the discipline has become more rigorous and focused on theory; nonetheless, its author warns of "counterproductive tangents that have seduced other areas of international studies, most notably the 'post-modern' approach ... to date, these works are mostly criticism and not much theory" (ibid.: 223). A note of confidence is struck that security studies are undergoing a renaissance. Further along, there is acknowledgement of a "widespread belief that the end of the Cold War has decreased the risk of war [and] may temporarily divert financial support and research energies in other directions" (ibid.: 222).

The continuing fragmentation of the field *cum* loyalty to realism that concerns Ferguson and Mansbach is also evident in that security review article. We are told about: "third-image pessimists" who warn that the end of the cold war will fuel a multipolar restructuring of Europe that opens up the dangers of war; "second-image pessimists" who warn of "dangers arising from the weak democratic institutions in Eastern Europe" (ibid.: 226); and "second-image optimists" who maintain that European societies have changed and so have the prospects for war in that region. The two-to-one pessimistic predictions about the impact of the terminated cold war on issues of western national security shows both ongoing cleavages and the way the normative aura of ethnocentric realism dogs the field.

Dissident celebrations and skepticisms

A very different view of the field appeared in *International Studies Quarterly* when the journal was partly under the stewardship of a self-named dissident in 1990. Consider this:

> Whether one speaks of the "discipline of international studies," the "discipline of international relations," the "discipline of international politics," or the "discipline of world [or maybe 'global'] politics," the words manifestly fail, even as they promise, to discipline meaning. The words but broadly connote (they cannot denote) a boundless nontime and nonplace – a deterritorialized, extraterritorial zone of discourse – where the work of producing the subjects, the objects, and the interpretations of an institutional order and its limits visibly eludes the certain control of that order's supposedly reigning categories. (Ashley and Walker, 1990b: 376)

143

This passage is a statement of challenge to academic IR that takes both tradition and science to task for attempting to limit rather than expand possibilities of analysis and politics. It presents the quest for grand theory, however it is packaged, as an illusion that slips out from under the controlling lasso at the very moment when the beast seems secured and ready to be pulled home, scattering into a million pieces of dissidence, into scores of refusals to be tamed by theory, into resistances and lonely exiles that defy any sense that truth has been found and conquered.

It is a statement of poststructuralist or postmodernist IR,[2] the practitioners of which, in IR-related studies at least, call themselves "exiles." These dissident exiles are "marginal instances" that:

> resist knowing in the sense celebrated in modern culture, where to "know" is to construct a coherent representation that excludes contesting interpretations and controls meaning from the standpoint of a sovereign subject whose word is the origin of truth beyond doubt. In modern culture, it is the male-marked figure of "man." (Ashley and Walker, 1990a: 261)

They are certain that the time is right for dissident activity because all of us face a "crisis of the human sciences, a crisis of patriarchy, a crisis of governability, a crisis of late industrial society, a generalized crisis of modernity" (Ashley and Walker, 1990b: 377). The crisis is the "acceleration of social activity such that it strains, ruptures, overflows, or otherwise *transgresses* the institutional limitations of a social order" (ibid.). One cannot carry on as usual unless one is ignorant of the contributions that a business-as-usual attitude makes to the tumult. One cannot take refuge in some closed system of knowledge or fail to see that the very language one uses shapes, mirrors, and challenges the crisis.

An IR-relevant understanding of the crisis often points fingers at the long Cartesian search for foundational Archimedean points that could stand beyond social constitution as truth. The tool of choice in this search has been rationality, the agent of transcendence. Rationality enables a researcher to separate himself from "objects studied" and to control them in the name of objectivity. As long as such seek-and-control missions evoke little dissent within the community that undertakes them, the method can seem consensual. But there are always doubters, homeless people, skeptics, madwomen, who defy the logic and who refuse to be controlled. Their whispered, bellowed, or silenced dissent orchestrates into a crisis of knowing and then into a more encompassing cultural crisis when the truth begins to disappoint, and does so time and again. Just in the current phase of late modernity or postmodernity, we think of scientific progress and of bombarded people on Japanese islands, of smashed people in a crashed space shuttle, of "our" failure to kill enough people in Vietnam to make for a US technological victory. We cannot cure AIDS even though health sciences are biased in favour of improving men's health and many AIDS sufferers are men. Third world underdevelopment worsens and science cannot get a handle on it or sustain western development. Offering material progress as a substitute for old-fashioned spirituality, morality, ethics, poetry – for death – science has not tamed all frontiers of "ignorance." It has not fixed everything in the name of sovereign man. It has not even fixed the problem of homelessness in US cities. This is our crisis: one puts faith in the assurances of modern progress and finds the recurrence of the unexpected, the irrational, the taboo, rather than the triumph and transcendence of strategic reasoning.

In IR the signs of the general crisis creep into the disheartened but reformist efforts of Ferguson and Mansbach (1991) and into the new reflexivity *cum* defensiveness of the scientists. It can be heard in the clamorings of gay, feminist and men's groups, handicap-rights and cross-cutting peace-feminist movements. The pieces of these movements have been visible for a long time. The crisis makes it marginally safer for these marginal groups to speak out, and in speaking out the groups help to constitute (sometimes to heighten) the crisis. It is the *gestalten* of the times that "[t]he attempt to impose boundaries – to exclude the concerns of cultural and ecological movements from the political programs of worker movements, say, or to exclude feminist scholarship from international studies – becomes distinctly visible" (Ashley and Walker, 1990b: 377). These movements press on, transgressing "institutional boundaries that would differentiate, mark off, and fix time, space, and identity within a social order, including the identities of subjects as agents of knowing and the objects that they would know" (ibid.: 377–8). Now:

> there is no clear and indubitable sense of inside versus outside, domestic versus international, particular versus universal, developed versus underdeveloped, reality versus ideology, paradigm versus counterparadigm, fact versus fiction, political theory versus political practice, identity versus difference, progress versus regress, continuity versus change, father versus mother, rationality versus irrationality, system of communication and circulating exchange value versus nature, positivity versus negativity, maturity versus immaturity, seriousness versus play, sense versus nonsense. (Ibid.: 378)

The articles that comprise the issue of *International Studies Quarterly* edited by IR dissidents and exiles approach study and research in ways that differ both from science and from the many traditional reforms that would quell the crisis without responding to its specter. James Der Derian (1990), for instance, talks about the importance of simulation, surveillance, and speed as global forces that have eluded conventional second-debate IR because they are more of time than (geo)space, more transparent than discrete, and more bound up with signs that are exchanged rather than goods that exchange. Bradley Klein (1990) examines NATO as a set of practices that both constitutes the West and provides a network of intertextual representations of global political space. His method includes genealogy (examining mechanisms by which certain ideas and practices come to grip minds and rule actions as though they were natural and true) and deconstruction (which I think of, using a construction-industry metaphor, as pulling apart and looking in-between the cantilevers of knowledge and power that hide a host of meanings and identities at the movable joint, and that engineer the left beam [reading right] to be more reliable, solid, active, normal than the other beam).[3]

Michael Shapiro (1990) provides an account of strategic discourse as transected by a variety of practices (including commercial practices) "with which American policy is thought, expressed, represented ... understood" and increasingly scrutinized by the media "which creates the need for another level of strategy, a media or representational strategy, for both the official strategic discourse and its various contenders" (ibid.: 329). William Chaloupka (1990) leans on Foucault and Baudrillard to consider the partial interventions into US foreign policy that come under the guise of "lifestyle politics," a "moment of difference ... located by a specific characteristic: the *self* has become crucial to every political critique" (ibid.: 342). Finally, Cynthia Weber (1990) takes us into an analysis of third world debt as the constitution of a foundation of interpretation for speaking positions on the claims of obligation. Her illustrative case is Peru and the foundations she uncovers are theological metaphors that lead, she says, to contrasting claims of debt-servicing obligations by two Peruvian presidents.

These pieces and others that make up the lexicon of dissidence problematize the modes of social and political discipline that modern subjects have imbibed with the morning newspaper, taught our students, believed, and defended. They interrogate present knowledge through an evaluation of practices that have built up our sense of what is normal. They listen for critical voices that have been drowned out by official discourses. They read "the textual interplay behind power politics" (Der Derian, 1989: 6–7). They exemplify a postmodernist philosophical approach to late or post-modernity.

In and around the field of IR, this approach is treated as a playful-mocking-irresponsible-nonserious long dangle on a bungee line without thought to whether the line is strong, there is equipment below to break a fall, or there is a way of making sense of the activity in any larger context than yahoo adolescent rebellion (e.g., Walt, 1991). Indeed, there is a form of postmodernism that Pauline Rosenau (1992) calls the skeptical mode. It seemingly abandons theory building as a legitimate goal in the social sciences in order to avoid incessant encrustations of rationality. She summarizes the skeptical position this way: "Feeling no need to be logical, to reconcile oppositions, to test, or to choose between theories, it accepts inconsistency and contradiction." The writers she textually associates with this position are Richard Ashley and James Der Derian, both from the dissident wing of the third debate in IR.[4]

But there are other aspects of postmodern philosophy that celebrate the opportunities that the crisis presents to decentralize and democratize knowledge and power by dememorializing old sovereignties and exploring the borderlands of difference. Pauline Rosenau (1922: 83) depicts this orientation as affirmative postmodernism and characterizes it as "unsystematic, heterological, decentered, ever changing, and local. Nonrepresentational, it is personal in character and community-specific in focus." She does not authorize any of the IR postmodernists for this group. I think this is an oversight. Ashley and R.B.J. Walker are skeptical and affirmative, attracted to the cusp of Rosenau's binary categories of dissidence. In fact, defending themselves against claims that dissidence can only tear down and not build up a more moral set of behaviors, these dissidents say:

> It is true that we cannot represent, formalize, or maxim-ize deterritorialized modalities of ethical conduct. We cannot evoke a juridical model, define the good life and lay down the code crucial to its fulfillment, as if bespeaking some universal consensus formed according to rules of discourse already given, without at the same time covertly imposing a principle of territoriality that these modalities refuse to entertain. But our inability to represent human beings does not prevent us from talking about it or from trying to understand how it might orient deterritorialized ethics in the valuation and disciplining of their activities. (Ashley and Walker, 1990b: 391)

At issue for Ashley and Walker (1990b: 403) is whether "those engaged in international studies will exercise their resources and their freedom to test limitations and open up possibilities, thereby both exploiting and expanding spaces for thought and action in reply to the contemporary dangers and opportunities of global political life." This is the type of strategic concern that Braidotti (1991: 2) sees as "the sign of an irrespressible theoretical vitality," of "the will to go on theorizing, that is, to engage in philosophical discourse by all possible means," rather than abandon it.

One summarizer celebrates the third debate

Josef Lapid (1989) steps back from the disappointments and refusals of disappointment in the field to summarize the third debate in terms of three main tendencies. I think he misses at least three other tendencies but will start with his concerns first.

The first tendency he sees is to construct long-lived, large-scale, and multitiered paradigms or research programs that "qualify as basic knowledge-producing, knowledge-accumulating, and knowledge-conserving units" (ibid.: 239). This paradigmatism replaces much of the second-debate concern to craft middle-range theory and yields research that can be compared across large organizing frameworks. Recent comparisons of realist and neoliberal institutionalist views of cooperation (Grieco, 1990) illustrate this trend as do debates over modernist versus postmodernist discourses. Ferguson and Mansbach (1991: 364) are *aficionados* of paradigmatism in that they want to build a research scaffold for IR that enables its users to take "seriously the claims of [the] 'dissidents' while continuing to be precise in setting forth values and assumptions, defining terms, clarifying variables, and collecting evidence for generalizations."

A second tendency in the current debate, according to Lapid, is for mainstream scientific analysts to evaluate the premises and underlying research assumptions in their work rather than accept the custom of posing some propositions as unquestionably given or as given because they are of heuristic value and "work in the 'model'" (for example, assume perfect competition). As a result of this perspectivist trend, fortress "anarchy" has been under scrutiny as a problematic realist assumption (Jervis, 1988; Suganami, 1990; Wendt, 1992; Milner, 1992; Powell, 1993), as has the discipline-establishing claim that there are important differences between domestic and international arenas of politics (Stein, 1990; P. Haas, 1990; R. Walker, 1989; Putnam, 1988; J. Rosenau, 1990; Ferguson and Mansbach, 1991). By implication, the levels of analysis theorem is losing ground and down with it comes the assumption of unified states as actors: "states do not 'behave' ... [i]ndividuals and a wide variety of groups within, without, and extending across state boundaries act" (Ferguson and Mansbach, 1991: 370). Sovereignty takes a beating as a synonym for authority to pronounce IR (Ashley, 1989) or as a specific concept that gives "states" far more autonomy, cohesion, and universality than "they" deserve (J. Rosenau, 1990; Elshtain, 1992; R. Walker, 1992).

Finally, Lapid argues that the third debate features methodological pluralism, which is the drift toward an "intriguing eclipse of consensus as a prime desideratum in social science," a "massive move toward relativism" (Lapid, 1989: 243). Unlike the previous two debates, more elements in the third debate disavow "exclusive epistemological principles and prescriptions" (ibid.: 244). But lack of consensus is not itself consensual or we could not find the scientists currently in charge of *International Studies Quarterly* hoeing such predictably straight rows without calling those rows "the special issue on science in contemporary international relations."[5] We can think of a fourth characteristic of the third debate, therefore, as the lingering on of second-debate issues into the third era, which means that the third debate is also – and this is characteristic five – an arena of debates-within-debates about how to proceed to find method, how to keep method at bay, how to deal with all of our bounded and/or differently configured rationalities.

The sixth characteristic, unmentioned in Lapid's summary, is that feminism is present in the third debate.

Feminism: present if not consensually accounted for

Ferguson's and Mansbach's 1991 version of the third debate mentions two feminist debaters but joins them at the hip with Robert Keohane, who is referred to as a neorealist. The text reads (Ferguson and Mansbach, 1991: 364): "NeoMarxists and feminists clash with neorealists (see Keohane, Molyneux, and Whitworth, 1989)." In fact, each of these analysts contributed a separate and distinct piece to the particular debate in *Millennium* that Ferguson and Mansbach recognize (Keohane, 1989b; Molyneux, 1989; Whitworth, 1989). Moreover, there are many other feminists in the third debate. As I pointed out earlier, there was a special issue of *Millennium* in 1988 that was packed with feminist contestations, and feminist articles and books stretch back several years (e.g., Elshtain, 1987; Enloe, 1989; Sylvester, 1987; Mies, 1986).

This is not the only example of a selective naming of feminists. Ashley and Walker (1990a) report that feminism is a worthy dissidence and that "women" too are in exile from IR. They even present the sovereign voice which they find offensive in IR as the male-marked figure of "man." But then they mimic that sovereignty, even as they very seriously critique it in other ways, by finding it unnecessary to enable even a single feminist "marginal instance" to analyze at length the implications of sovereign man for people called "women," for her-selves. One might say that the editors represent feminists without giving one among us voice(s), interpretation(s), writing(s), word(s), brush and canvas. One supposes that in their minds this presentation is fully permissible on the grounds that in a crisis of representation, such as we are experiencing, "there is no possibility of a well-delimited, identical presence of a subject whose interior meanings might be re-presented in words, for it is impossible to exclude the contesting interpretations of subjective being that must be absent if the presence is simply to be" (Ashley and Walker, 1990b: 378).

Where are we in the third debate when "we" are so tokenized in the main debate and lively in our own quarters? There are at least three feminist perspectives on where we might be. One suggests that we are part of the dissident exile group of postmodernists. Another maintains that some of us are in the feminist third wave, which focuses more on epistemology than theory building, and in that role we are akin to participants in the IR third debate; others of us are more properly second-wave, for good or ill. A third position is that it is unnecessary to rehearse these boundary questions because the drive to fix location misses an important point about the importance of "incommensurable" voices in this era of change.

Feminism: necessarily a dissidence

Jane Flax (1987) makes the argument that contemporary feminism, the feminism we have been tracing in previous chapters, is a postmodern historical phenomenon and part of postmodern philosophy.[6] It is always and necessarily a dissidence.

Feminism is a postmodern phenomenon in the sense that the transitional state Flax believes the western world is in, "makes certain forms of thought possible and necessary, and it excludes others" (ibid.: 621–2). Feminism, a product of transition, has itself made possible the problematizing of gender. Gender was intermittently problematized in the past, but today's variants of feminism unfold in a global context that is marked by considerable questioning of "the appropriate grounding and methods for explaining and/or interpreting human experience" (ibid.: 624). We used to claim to know for certain that real women existed: you knew them by bodies and social roles as (fill in the blank) – mothers, wives, passive people in skirts, bitches, nags, tramps, little old ladies in tennis shoes, bad at mathematics, the ones who carry the wood and fetch the water and so on. Now the analogic statement

150

"women" is to "____" can have virtually any referent. The proliferation of markers shows up in more open public acknowledgement of
what society used to pretend not to see, or to trivialize if it did see it –
women novelists, women road workers, women police, women
department chairs, women dentists, lesbians in the next office, women
weight lifters, women guerrillas. Simultaneously, there is a backlash
against the inverted-comma-ization of "women" (Faludi, 1991) and
debates within feminism about how to respond to onslaughts of
commercialized "new women" that mock feminism. If the postmodern is, as Wendy Brown (1991: 65) contends, a "time, circumstance, and configuration rather than an intellectual tendency or political position," then these feminist questionings of place, these
backlash nostalgias of gender, these fragmentations and heterogenei-
ties, deterritorializations of women and decolonized spots for feminism, this feminist and antifeminist and postfeminist in-your-face is of
this time.[7]

As for the relationship of feminism to elements of postmodern
philosophy, Flax argues that "women" possess and want to claim
certain traits that modernity denied us, such as reason, sovereignty,
progress, self-emancipation, and science. Therefore, if we become too
dissident and deconstructive, those reclaimed traits must be revealed
as bogus and relinquished as undesirable for everyone. Flax (1987: 625)
works through this contradiction by posing another. She says that
"[f]eminist notions of the self, knowledge, and truth are too contradictory to those of the Enlightenment to be contained within its
categories." When we talk about gender, for instance, feminists soon
realize that gender is linked to other subject statuses and wonder if
there can be "gender" apart from race, class, sexual preference, historical era, locale, generation and so on. We wonder about "women"
within "gender." Should we, for instance, emphasize the insights that
come to us through mothering when, in fact, mothering is a social
assignment that conflates biology with culture? Flax "solves" these
dilemmas of ontology and epistemology by arguing that feminism is a
postmodern philosophy because feminists stub our toes, feel the pain,
and dissent from modernity's tropes whenever we seek to imitate
them.

We should not construe from this position, however, that feminism
can simply imbibe postmodern philosophy without exercising considerable caution. Flax (ibid.: 632) questions whether feminists should
even rely too heavily on the postmodernist French *feminists* who,
like the IR postmodernists, place considerable emphasis on texts. She
says:

> A problem with thinking about (or only in terms of) text, signs, or signification is that they tend to take on a life of their own or become the world, as in the claim that nothing exists outside of a text; everything is a comment upon or a displacement of another text, as if the modal human activity is literary criticism (or writing).

Flax also faults postmodernism – which she paints with broad strokes – for obscuring "the projection of its own activity onto the world and den[ying] the existence of the variety of concrete social practices that enter into and are reflected in the construction of language itself (e.g., ways of life constitute language and texts as much as language constitutes ways of life)" (ibid.: 632). To relate this to IR, there is in the otherwise laudatory projects of dissidence a politics of sometimes forgetting that even exiled "men" have a social context that affects what they say and that opens up to them certain vehicles for voice that remain closed to others. That is, Ashley and Walker may lament their exile and the exile of many dissidents from IR, but some among them do have voice and the power to decide who to voice.[8] Indeed, efforts to avoid complicity with privileged identity by deconstructing the way identity has been used by (other) men to oppress, may be what leads some postmodernists (like Derrida) to "metaphorize their crisis in the guise of discourses about the feminine" (A. Maugue, 1987 in Braidotti, 1991: 135).[9]

The postmodernism Flax (1987: 640–1) encourages for feminism is not naive:

> The enterprise of feminist theory is fraught with temptations and pitfalls. Insofar as women have been part of all societies, our thinking cannot be free from culture-bound modes of self-understanding. We as well as men internalize the dominant gender's conceptions of masculinity and femininity ... We need to (1) articulate feminist viewpoints of/within the social worlds in which we live; (2) think about how we are affected by these worlds; (3) consider the ways in which how we think about them may be implicated in existing power/knowledge relationships; and (4) imagine ways in which these worlds ought to/can be transformed.

What Flax implicitly calls for is a feminism within postmodern philosophy that is multistandpointed and "women"-aware. She wants a postmodern blasphemy that enables feminists to be on several (assigned and el(l)e-phantly painted) shores at once and to see around us with an owlish sweep of vision that never loses sight of embodied women even as it casts a skeptical eye on the constituted subject status "women."[10]

This perspective has a sonorous timbre in certain feminist contributions to IR's third debate. Jean Elshtain (1987), for one, is well known for her efforts to homestead war and peace with blasphemous "women" and "men," whose standpoints once revealed are no longer easily corralable onto "a" shore. She says, for instance, that:

> By speaking of women *and* war – rather than presenting a chronology of women *in* wars or a paean to the notion that women have not been in the thick of violent things, not eagerly anyhow – I signal my intention to explore diverse discourses and the political claims and social identities they sustain. Women have played many parts in narratives of war and politics ... Although some men no doubt conform to the image of adolescents itching for a fight, many others seek ways to constrain and limit violence and find nuclear weapons repulsive. *Women and War* is the result of overlapping recognitions of the complexity hiding behind many of our simple, rigid ideas and formulations. (Elshtain, 1987: x–xi)

Here, there is a simultaneous acceptance of women as real – their bodies can die in war or mourn the loss of others – and a sense that "women" have been constituted, created, invented, and imagined through war and peace narratives that are repeated and repeated.

A different angle on the problematique of sighting and unsiting women in IR is revealed in Anne Sisson Runyan's (1992) review of "The 'State' of Nature." Runyan provides a critical picture of the intricate relationships to which "women" are assigned (or assign themselves) vis-à-vis "nature": Mother Earth tending her flock well if only she is allowed to do so by the fettering forces of capitalist-industrial-statist-industrial politics; witches associated with nature's presumably dark and disorderly side; gardeners of nature (for man); whole-earthers who offer "a sterile and harmonious picture of Mother Earth by denying man-made disasters and natural forces of death and decay" (ibid.: 133). Her owlish vision takes her to "fractious holism" understood, following Jane Bennett (1987), as a politics that "refuses to see the natural world as organized either around human ends or around the needs of the state, and refuses to see women's bodies and lives organized around the needs of the white man's state or as subsumed by the images and claims of an anthropomorphized, state-centric "environment" (Runyan, 1992: 136).

Some feminisms are second and some are third?

A second perspective on feminism's place, as it encounters the third debate in IR, can be deduced from feminist discussions about the pros and cons of second- versus third-wave approaches to knowing. The

153

question of which wave of feminism has been better for "women" has two-ish positions.

Hester Eisenstein (1984) makes a definite distinction between the waves of feminist thinking. She argues that feminist approaches to knowledge and action shifted in the 1980s from a modernist-resonating effort to correct analysis and public policy finally and once and for all, to a concern to explore epistemology and the existence of the subject. One can indeed make the argument that the liberal, Marxist, radical, and socialist feminisms of the 1960s and 1970s were really feminist modernisms. After all, they seemed beholden to various preexisting philosophies that posited one cause of and answer to women's degraded status in the West if not Everywhere, and some among them were adversarial in denouncing feminists who did not see things their (one) way. In chapter 1 I suggested many distinctions between feminisms that could, at first glance, make it textually difficult for some of them to ride the third wave rather than be stuck behind it. But I did attach each second-wave body of thought discussed to a third-wave epistemology, thus smudging the boundaries between waves, which I think is a more accurate depiction of overlapping waters.

Braidotti's (1991) second, more complex way of understanding the relationship between second- and third-wave feminist thinking smudges boundaries in a different way. She claims that "some feminist theorists, too often and too hurriedly labelled as 'difference thinkers,' have moved towards ideas of multiplicity and difference in order to avoid the trap of ready-made dualism" (ibid.: 130). They have, in effect, reinvented "an" enemy in the binary opposition even as they strike out against the notion that there is a unitary logic to anything. Second-wave feminisms made "women or the feminist the new master, or patroness, or protector of a new form of normativity ... This would ultimately result in rationalizing women's counterknowledge, experience and discourses, but it would basically leave untouched the framework of power within which they operate" (ibid). Yet the second wave, says Braidotti, was utopian, full of political blueprints that specifically addressed frameworks of power and justice. It produced a feminist literature that was inspiring, unconventional, irreverent, humorous, fun to read – "free from the specialized tone of later feminist scholarship" (ibid.: 153). It was linked in struggle and in tension with workers, lesbians, third-worlders, people of color, Marxists, students – all subjects claiming subjectivity. It revolted too – against reformist and revolutionary doctrines of the day that could not extricate themselves from gender-occluding formulas and from

154

complex patriarchy. It radically rejected master narratives even as it accepted certain subject positions as real. It was in your face.

The point to recuperate from Braidotti's analysis is that to be second-wave need not mean that one has lost the race for progressive knowledge. It need not signify a banishing of the second behind the third in a patronizing rehearsal of the modern sense that to move to a new way shows some freeing of ourselves from the past. Second-wavers are not necessarily in some rhapsodic state of numbed thinking. Their movement politics in the 1970s empowered some women relative to the hyper-intellectual, hyper-epistemological third wave of the 1980s. When second-wave politics became (prematurely) passé, away went a certain permission to be outspoken, outraged, and out on the streets – as subject positions with power and confidence. Out of fashion went the empowering old ways of reading the radical oldies – Mary Daly, Sonia Johnson, bell hooks. Too bad. I still believe that the "radical feminists" pushed feminist thinking the farthest the fastest and with the most KAH-POW(!!). Now "[t]he 'problem without a name', as Betty Friedan called it in the sixties, has gradually been transformed into a movement without an ideology, and against all ideologies" (Braidotti, 1991: 157). It can seem to be struggling against power as a thing to struggle for.

Ah, but that is nostalgia for you. The second wave was also mean-spirited at times, rejecting, violent, and not for the terminally shy. It was knowledgeable, but knowledge was not always translatable into power for us. Ultimately, we did not ride the second wave to our way, however many ways that way was articulated. Some "women" hated us. Some of us mingled with the popular texts of burn-out. And so the cautions of the third wave.

All feminisms are percolating through our postmodern time, debating each other and all others, scripting and rescripting their own texts and identities as they confront a world that once fixed us and now is a bit unhinged. Accordingly, I have placed all the waves of feminism in all the debates of IR, whether they belong there in linear time or not. I am placing them again, in ever different ways, in the third debate. This is not a refusal to see feminist differences. It is a flexibilizing move that recognizes mobile subjectivities. But not everyone will agree. There will be debates about which wave does it better and why all these labels anyway.

As for flexibilizing feminism in its encounter with IR's third debate, ponder the intellectual journey some feminists have taken as they consider and reconsider the relations of (second wave) women to issues of (third wave) epistemology.

Rebecca Grant and Kathleen Newland (1991: 2) open their collection on *Gender and International Relations* with this statement:

> From the start international relations has had difficulty drawing the connections between individual citizens – male or female – and the states system. The focus on events and behaviour has not been conducive to feminist thought because the role of women has long been muffled. At the same time the competing influences of realism, idealism, Marxism, behaviourism and so forth have had one particular effect in common. These intellectual concepts which helped define the discipline also gave the appearance of transcending gender issues.

Here, "women" and "gender issues" almost converge textually. In the special issue of *Millennium* that first highlighted the feminist IR link, and from which most of the chapters in *Gender and International Relations* were taken, there was a very definite insistence on the part of the editors, Grant among them, that "'women and international relations' is a viable subject of intellectual significance, in its own nascent terms and within the discipline of international relations" (1988: Editors' Introduction). And we "know" that studying unproblematized women is second-wave.

In a recent piece, Grant shows us how a foot in second-wave feminist thinking may be needed to negotiate the third debate in IR. Her concern is to think through what a feminist epistemology can do for security studies. This is her view:

> What a *feminist epistemology* must do in time is to include tools for confronting the gender bias structured into the theories of security in international relations. It must also resolve the conflict of values between women's experiences in combat, and feminist assumptions about security that feed a feminist epistemology. Finally a feminist epistemology must define how it functions given the presence of other epistemologies that cover the same agenda of war and security. (Grant, 1922: 96)

The emphasis on "bias" and the need to "resolve the conflict of values" and "to define" and delineate epistemologies is different from pondering whether "women" exist, whether bias can be corrected without dissenting from the inherited intellectual-power order. It is different from asking whether a conflict of values is necessarily as undesirable as she suggests. Yet Grant's approach resonates with third-wave efforts to move "beyond simply criticizing established ideas ... [to] a critique of the status of theoretical discourse itself" (Braidotti, 1991: 174). So where is the boundary between the second and third wave?

156

Again, that differences mark feminist contributions to IR's third debate should not be refused. But our discussion of points of overlapping waters suggests that there is little reason to engage in acrid and enervating debates about which feminism is the best for IR. Our waves unfold around, under, on top of each other, blurring the borderlands into that "mestiza consciousness" that enables us to be on several shores at once. In effect, we are drawn away from the liberal convention of dialogue or debate, where one side tries to display such brilliance that the other side is cowed into publicly conceding the point, while privately, perhaps, dissenting. The postmodern in feminism is conversational, fluid in identity, and comfortable with a certain degree of unpegged ontology. It comes around once again.

Postmodern feminism – again

Kathy Ferguson offers us a third perspective on where feminism could fit that takes us around and through and into the others and back to postmodern feminist borderlands – yet another time.

She writes about the "important tension within feminist theory ... between articulating women's voice and deconstructing gender" (Ferguson, 1991: 322). This standpoint versus postmodernist tension has a flaw on both of its sides that makes righteous side-taking somewhat pompous. The standpoint flaw is this: "expressions of women's voice usually call for respect for differences among women (and sometimes among men as well), but the logic of the search for a founding experience tends to elide difference nonetheless" (ibid.: 323). Thus Grant (1992) has difficulty reconciling her sense of women in combat with "a" way of thinking about "women's" experiences, although she sees no reason to doubt that some founding experience is authoritative in establishing the existence of women and men. The flaw in the postmodernist project of deconstruction is that it is "parasitical upon the claims it seeks to unfound, including claims about sexual difference, both those of the patriarchal order and those of feminists" (Ferguson, 1991: 324). Thus, one could argue that Elshtain's (1987) approach to women and war, although ungluing in its refusals to accept the authority of inherited war narratives, depends on war for a starting point (indeed, it is more complicated than this because Elshtain also critiques peace as being a piece of the war/peace dichotomy).

In Ferguson's mind, the tension between the two feminist approaches, both of which seem to straddle the second and third waves, can be overplayed to the point where we fail to see that the deconstructionists keep the standpointers honest by reminding them

157

that the subject "women" is constructed and must be decolonized; meanwhile, the standpointers give the deconstructionists a direction to land political action and moral claims in a postmodern world. At the borderland of the two feminisms there can be mobile subjectivities that "multiply the levels of knowing and doing upon which resistance can act" (Ferguson, 1993: 157). Rather than move from the stable resting place of interpretation to the destabilizing place of genealogy, or vice versa, mobile subjectivities help us to interrogate the "contours of the resting [or the homesteading] one does" (ibid.: 158) and to negotiate among "needed incompatibles."[11]

Such negotiations in the field of IR (or other fields) would not be grand in theoretical aspirations. Rather than produce something consensually new and global – a novel homestead designed by "the" new committee (or an offering of two homesteads that we can then debate the merits and demerits of), the conversations would be different across places and similar where there were shared circumstances. The point is that "[m]obile subjectivities must negotiate their incompatibilities" (ibid.: 165) – and their compatibilities. Those involved must decide and not simply rest content to derive knowledge. They must also be attentive to the shrapnel that their decisions unleash on those who prefer deriving over deciding and on those whose concerns may be excluded, once again, from the field of negotiation (Sylvester, 1993d: 116).

In a spirit of encouraging conversation among feminism's potential allies in IR's third debate, I roam two texts that would, that could, but that do not quite include the local concerns of this particular feminist. What follows are the contours of my initial input to a would-be empathetic negotiation about Ferguson's and Mansbach's (1991) "Constructive Suggestions for Future International Theory," and R. B. J. Walker's (1992) dissident view of the place of "Gender and Critique in the Theory of International Relations." The outcome of such a conversation cannot be known in advance because processes of empathetic cooperation promote some slippage in positions on all sides.

Between celebration and despair

Ferguson and Mansbach contend that the third debate is now in a feedback loop that debates-the-debates-within-the-debates. The two analysts want very much to get out of this "anarchical" loop and find a constructive stand for the field that allows, as noted above, the claims of "dissidents" to be taken seriously while continuing to press on for the rigor and precision that is associated with strategic reasoning, with the reproductive fitness of IR. They suggest that we proceed as follows.

The most important step is to rethink the concepts we generally use to ground the field, replacing unitary states, bounded rationality, and anarchy (with or without cooperation) with a more fluid and encompassing focus on authority. They understand authority to mean effective governance resting on "the loyalties of those who are governed and on their willingness to provide resources to the collectivities of which they are part" (Ferguson and Mansbach, 1991: 376). This starting point is somewhere near the place where neoliberal institutionalism posits we might end up if diffuse reciprocity becomes a basic convention of the anarchic international state system. But Ferguson and Mansbach do not interpret the problematic of the field as cooperation under anarchy to defeat anarchy. Rather, they want analysts to focus on "questions of how authority patterns and attendant human loyalties evolve, overlap, and interact" (ibid.: 377). They want us to broaden the human loyalty groups that are considered relevant to international relations, to families and kinship groups, nations, religions, and other authoritative lightening rods for value allocation in certain issue areas. There is no such thing, they say, as an actor whose positions summarize a society or single political system. There is no decision maker who acts for a state and no realistic realist imaginary of states acting. There are only micro–macro continuums that researchers can probe in order to know (following Dina Zinnes [1980]) the following about them: their number in an issue-area; their distribution of resources; their issue-positions; the location of their power; their patterns of affect; customary rules that govern their interactions; and the accorded status of competing authorities.

Along the way, we must abandon a strict levels-of-analysis reading of societies as hierarchically arranged: "Family-level groups tend to be subsumed into local polities, and these into regional polities, but the different strata neither completely disappear nor achieve full autonomy" (Ferguson and Mansbach, 1991: 380). And we must abandon the notion of unilinearity once and for all and realize (as I would say that most area-studies scholars focusing their work on the third world already realize) that the "fact that older entities have been absorbed into newer and larger ones does not mean that the former are irrelevant but may merely mean a shift in the political venue and a new set of rules for waging conflict" (ibid.). In sum, we must become comfortable with the idea that "there is no 'sovereign' player" but only various contests among authority patterns (ibid.: 382).

Having gagged the state, Ferguson and Mansbach admonish us to break from Eurocentrism and from the focus on our own time of international relations as the fascinating point of study. They admonish us to break off, as well, the endless discussions of epistemology and the tiresome battles over disciplinary turf to get on with the agenda they have laid out for us. But in other areas, they seek connections. They claim that we must "venture beyond our field's familiar boundaries" and learn to "tolerate the effrontery of others messing about in *our* intellectual territory" (ibid.: 383), because (they do not quite say this) the cross-dresser performs best:

> Only then can we begin to integrate the apparently disparate insights of geography (e.g., location, climate, population, natural resources), biology (e.g., disease), technology (e.g., weaponry, communications), economics (e.g., production and markets), sociology (e.g., social strata), archaeology (e.g., non-historical evidence), anthropology (e.g., social mores), philosophy (e.g., religion, ideology), psychology (e.g., personality, group identity), language (e.g., concepts) and others into a broad understanding of politics. (Ibid.)

In effect, Ferguson and Mansbach argue that the dissidence–empiricist impasse, which is their understanding of the third debate, is really all about displacing some misconnected compatibles (Europe, the state, anarchy) with "needed incompatibles." They grant the dissidents their point about the benefits in lifting disciplinary blinkers. They think the empiricists have a point in wanting to traverse the canyon of doubt and get to another side rather than fall into a void or dance merrily back and forth on a tightwalk. The two sides are parts of a field in transition. The third side is the venture beyond the usual turf to make many strange bedfellows our constant companions.

Ferguson and Mansbach make the point that there is relevant political activity – a world of "we" – that We have not examined. Feminism is made part of that world, but only through a mention so brief and limited in scope that it is clear Ferguson and Mansbach have not yet begun to follow their own advice to look farther afield. I wonder if this is what feminists can expect in a new, authority-focused IR: as the truly exciting fields "out there" are approached for insights, feminists will be out beyond the "out there." Other questions come to mind. Will turf journals refuse to read certain unfamiliar forms of IR as IR, refuse to break the conventions of cooperative autonomy from "women" that seep into their regimes? Might we expect that there will be pressure to integrate on terms other than our own, that is, by abiding by conventions of speech and analysis rather than taking on IR in different ways? Whose norms, rules, and expectations will comprise the standards into which others must integrate? Which feminism will be integrated with which IR? The possibility surely exists that "integration" could be synonymous with "assimilation," which is an old-style project of colonizing local differences.

These questions address the authority-patterns in academic IR and raise points about gender as fully eligible for investigation under the Ferguson and Mansbach agenda without the processes of empathetic cooperation that postmodern feminism advocates. I might extend those questions by asking, in addition, whether gender can be considered an issue-area, authority-pattern or both – from a Foucauldian perspective, the differences between these concepts are not real. Also, where would gender be studied – in global-domestic politics *and* also "in here" in the field of IR among our analysts and practitioners? Without addressing the local roosting place for gender in IR, it would be difficult to see, let along study, gender in more distant places.

I suspect that Ferguson and Mansbach would not endorse integrations that recall the days of Westward Ho refusals of self-reflexivity. More likely, they have in mind what William Connolly (1991: 473) calls a "politics of disturbance," by which he means "efforts at projecting new challenges to old relations of identity and difference, disrupting the dogmatism of settled understandings and exposing violences and exclusions in fixed arrangements." If so, there should be more attention paid to a postmodern feminism that disturbs by not-inserting women into IR or IR into women, but that looks instead for places in overdefined subject statuses where many differently constituted "women" are deciding authority rather than resting content with authority-patterns-issues derived from gender-encumbered mapping operations. IR needs to look for creative and mobile acts of homesteading, rather than confine its new inspiration to conventional academic disciplines, where there is no guarantee that feminism and "women" have been treated any better than they have in IR.

Where would this search take us? Ferguson and Mansbach mention the power of the Catholic Church to deauthorize abortion in the Republic of Ireland: "In the Irish Republic ... it is virtually impossible for any government to challenge the Catholic Church on abortion or birth control, where the loyalty of many citizens is to the Church first" (Ferguson and Mansbach, 1991: 381). But what about disloyal citizens? We should want to hear from and about people who defy that authority-pattern, who travel to Europe for abortions in countless acts of unmentioned international relations, who petition for change at home in order to make the absolute right to life, as defined by the Catholic authorities, far less solid as an old-style homestead, far more open to public discussion than it has been. If the efforts of these challengers to Catholic authority do not prevail, certainly this cannot

161

mean that there is nothing for IR to study, owing to the fact that the challengers have not displaced the authorities to become authority-patterns themselves. Indeed, abortion suggests an international relations of reproductive relations that is begging for investigation.

Ferguson's and Mansbach's Agenda allows us to see this possibility for research and that is laudable. Yet I do not seek "an" agenda that could foreclose those that can be empathetically formed and cooperatively decided. If one looks at feminist theorizing across all forms, one can see a model of practice that enables competing research agendas to flourish in a spirit of critical checks and balances on what constitutes the new versus the recycled. This does not produce conceptual anarchy so much as it keeps us appropriately unsure-footed in an era of uncertainty while not forsaking "women." Anyway, anarchy is now a contested concept. Ferguson and Mansbach themselves question the existence of "anarchy" in international relations and I question anarchy in a field of study that shows considerable cooperative autonomy from "women." Is it anarchy we fear in third debate theorizing or loss of authoritative issues?

Gender and critique in the theory of international relations

In Spike Peterson's (1992a) collection on *Gendered States*, one male-bodied person has joined the "All-Girls" to see, critique, reformulate, and decide gender issues in IR. I read Walker's analysis and am fascinated by its intricacies, its powers, its moments of sympathy: "feminist voices have begun to make themselves heard in what has been one of the most gender-blind, indeed crudely patriarchal, of all the institutionalized forms of contemporary social and political analysis" (R. Walker, 1992: 179). I am also saddened, however, by the many insights of feminism that Walker does not see but would throw away anyway.

Focusing on problems that arise when we juxtapose "claims about feminism and international relations theory". (ibid.: 180), Walker takes up (implicitly) where Ferguson and Mansbach leave off:

> What is at stake, I believe, is not just the possibility of adding certain excluded voices to the discipline of international relations as it is presently conceived. It is, rather, the possibility of challenging the grounds on which the theory of international relations has been constructed as a constitutive margin that simultaneously limits and affirms an historically specific account of political identity within a spatially bounded community. (Walker, 1992: 180)

Walker advocates an IR that acknowledges "world politics" rather than "international relations" as its *modus operandi*. "World politics," he argues, communicates the sense that there are politics occurring "out there" in the world that are "rather more complex and puzzling than the available categories of explanation" (ibid.: 182). Think of the post-1989 politics of surprise that disturbed conventional IR by spilling out of political communities, where "it is possible to aspire to Justice, Reason, Enlightenment, and History" (ibid.), into the realm of mere relations of order or crude power-plays. As well, think of the politics that "repudiat[e] the Brezhnev Doctrine here and ... reassert ... a Monroe Doctrine there" (ibid.: 181). Think of "women" pushing baby carriages through the Berlin Wall in defiance of cold war jeremiads. The discipline of IR hangs its hat on various distinctions between relations – its realm – and politics. Ergo, it must capture these odd politics to survive.

Walker says that "the diversity of women's experiences is captured and simplified in the same way as the diversity of all those events that might be interpreted as an aspect of world politics" (ibid.: 183). In this case, the simplification is that "women" "have their only effective political expression in the sovereign state" (ibid.: 182), irrespective of whether we ever notice their politics there or incorporate them into our theories. Through this commonplace assumption of place, "women" are evacuated from international "relations" and, although assigned place in the domain of the sovereign state, are effectively evacuated again through refusals of equal political recognition there with "men."

Several reasons for the evacuations of politics and "women" from IR are on Walker's mind. He says early modern political philosophers tried to define autonomous subjectivities against God, Nature, or Humanity. Thereafter, there was concern "to find ways whereby the autonomous individual, the knowing subject, and the inner conscience might be reconciled with the world from which they had been, ambiguously, alienated or freed" (ibid.: 186). IR theory tried its own reconciliation of knowing subject with the world and came out with a negation of such reconciliation:

> The world has become populated by individuals who know them-
> selves politically only as abstract subjects; free yet constrained by law;
> citizens, but humans only to the extent that they can realize their
> humanity through the twin sovereignties of state and subjectivity –
> the abstract autonomies whose conditions of production and repro-
> duction have simply vanished from sight. (Ibid.: 188)

As Walker realizes, the "individuals who know themselves politically only as abstract subjects" are ultimately summarizable as citizen "men." What he may not see clearly is that "men's" autonomous

163

subjectivity was never separated from humanity or from the state, at least not in Hobbes's rendering of Leviathans. Walker claims, as do others (Suganami, 1989; Bull, 1977) that Hobbes did not intend to equate individuals with states – "[h]e clearly understood that states are not like individuals; they are less vulnerable to violence than are individuals and they are unequal to each other" (Walker, 1992: 186). Walker also asserts that "[c]onsiderable interpretive tenacity is required ... to locate asymmetries of class, culture – or gender" (ibid.: 188) in Hobbes's work. But there are individuals and then there are "women" in Hobbes (Pateman, 1988; Di Stefano, 1983). Hobbes hobbled "women" politically by setting them up with children for likely conquest before they ever entered the jurisdiction of the sovereign state.[12] The state then made it difficult for the gendered citizens it sheltered to reconcile with the rest of conquered humanity. As Walker says, following a parallel path:

> [D]espite the appeal to principles of universal reason, the reconciliation of the autonomous individual and other autonomous individuals in a particular society does not lead to a reconciliation with humanity as such. On the contrary, the reconciliation of particular and collective on the terrain of the universalizing appeal yet particularistic authority of the sovereign state affirms the irresolvable conflict between the claims of citizenship and the claims of humanity. (Ibid.: 187)

Walker claims that sovereignty is "the key constitutive moment of modern political life" (ibid.: 188), a "particular rendition of rational man" (ibid.: 191), and yet "the most enduring silence in modern political discourse" (ibid.: 188).[13] I agree but see no puzzle here as to why it is so. Sovereignty seems "natural" and unspoken once a particular gendered composition of it is crafted in the early modern era. In answering "questions about political identity – about who the 'we' is that engages in political life" (ibid.: 189) – sovereignty countenances minimal processes (at best) for deciding and redeciding identity as part of humanity rather than, or while part of, the state.

The problem facing us now, Walker argues, is that "[a]ccounts of gender identity – and of all other identities, not least those that might be articulated in relation to concepts of class and culture – are *already* incorporated into the most fundamental assumptions that permit an account of international relations to be constructed at all" (ibid.: 190). And the incorporation is problematic. As I see it, we need to take feminist challenges to these forms of incorporation as seriously as we have taken the whole implausible device of constructed IR and its levels of analysis-defying conflations of "individuals" with "states" with "relations." Walker knows that challenges must be made, albeit "problems arising from the expansion and proliferation of theoretical perspectives seem less pressing than the sheer difficulty of establishing the relevance of *any* form of critique" (ibid.: 192). But, in a *trompe d'oeil*, he actually refuses to attempt "to apply insights from contemporary feminist theory directly to the theory of international relations ... [because] feminist theory is not a collection of insights that may be applied [so much as it is] a fractured and heavily contested discourse [and] site of active political struggle" (ibid.: 196).

I do not think Walker has carefully considered the potential contributions of feminist theory – fractures, contestations, and all – to the issue of identities, politics, and relations. Feminist psychoanalytic writings, for example, tell us that "relations" are produced by the conventions of human birth and caretaking and then downplayed as boys become gendered. Adult "men" routinely act in ways that deny human relations and that affirm polarities in which some of us seek freedom and the women seek connections. In the feminist psychoanalytic school of thought, "relations" connotes closer bonds of sociality than the interest-group manipulations, rules, and competition of "politics." To valorize "politics" is possibly to ratify activities that evade "relations" national–international and that keep us, intentionally or not, enthralled with the liberal imaginary that "individuals" still count in politics and these individuals can only connect through rights rather than through relations.

If we consider that even among feminists "politics requires ... cultivated political *spaces* for posing and arguing about feminist political norms, for discussing the nature of 'the good' for women" (W. Brown, 1991: 79), then we realize that relational memories, are useful when we begin a process of empathetically cooperative politics in IR. Relations are also needed to negotiate those "cultivated political spaces" that emerge once the discussions begin to leave us feeling a bit homeless vis-à-vis our former identities and positions on "the good for women." This means that we need not choose between relations and politics. The empathetic cooperation I associate with postmodern feminism joins the two in ways that do not simply rehearse old inclusions and exclusions or reinforce old readings. Empathy leads to listening to the excluded, listening to their sense of the good, knowing that they will present a fractured and heavily contested discourse because they have been simultaneously inside and outside a master narrative. Cooperation comes in rescripting agendas to reflect the subjectivities that have been etched into the identities of empathetic listeners.

Postmodernists in IR, like Walker, sympathize with "marginal instances" and investigate the textual ways that exclusions have been nativized historically. The postmodern feminist insight, however, is that sympathy and empathy are not the same. Empathy brings the heretofore "instances" into politics on their own (fractured) terms and it also makes us think critically about our relations to the stories we hear, our social constitution as men and women, our I-to-i connections. Above all, empathy is the capacity to participate in another's ideas and feelings. Sympathy is a more distanced, socially correct response mediated by a constant "I," an immobile subjectivity. It represents another's situation through compassion and pity without losing much in the way of personal control. Walker sympathizes with feminists, but he says that "the aspiration for a feminist theory of international relations is fundamentally misguided" because it perpetuates the two-realm imaginary of gender. "A feminist theory of world politics ... might be understood as a different matter" (Walker, 1992: 197).

Walker's sense of feminism is inappropriately heroic – "brave intellectual explorers [like] a de Beauvoir, for example, or a Kristeva" (ibid.: 183) (are they all French?). It is also unnecessarily paralyzed in its incapacity to generate a method that enlivens politics and relations and challenges "the grounds on which the theory of international relations has been constructed as a constitutive margin that simultaneously limits and affirms an historically specific account of political identity within a spatially bounded community" (ibid.: 180). We are thus left with chiaroscuro at the end of his chapter in the form of a curious "metaphor of domesticity that nonetheless suggests a possible reading of at least some aspects of contemporary world politics" (ibid.: 198). The metaphor is this: "A woman's place is in the kitchen" (ibid.) What the woman is doing there is obliquely working amidst the unplugged freezer that is now Central Europe, ignoring the microwave that cooks and transforms "everything within range" (ibid.). We are – this is not clear – also over there in some red light district or in zones of exclusion that include the garbage pail where "one would not want one's children playing" (ibid.).

This playful-serious woodcut portrays a world that is turning out to be disgusting by standards of IR theory because no one is doing the usually unacknowledged support work necessary to sustain relations as usual: In our liberation, we leave Siberian freezers unplugged and offensive odors and rotting remains around to be transformed. It can also read as a "backlash" against women who have become so alienated from kitchens, so prone to abandon responsibility in favor of the zones of red-light behavior, that they cannot even remember simple things – like to plug in the freezer after defrosting it or to clean the garbage pail on the inside as well as the outside. Foolish women. Lazy women. Reckless women. Mindless captives of gizmos they do not have the brains to use properly.

Women relating to the kitchen. "Like all metaphors, no doubt, this one has serious limits" (ibid.: 198). It is time to move beyond analysis by metaphor. Metaphors *are* limited. They are funny reminders of the not-so-funny. They are stories about action that take the place of action. We need metaphors to instruct us. But we need a more active method to disturb the intractabilities of IR.

Rethinking third

The third debate is our debate, our place in time, our space, our moment, our tree to climb, our queue to form. So where are we? The fascinating point about where feminism is in the third debate is that we were in-scriptively of the first and second debates of IR, and we are in and ahead of the third debate as it is structured in the pages of various IR journals. Feminists are becoming more and not less comfortable with their needed incompatibles, with their disagreements, mobilities, and internal critiques. This does not mean that feminists on postmodern terrains do not sometimes blast the standpointers and the empiricists among us or vice versa. The point is that the terrains are blurring for us while the various immune systems of late modernity (some cast as postmodernism) maintain some respectable boundaries separating feminism and IR.

Immune systems. Are they metaphors? Or are they more than that, being living lines that exist to:

> construct and maintain the boundaries for what may count as self and other in the crucial realms of the normal and the pathological. The immune system is a historically specific terrain, where global and local politics; Nobel Prize-winning research; heteroglossic cultural productions, from popular dietary practices, feminist science fiction, religious imagery, and children's games, to photographic techniques and military strategic theory; clinical medical practice; venture capital investment strategies, world-changing developments in business and technology; and the deepest personal and collective experiences of embodiment, vulnerability, power, and mortality interact with an intensity matched perhaps only in the biopolitics of sex and reproduction. (Haraway, 1991: 204–5)

Postmodern feminist theorizing is, by this understanding of the immanence of immune systems, immunomodulative and more.[14] It is cyborg active as "text, machine, body, *and* metaphor" (ibid.: 212

[emphasis added]) and as motoring agent exiting the garden of state and nature and de-longing for a home, for assimilation and normalization. It asks "who and what constitutes 'we' in our conceptions of political community" (Runyan, 1922: 137). It also leads us to ask: Who is left in "nature" at all?

Someone is still there. International naturalizations crop up in places that an active and less metaphorical concern with multistandpoints has only begun to enable us to see. Consider this. It is forbidden to import cross species relations of affection into the geospace called Australia (New Zealand too) if one species involved in the relationship is "bird." The text of immigration says: our nature here in Australia must be protected from outside nature that could break down our immune system and destroy our birds. (Advances in veterinary medicine are quite ignored in this statement.) What we see in this case is an international relations of naturalization that labels and differentiates and links "birds" to "human" geospaces of nationality as a way, supposedly, of protecting Mother Earth's thin and locale-specific immunities from sovereign diseases "out there."

With such very real sightings, which also happen to be the flying metaphors of "women" (as well as AIDs) in IR, feminist theorizing presses on. Our toolboxes of knowledge at our sides, we keep up the effort to unravel the fences and to hear the unsung. On bad days we hope, as Braidotti (1991: 283) puts it, that "the male death-wish is proving to be the greatest enemy of today's civilization, and that by comparison with this destructive drive, feminism is shaping up as the one possible new ethical system of postmodernism." Knowing about the immune system, though, we know better and paint in defiance of nature and homestead in defiance of various strategic cavalries. It is to some of our specific postmodern paintings of homesteaded IR that we now turn.

5 FEMINIST HOMESTEADINGS OF SECURITY AND COOPERATION

The encouragement of a scientific, detached impassivity struck directly at any link with the emotions. And in a conscientiously reportorial notation of natural phenomena there was no place for the imagination or fantasy. (Sweeney, 1934: 6)

One can claim, as this art critic did, that attention to light and color is quintessentially scientific and, therefore, that impressionist art has no imagination or fantasy. One can claim that impressionist art is quintessentially feminine and, therefore, it has imagination and fantasy. Either way, one creates a mirror-imaged aesthetic with little room for the in betweens of el(l)e-phants painting *en plein air*.

Security is a neorealist concern of highest importance. Cooperation is the neoliberal institutionalist *raison d'etre*. Strategies encircle them both and strategic thinking is endemic to IR. My task is to make good on postmodern feminism, on empathetic cooperation, on the creative homelessness from constraint that accompanies mobile subjectivities, on mestiza consciousness, owlish vision, feminist homesteadings – making face and making something postmodern and feminist that paints security and cooperation in multihued multistandpoints that may be discredited as monstrous by modernists but that will not go away.

The following discussion centers first on the IR zone of security as a realm of strategic vision that would immunize protected spaces from unwanted penetrations. Putting metaphor aside, as eventually we must, the discussion then takes the reader on a journey to two alternative locations of insecuring immunomodulations: Greenham Common Peace Camp in England, 1980–9; and two women's producer cooperatives in the high-density townships ringing Harare, Zimbabwe, 1988–90.

Securing an immune system

Security studies is one of the most encompassing components of modern IR theory. Its umbrella shelters studies of national security, international security (security interdependence), global security of the planet, and, some would say, peace studies.[1] It is a field born in the US and born-again, in both a military role and the political role of preserving certain western values, in Europe through NATO (Klein, 1990). It is a field full of debates; but it is also sketchable as a multicentered community that tacitly cooperates within itself to reproduce a strategic culture (Klein, 1988b), despite appearances of grave difference between some members who dedicate themselves to maintaining an immune system around a particular national, regional, and professional turf-space and those who would like to immunize us from this hard perimeter of defense.

Postmodern feminism insecures this immune system and even some of its more porous boundaries by introducing knowledges of security and cooperation by those ignored or "protected" by purveyors of particularistic immunities. It too comprises a multicommunity – of radical doubters, tolerant dissenters, seekers of knowledge at the hyphens of lived subject experiences, and resisters to the social constitution of secure identity, whose home-breaching activities make it difficult for the privilegedly secure to carry on. Turned toward "women" and away from Woman, there is alertness in this community to *many* subject groups that have been in-secured by the strategic immunities of security, including those outside the Americo-European deterrent umbrella who are, therefore, seemingly outside the western way of life.

To date, the security studies and postmodern feminist communities have had relatively little social interaction.[2] It is not for want of feminist security analyses. Rather, mainstream IR security specialists can be skeptical about any analysis that has the word "postmodern" in it (e.g., Walt, 1991: 223). In addition, differences within that community hide a certain degree of similarity in gender-insensitivity, as some concern themselves with techno-strategic vigilance, others more open to new understandings of security show spotty records on gender awareness, and critics of modernist projects to secure all ports shy away from feminist projects. Feminist homesteaders face a challenging prospect of probing the possibilities for empathetic cooperation across mutually discrediting, but in some sectors similarly gender-insensitive, communities to enable rescriptings of security and cooperation that avoid mirror-imaging a pregiven aesthetic.

170

Hardline sketches

There have been many malevolent "hawks" in the metaphorical kingdom of security, many hardliners who would damn those torpedoes at a drop of an insult or at a hint of a cause. They are easy targets of criticism, the stuff of political cartoons and of horror on the ground. I will let them goose-step by in their silly-fearsome uniforms. We know about their security and we know that most contemporary hardliners in academic IR are not of this ilk. As Walt (1991: 212, 224) tells us, "[s]ecurity studies assumes that conflict between states is always a possibility and that the use of military force has far-reaching effects on states and societies"; but at the same time, "most theories about the causes of war are also theories about peace ... and exploring ways to reduce the risk of war has been part of the field since its inception."

The hardline community I want to sketch centers first on members of the nuclear techno-strategic community – the immunologists who talk about missiles, throw-weights, payloads, verification, TERCOM and the like in a seductive, pornographic, and controlling language that highlights missiles more than issues of war, peace, and "women's" security (Cohn, 1987). In this group are "men" of the Golden Age, who comprised the first wave of hardline security studies (Walt, 1991), and who carved homes for themselves within various academic institutes; genealogically, one might say that the Golden Age community coalesced at the Rand Corporation in the US (B. Smith, 1966) and the Institute for Strategic Studies in London. My understanding of hardline includes but also reaches beyond that group to, as a second point, all analysts for whom security is a "strategic vision of international life" (Klein, 1988a: 297). This encompasses most security-studies specialists of· the so-called Renaissance years of the mid-1970s to the present, many strategic softliners, and even the seekers of the rules of strategic interaction to enable cooperation between states (Keohane, 1989a; Stein, 1990). The Renaissance brought security to academia, integrating it in its many forms into social science programs under the command of a new generation riding the wave of the second debate in IR. This generation brought: neorealist analysis to the speculative work of the Golden Age; historical analysis in the form of comparative case studies of security; evidence of bounded rationality to bear on deterrence theory; debates about grand strategy and peace studies to the field (Walt, 1991); and "strategic interaction" as the bridge between the systemic assumption of anarchy and decision-making approaches that stress self-interest and perception (Stein, 1990).

Before proceeding to some of the paradoxes of these eras,[3] one

171

might pause to consider the terms "Golden Age" and "Renaissance." Here are two very upbeat and epoch-resonating concepts. Taken together, they suggest that security studies is one of those great moments in western civilization, like the Golden Age of Rome or the Italian Renaissance. The use of these terms (principally by Walt, 1991) throws down a gauntlet for feminists who are familiar with the touted historical epochs of human greatness that have often been eras for "men." Joan Kelly (1984: 19), in particular, has warned us, as noted earlier, that "[t]o take the emancipation of women as a vantage point is to discover that events that further the historical development of men, liberating them from natural, social, or ideological constraints, have quite different, even opposite, effects upon women." Donna Haraway (1989), we have also noted, reminds us that usual studies of evolution put a vast game of strategic reasoning at the service of reproductive fitness. Indeed, the Renaissance of strategic studies seems merely to reproduce and perfect strategic vision as the emblem of IR across all eras and in-house debates. It protects missiles, nations, hardliners, softliners, and no-liners by liberating them from the limitations and lacunae of the earlier Golden Ages of strategic vision. Immune again.

California dreaming

Fred Kaplan (1983) provides the overarching metaphor for the techno-strategic Golden-Agers as Wizards of Armageddon. He describes them as an intellectual elite of men "whose power would come not from wealth or family or brass stripes, but from their having conceived and elaborated a set of ideas ... about the bomb: how to prevent nuclear war, how to fight nuclear war if it cannot be deterred" (ibid.: 10). Corporate financing facilitated wizardly escape from everyday insecurity into the world of deterrence, coercion, and escalation, and the Defense Department provided outlets for the wares as long as the emphasis was solidly on military forms of securing national space.

Through economist Thomas Schelling's (1966: 134) words – he was a member of the Santa Monica-based Rand Corporation in the 1960s – we can locate a guiding motto for this era in the principle that postwar weapons are different – "by *convention* – by an understanding, a tradition, a consensus, a shared willingness to see them as different – that they are different." With the bomb, if you could defeat the enemy by force, the dying society could, and conceivably would, use its last breath to deliver a deadly nuclear blow against you, the winner. Recognizing the dangers of this new technology, the mission of postwar nuclear strategists became to plot ways to impose some order

172

on the newly extreme disorder of an always unruly "out beyond"; supposedly there was little that prenuclear strategic thinking could teach about this new difference.

One element of order came in conceptualizing the nuclear age, which, of course, was also the era of the cold war, as not only about new weapons but about "the presumed hostile intention of the adversary" (Snow, 1989: 4). Hostile relations with adversaries owning nuclear weapons were survivable only through declarative and operational strategies of deterrence. Understood by some as a diplomacy of violence emphasizing the coercive use of power to hurt rather than destroy the enemy, deterrent power, it was said, is "most successful when it is held in reserve. It is the threat of damage, or of more damage to come, that can make someone yield or comply ... The threat of pain tries to structure someone's motives, while brute force tries to overcome his strength" (Schelling, 1966: 3). Thus, the emphasis was on "how different force postures could alter the incentive to strike first" (Walt, 1991: 215). And the force postures were products of the rational realist state unaffected by organizational maneuverings and domestic politics.

There is a paradox in the work of the early techno-strategists. Nuclear weapons are presumably different from conventional weapons and yet they are also presented as being of a piece with the weapons of the past, in that one can think strategically about how to use them to achieve the concrete political objectives that wars have always been fought to achieve. Thus, there has been concern to know "what war plans will best convince the opponent to desist from nuclear attacks and, should deterrence fail, allow war termination on the most favorable (or least unfavorable) terms" (Snow, 1989: 3). Should we threaten use mostly against enemy cities or military forces? How many weapons are required to survive a serious first use by the enemy and then deliver a decisive yet measured and proportional response? Does counterforce strategy, as opposed to counter cities, provide a form of mutual deterrence, something that can structure stability, or is it a war-fighting strategy? If the latter, how many deaths and how much destruction constitute a certain win? How vulnerable are we to their arsenals? Should we protect ourselves with ABM's or would this reduce mutual vulnerability?

Those subscribing to the view that nuclear weapons were continuous in some ways with the weapons that came before, formed "a causal succession," as Michel Foucault (1972: 3) would put it, as a rationale for continuing the Grand Tradition of war. Other community members were more willing to "tolerate the incommensurabilities" (Lyotard, 1984: xxxv) of new and old weapons and recognize

173

differences in defense requirements. They could see that nuclear weapons changed history; but even the tolerators could tolerate only to a point because of the need to ensure that internal incommensurabilities did not produce incoherent policies. Deterrence bridged the gap to strategize away strategic uncertainty.

But, owing to the basic paradox, Golden Age techno-strategists were never fully comfortable with the stable deterrence they wrote, and some among them devised ways to gain advantage by forcing the enemy to be the "chicken," "sucker," or "saint," to use game-theoretical terms, in smaller-than-nuclear encounters.[4] As Robert Jervis (1984: 31) puts this, in the nuclear age, "to the extent that all-out war is unthinkable, states have greater opportunities to push as hard as they can." Hence, the Golden Age strategic vision extends to and encompasses the era of "dirty little wars" of nerve and risk-taking that take place in the no-man's land between Golden Age and Renaissance – the land of Vietnam. Supposedly, theoretically, the "hurt your enemy" principle becomes a form of diplomatic bargaining in which the weaker side backs down, partly because of the actual hurt being imposed on him through conventional weaponry and in part because he fears the consequences of military escalation. To quote Schelling (1966: 132, 135) on this, "there is a simplicity, a kind of virginity, about all-or-nothing distinctions that differences of degree do not have ... what we have is the phenomenon of 'thresholds,' of finite steps in the enlargement of a war or a change in participation."[5]

A threshold was a decisional point, a moment in the continuous conflict when the enemy tripped the wire or crossed a fine behavioral line, leading the strategist to reevaluate his prevailing position. It was a moment when the strategic vision needed to take on board a new policy. We can also think of a threshold as signifying ruptures, discontinuities, transformations, and entrance points of homesteads. If one subverts and disciplines rupture in order to make it fit a unified notion of history, then, to quote Foucault (1972: 13), "one must obviously deny in the historical analyses themselves the use of discontinuity, the definition of levels and limits, the description of specific series, the uncovering of the whole interplay of differences." Transformation of system structure then becomes nigh to impossible. The game continues even in the open knowledge that there are risks in using and threatening to use nuclear weapons, and in "dirty wars," that strategism could not readily predict and control.

Not so parenthetically, the Golden Age strategic vision of "dirty little wars" seemed to guide behavior in the inner circles of the community itself. F. Kaplan (1983: 21) describes the tight group of

Chicago and Yale academics who promoted each others' careers and worked under "a shared conviction that its members were pioneers of a new age, riding on a crest that most others of their profession – including many of their non-Institute colleagues down the hall – chose not even to paddle through." At Rand, it was common and considered fun to test one's new ideas through colloquia so brutal in their competitive gamesmanship that one colleague once fainted from the barrage. Physicist Herman Kahn, on the other hand, was the ultimate defense intellectual at Rand – "cool and fearless, asking the questions everyone else ignored, thinking about the unthinkable" (F. Kaplan, 1983: 222). He was the impassively detached scientist who "struck directly at any link with the emotions." By contrast, Roberta Wohlstetter was the only female-bodied person on board for many years. She was known for her soufflés (ibid.: 122).

Getting real

Hardline strategic thought has not died. We can see elements of it in the concerns raised by Gorbachev's leadership of the used-to-be Soviet Union. It had been axiomatic to many Golden-Agers, mainly the Sovietologists, that the USSR was the ultimate other to the United States. As time passed, that other was perceived as less hostile in intent and more "self-deterred" (Jervis, 1984) or "existentially deterred" (Bundy, 1983) by "the objective reality of assured destruction in an all-out nuclear war" (Laird and Herspring, 1984: 5). With Gorbachev, it appeared that the distance between the two superpowers was really closing, even as he insisted on maintaining some differences that would foreclose a complete merger with the western way of security. This presented the Renaissance strategists with something unexpected in their period of certain reawakening – a postmodern problem. The immediate hardline Renaissance responses to it now make for interesting memories.

Graham Allison (1988: 18) argued, as did Francis Fukuyama (1989), that we in the US were responsible for changes in the USSR – our policy of containment worked. What we now needed to do was to put Gorbachev to the test and see just how similar his country could be to ours: "The failure of American policy makers to develop any concept or strategy for dealing with the 'new-thinking' Soviet leadership forfeits what may be a historical chance to push actively for specific and major steps by Moscow that advance Western interests." In effect, Allison was saying that the acknowledged differences between the US and the USSR had to be disciplined rather than mined for their

175

multistandpointed opportunities to forge a new framework. The USSR had to be made into the "chicken," even as it pursued moves more akin to saint (albeit some of its moves were inconsistent and difficult to read). The possibility of homesteading the cold war with hyphenated identities was subordinated to the certainty associated with some continuous hostility. It was more secure, more immune, for the US to resist reorienting its strategic thinking simply because there was a new and more softline head of state in the USSR; for, the motive for Soviet cutbacks in military spending could have been to resurface down the road as a more competent competitor.

Thus the hardline strategic vision, carried into the Renaissance period, moved forward the notion of Man-as-Strategist, the community's calling card.[6] Not all people called men fit the bill: The strategic man in a deadly age was an abstract thinker who could draw sharp lines between himself (and people like him) and others and maintain those lines by assuming that the others "out there" were playing the game by nearly the same rules.[7] This belief lent itself to a certain camaraderie among strategic thinkers that has been akin to the camaraderie of the battlefield, where intimacy is established in the act of strategizing to secure the hill – whether that hill is worth securing or not.

This camaraderie showed up in the Golden Age through a tendency for "men" of weapons to appropriate/reverse motherhood for their inventions – Golden-Ager Edward Teller proclaimed the hydrogen bomb a BOY. It also came in the form of a Thanatosian sexuality: General Jim Walsh, while director of Strategic Air Command (SAC) Intelligence, talked about war between the US and the USSR as having the goal of knocking their balls off; Bernard Brodie likened his plan for no cities/withhold as "withdrawal before ejaculation, while the SAC war plan was like going all the way" (F. Kaplan, 1983: 223).[8] Although dedicated to discovering and ordering the world of war and peace through rationality and the disembodied knowledge it often assumes, identity in this community always seemed to require these certain other qualities as well.

In the Renaissance era, those certain other qualities of the hardline were to include the ability to remain hard while training soldiers for nonnuclear combat:

> Militarists use the myth of war's manliness to define soldierly behavior and to reward soldiers. Boot camp recruits are "ladies" until, trained in obedient killing, they become men. Misogyny is a useful element in the making of a soldier, as boys are goaded into turning on and grinding down whatever in themselves is "womanly." Women are dinks. Women are villains. (Ruddick, 1989b: 77)

176

General Robert H. Barrow, former commander of the US Marines, reiterates the hardness:

> War is man's work. Biological convergence on the battlefield would not only be dissatisfying in terms of what women could do, but it would be an enormous psychological distraction for the male, who wants to think that he's fighting for that woman somewhere behind, not up there in the same foxhole with him. It tramples the male ego. When you get right down to it, you have to protect the manhood of war. (Wright, 1982)[9]

Should it escape our attention, we find in the security hardline – whether California dreaming or getting real – a rationality that immunizes the security specialists from mundane insecurities and allows the immunized to flaunt their bodies and to penetrate "others" in the spread of dis-ease.

Immunizing the immunologists

Consider now the report of Daniel Yankelovich and Richard Smoke (1988) on US public opinion on the new Soviet Union:

> It has been a bedrock perception, endorsed for a long time, by enormous majorities, that the Soviet system differs from the American one in the most basic ways. If that perception starts changing in the years to come, the implications could be profound. If Americans came to the conclusion that the USSR differs only relatively, not absolutely, from the US, the ideological core of the conflict could start to melt away. (Ibid.: 11)

From their survey research, the analysts conclude that "the average American wants to explore new possibilities but cannot easily brush aside forty years of hostility and mistrust" (ibid.: 1). The proof they offer is the volatility of public responses to new information on the Soviet Union and the distinctions the public draws between short- and long-term policies.

This Renaissance-era analysis draws on social scientific methods. It is also, supposedly, the softline at work – exploring the views of the public rather than assuming them away as the Golden-Agers did. Yet we face two problems in this work. First, Yankelovich and Smoke report findings about "the public" without explaining precisely who is included in and excluded from that group, except to equate "public" with "registered voters." Second, they measure the so-called public view with either/or, long-term/short-term questions (for example, should we seek agreements as rapidly as possible or proceed cautiously, step by step?). In the spirit of the rationalistic hardline, we see here a transcendence from the messy study that would have ensued had inter-views and positions of intersubjectivity been established between opinion pollers and people with stories to tell about their perceptions of the USSR (which is somewhat more than the contact group research strategy).[10] Instead, there is the easy retreat to an irreal "public" as a convenience; unintended perhaps, it is also a way of submerging "women" in the implied category of citizensand-states when, in fact, they are apart from that group in terms of the social contract (Sylvester, 1993a). The study reproduces strategic reasoning as a western way of securing life that soulfully "forgets" that "women" are not entirely "public" nor secure in the spaces that strategism would secure for us.[11]

This point leads into the question of tacit cooperations across soft and hardlines. Softliners endeavor to distinguish themselves from, to valorize the inverse logic of, or find options gentler than, hardline strategism. They are the minimum-deterrence people calling for arms control and reduction; some go farther and call for nonnuclear deterrence through conventional and unconventional military means, or for scrapping the war system and with it the logic of deterrence (categories from Buzan, 1987). Many simply want a nuclear policy that takes academic strategism into account, that accords with "the greater expertise and information available outside official circles" (Walt, 1991: 218). Klein (1988a: 301) calls softliners the keepers of an ironic streak in strategism, because they "take seriously the military strategic enterprise while posing some important political challenges to the politics of prevailing arrangements." We can also think of them as taking seriously the notion of strategy and applying it in other areas of the field under the supposedly soft guise of (neoliberal) institutionalism.

There is a wide range of ironies in this line. Jervis (1984) carefully outlines the *Illogic of American Nuclear Strategy* even as he dedicates his book to distinguished hardline immunizers (an act of community camaraderie) and designs a successor strategy that has as a first principle that "American nuclear forces [must] ... provide the unquestioned ability to destroy the Soviet Union even if the Soviets stage a skillful first strike" (ibid.: 168). Robert Johansen (1987) takes the language of hardline security as the point of departure in talking about "Global Security Without Nuclear Deterrence," and offers advice to existing decision makers, those who have an ear tuned to the Pentagon rather than those who may resist the Pentagon in their daily lives, on how to modify elements of the military immune system. Robert

Keohane (1989b) likens strategic interaction in the pursuit of diffuse reciprocity among states to the empathy people feel for one another, to an ethic of care or to the connected self that some feminist standpointers discuss. All the while, he fails to realize, as I pointed out in chapter 3, that states and their regimes connect with people called women only to ensure, tacitly at least, that the benefits of regime participation will flow from "women" to "men" and not ever the other way round.

There are also efforts to substitute citizen-based (Clark et al., 1984) or nonoffensive defense (Forsberg, 1992) for nuclear strategic reasoning. These endeavors tend to submerge security in defense, as if the cure for a dangerously overwrought immune system simply entailed sitting on the fences of defense. There is an irony within an irony here: Greenham Common peace campers, who I will discuss in greater detail shortly, did challenge national defense at the international fences of a cruise missile base in England; indeed, they did more than that and yet their efforts have received relatively little attention in the "substitute" softline literature. *A propos* of that omission, Helen Caldicott (1984) imagines the security community as a "patient" suffering the pathogenesis of the arms race (with "germs of conflict in the Third World") and the "missile envy" that could lead the world to "the terminal event" of nuclear war. Neither her almost immuno-metaphor nor her detailed discussion of security, although very effective, acknowledges feminist practices that homestead the terrain of the modern "tribal mentality" writ nuclear. Caldicott is brief and acerbic about women as the difference between what their bodies tell them to do and what they do in the realm of political practice: "In the United States, women won the vote seventy years ago, but they have done virtually nothing with it" (ibid.: 293), even though "[w]omen are nurturers" (ibid.: 294). She presumes that socially constituted characteristics (e.g., nurturing) are facts of life, just as the Golden-Agers imagined that military strategy would be a fact of life as long as war was possible. It is regrettable that Greenham Common women, who camped outside a cruise missile base in order to problematize many "facts of life" managed to escape her notice and comment.

Caldicott's less than thorough portrayal of "women" and security reminds us of the gender assumptions scattered throughout the softer line. Some of this literature is itself strategic in posing the rationality of minimum deterrence, or disarmament, or citizen defense as the perfect obverse of the hardline. It differs from the hardline in simultaneously disembodying and embodying rationalism. That is, rationality often stands out in this literature as a human characteristic for which there is no call to socially constituted gender (Reardon [1985] talks about this),

179

and we know that humanism has been a "women"-eclipsing slogan of modernity. However, some softliners assume that body–sex differences *are* directly constitutive of political orientations. Caldicott calls, in effect, for women's rationality to replace men's rationality. She presents "woman" as nurturer, because of a biological probability of giving birth, and is annoyed that women's political activities have not kept pace with their sex-based capacities. Think of Rousseau painting "women" as captives of irrational uteruses who could not enter the cerebral world of rational citizenry.

Softline interest in feminism, as a vehicle by which "women's" lot can be improved and more gentle public policies promoted, has often been linked to the implicit hope that a softer humanism will eventually amalgamate feminism and other movements opposing the security hardline into "a" new way of life. Says feminist peace educator, Birgit Brock-Utne (1989: 38), "I envision a world freed from sexism and racism, class oppression, and oppression on grounds of caste, color, or creed." And yet, even as they urge women on to peace efforts, feminist peace researchers and educators know that there are authority patterns in the softline itself that make it difficult to envision a new humanism that will not, once again, be tilted to one side. Betty Reardon (1985: 5):

> virtually no peace researchers or world order scholars, other than those few feminists in the field, have advocated the need consciously to conscript women into peace research and world order studies or to include feminist perspectives or feminist issues in the field. Most tend to view women's issues as secondary or collateral issues to the central concern of peace. Some still maintain that the subject is a distraction from the more important and core issues involved in the reversal of the arms race and militarization, and the abolition of war.

Recent feminist challenges resist invisibilizations and happy expirations at the hands of softline executioners. I have already spoken about Rebecca Grant's (1992) concern to think through the possibilities of a feminist epistemology in the area of security studies (see chapter 4). Some new anthologies of peace research now include feminist chapters that hold their own against a peace humanism (e.g., Forcey, 1989). Books specifically on feminist security concerns continue to appear (e.g., Harris and King, 1989; Macdonald, Holden, and Ardener, 1988; Brock-Utne, 1989), and articles reviewing the contested terrain of feminist peace studies now find their way into peace journals (Forcey, 1991).

Nonetheless, the feminist empiricist concern to integrate women into "the" softline way of security through the door of (a feminist standpoint-based sense of) natural womanly emotion (as opposed to security's scientific, detached impassivity) survives as an important theme in the feminist line. It reigns as though it were strategically crucial to tidy up feminist-peace mestiza messes by incorporating them coherently into a peace project. Unitary knowledge exists. There is one monolithic enemy against whom we must join hands (see discussion in Sylvester, 1987; 1993d). Linda Rennie Forcey (1991: 350–1) captures these themes when she asks us to remember the special role of women in any peace endeavor:

> For peace researchers, a feminist perspective that focuses on caring, nurturing, feeling, intuiting, empathizing, and relating remains an important new catalyst to challenge militarism. This contribution of essentialist thinking to the field of international relations and the peace endeavor is refreshing, comforting, energizing, and affirming for women. Thus it is with more than a little ambiguity and hesitation that I myself have come to see its limitations and weaknesses, and the need to move on. Who among us can say that there could ever be too much *caring* in this violent world?

By contrast, Jean Elshtain (1988) reminds us that to join peace is to join war because both are configured from the perspective of war.[12]

The softline community knows no clear boundaries with the hardline but is, nonetheless, reluctant to probe the in-between securities and insecurities that could mark points of empathetic cooperations. It is a softline that often does not appreciate the value of "bringing Artemis to life" by valorizing the prospect of feminist aggression and hostility (Harris, 1989). There is a nostalgia in this literature for a time in the future when right-thinking women will get to call the plays and to install the peaces. But even if women get the part, these writings suggest that war and peace could remain strategically dichotomized rather than owlishly linked in scope of vision and mestiza in identity.

The lineless strategist

Postmodernists problematize the hardline position and its softline variants in a number of creative ways. Timothy Luke (1989: 226), for instance, takes on deterrence theory as a paradox of "postwarring": "Since nuclear war probably could not settle conflicts or realize beneficial systemic changes, postwarring involves contradictory preparations for a 'war' that never can be fought." Michael Shapiro (1990) views all discourse as strategic and all weapons as commodities wrapped in a linguistic political economy. Klein (1988a), looks forward to a postmodern theory of peace based on a poststructural theory of

181

violence, and Ashley (1989) and R. Walker (1987, 1989) take on the related task of identifying the decentering elements of realism that undermine strategism as a form of sovereignty (also Luke, 1989).

This lineless approach, however, is not without perspective. When it is not reporting on the doubleness in standard texts, revealing contradictory security immunities that rarely draw comment, it can herald the dissolution of the social into personal lifestyle politics (Chaloupka, 1990). It can take on the strategic, as in asking us to cut "all ties and become a stranger to country, language, sex – indeed, any notion of a sovereign identity of men" (Ashley, 1989: 313). To cut ties to socially constituted sex at this time is to risk leaving certain subjects out of the future by virtue of ignoring any of their stories that revolve around gender experiences. To say the social has evaporated into self-centered lifestyle politics (or media politics) is to neglect the Greenham Commons, the organized cooperations of "women" in cooperatives, the social life of "women" before we have even seen all of it. Haraway's (1991: 208–9) words of warning ring, once again, in our ear:

> neither the immune system nor any other of bio-medicine's world-changing bodies – like a virus – is a ghostly fantasy. Coyote is not a ghost, merely a protean trickster ... Perhaps our hope for account-ability in the techno-biopolitics in postmodern frames turns on revisioning the world as coding trickster with whom we must learn to converse.

Learn to converse with tricksters rather than cut all ties with ourselves and them. Arguably, there are latent realms of tricksterism in postmodernist currents if IR. Analysts from that lineless line may be bound just enough to the community they critique that they do not directly, or perhaps I should day publicly in print, converse with their own experiences of sexual–gender privilege.[13] Accordingly, they can be very sympathetic with dissident "women" while also finding it acceptable to represent "us." To be partially free of this problem may require some floating in gender limbo, as Ashley (1989) suggests in his discussion of statecraft as mancraft. But here is a challenge: Can their cutting of ties with gender be done in appropriate ways without cooperative discussions with people who are already homeless in IR but who may have political reasons for holding onto their gender identities as part of a mestiza consciousness that gives one a wide sweep of owlish vision? This challenge must be taken up to re-vision the strategic vision of international relations and other modern framing moves.

182

Postmodern feminist immunomodulations

Germaine Greer (1970: 341), a key agent of feminism's first wave of annoyance at constructed womanhood, once pithily announced: "security is a chimera." She still seems to maintain that position.[14] Here is the starting point of homeless homesteading. Whether challenging the foundational realism of IR or the various strategisms to which it gives rise, there simply can be no coherent statement, inscription, or morality that makes the definitive home, covers all the contingencies of contingent existence, and thereby ends insecurity. Security is always partial and Strategy is always, as a result, somewhat undecidable. This piece of knowledge is known by mothers, peasants, career women, and the working class, by the tormented drug user and the securely rich. For all these people, security is both elusive and mundane.

To work with this elusiveness requires a recognition that it is intensified in the late or postmodern era by the number and types of insecuring actions that rivet our attention. This is a time of simultaneous struggles, of storms with many centers unfolding on many fronts at once. These struggles make many faces, stand on many borderlands of eagles and serpents, and homestead each other with many strategies. Some simultaneous struggles are relatively easy to see, as in South Africa, where efforts to homestead the acrid terrain of apartheid move in cross-cutting directions; there are similar struggles, it seems, in Peru, erstwhile Yugoslavia, Liberia, Canada, Angola. Other types of struggles are more difficult to follow, as in the see-sawing efforts to "secure" the international environment (Brock, 1992) or to secure reproductive rights or religious identities (Rupesinghe, 1992).

This stream of messy, contradictory incoherences with several overlapping and semi-permanent fronts means that no one is fully in charge or entirely successful in installing a new program, project, theory – for IR or for much of anything – and no struggling center loses absolutely in the sense of being finally "captured" and thrust "outside." There is, instead, instability in the home bases, the home ports, the homilies, the nostalgic homesickness, the hometowns, the homebound, the homebred, the homemade, the homecoming, the homeland, the homemaker, the homespun, the home truths – along with a variety of homesteading moves that are difficult to outline and measure, indeterminable as successes or failures.[15]

"Women" are variously located within these struggles – as armed warriors, feminist fighters against the oppression of women, homefront stabilizers, invokers of traditional values, party members, cooperators, counterinsurgents (Sylvester, 1989, 1990b). It is not so much where "women" are located and which causes they espouse (or others assign to them) in this era as the ways in which their cross-cutting struggles mobilize their subjectivities and rescript aspects of their identity while contributing to a general subversion of modern expectations and rules. Yet we face a dilemma: as un-surefootedness insecures "women's" and feminist knowledges and ways of knowing, does it not inadvertently open up roosting spaces for knowledges and practices feminists actively try to insecure? This dilemma leads to the worry that has been turned into a debate on epistemology, about how to measure gains and losses. How to know, amidst the certainty of immeasurable uncertainty, that something works for "women?" How to be mobile in our subjectivities and not yearn for the identity and authority that others may retain? How to settle on method, on something "we" can do?

Greenham Common

On August 27, 1981, thirty-six "women" and a few "men" and "children" left their homes in and around Cardiff, Wales for the 120-mile walk to Greenham Common in Berkshire, where ninety-six US nuclear cruise missiles were to be deployed. The walkers, evoking standard images of "women" as "nurturers," called themselves "Women for Life on Earth." Their message, however, was political: they wanted to bring pressure to bear on the Thatcher government for a parliamentary debate about the deployment of these missiles on British soil. They arrived at the base ten days later and, when the press and the British government effectively ignored them – perhaps because "women" are invisible in the politics of international relations – some walkers decided to remain and others joined them. In fits and starts they learned to be in-your-face in unexpected and still largely unheralded ways.[16]

Greenham Common deserves careful consideration for the lessons it teaches us about "strange" struggles with a powerful immune system, with a Western Way of Security in its Renaissance, that would protect "women" while refusing them political place. It teaches us about the postmodern condition of simultaneous successes and failures – success in coming into politics on one's own terms and failure to be the source of the missile evacuations to Arizona starting in 1989 (they were bargained away as the cold war began to wane under the impact of changes in the USSR). It highlights the ways that subjectivities usually refused place in IR can become the basis of negotiated actions that strike at the field's core – realist defense. As a place, the Greenham

184

Common Peace Camp epitomizes the law of "women's" homelessness in international relations in ironic ways that enable creative politics. That politics, in turn, provides object lessons on the sterile assumptions the field often makes about who is involved in decision making and how they proceed. Just as importantly, Greenham draws attention to activities in international relations that defy the "rules" of gender place, process, and political technique and therefore are not usually studied for the lessons they contain.

One does not know where to begin to describe the postmodern feminist politics of Greenham, and that is probably all to the point. The major actions for Life on Earth are fairly easy to chronicle: the "women" chained themselves to the fences of the base upon arrival; they later affixed signs of mundane security to that fence – pinning whole tea sets there along with diapers, recipes, tampons; they planted seeds, bulbs, and saplings around the dreary perimeter fence and, when threatened with evictions, they made a mobile garden in a pram to take with them; they danced the el(l)e-phant and teddy bear walk on the missile silos under construction at the base; they blockaded the base gates when missiles were sent on maneuvers; they had cruisewatches report every movement of the convoys, defying the official military line that the weapons could simply "melt into the countryside"; they domesticated the forces by sticking potatoes up the exhaust pipes of convoy vehicles. Throughout, some campers burned out, became angry, and left. Others stayed angry on, in, and around the fence – that emblematic boundary of security that could not keep them out.

In all of this (in)subordination, decisions took form and actions were forged in "strange" ways that slip through one's research techniques just at the moment one would like to specify them, calculate the moves, and assess policy outcomes. For virtually all of the "women," the first "strange" decision was to leave home for the homelessness of a walk that then turned into the trials of a wet and soggy makeshift camp served, after 1982, with daily eviction notices and actions. Ann Pettitt, usually credited with initiating the walk, says it started with a threshold breached in her mind, a point seemingly not unlike the decisional moment for strategists when the enemy crosses a fine line and precipitates a reevaluation of policy:

> There was just one day when I got fed up with cutting up newspapers and putting them in folders labelled "Nuclear Power, radiation, leaks, etc", "Pollution," "Third World," "Arms Race, weapons," and so on. That day, after the umpteenth "Minister rejects enquiry findings" and "radioactive leak denied" ... I sort of

185

blew a fuse, and I think I started shouting. (Quoted in Liddington, 1989: 223)

That threshold breached became a point, though, of creeping discontinuity as successive moves set in motion a turn toward "the whole
interplay of differences" that would render an initially centered group
increasingly removed from the alternative homes they had hoped to
build for Life.

Pettitt made posters out of old white wallpaper about a meeting to
be held on "Nuclear Power – Poisoning Our Environment." Thirty
people attended. They formed a small organization and set off down
the liberal path of writing protest pamphlets, in their case, calling for
nuclear-free zones. In the course of this softline strategic work,
however, they read about a march from Copenhagen to Paris led by
women against nuclearization. Pettitt says: "Immediately, we got off
on the notion of a similar march happening in this country ... marching to one of these damn military installations in the middle of
nowhere ... led and organized by women, with a women's 'core'
group" (quoted in Liddington, 1989: 224).

Here is the standard act of liberal protest with a twist. A "women's"
march, not a humanist march. For what, it was not clear. The "fanta-
sies" about marching together as women against the stereotypes of
impassivity were the palette of inspiration at first. Then a press release
was prepared and the goals of the march (momentarily) clarified: "To
show everyone that women are active and prominent in the peace
movement" (Press release from Women for Life on Earth, 1981). There
was an instrumental strategic element in that simple declaration:
women were creating a political movement for peace and leaving the
kitchens of NATO households to do so. A slide toward homelessness.
Also, the group would be comprised mostly of "women" because
"women" were less likely to incur a violent response from authorities.
(Of course, one thinks. "Women" are not even visible to authorities as
agents of international relations.)

Throughout this early maneuvering, feminism was more a distant
echo than the point: "[The walkers] had little interest in feminist
theory, and attempted to give voice to a wide range of women *without*
excluding men" (Liddington, 1989: 226). But by virtue of deciding on a
women's walk, feminist elements soon began to homestead peace and
life. Walker Denise Aaron recalls that the cross-cut crossing point of
her own identity threshold came as she watched the small band of
marchers from Cardiff come toward her: "I suddenly realized with
horror, going somewhere ALONE for the first time since I'd been

186

married thirteen years previously. It felt extraordinarily good" (quoted in Liddington, 1989: 229).

When the walkers arrived at the base, one among them suggested that they chain themselves to the fence in order to attract more media attention, in the manner of the earlier suffragettes. This action sent a ripple of alarm through the group and led to another brush with homelessness as "everyone was forced to reassess why they had come on the march." (Liddington, 1989: 230). Pettitt, for one, suffered an excruciating moment of personal indecision as she contemplated the action: "Oh, no, God, I knew it! ... This is not one of those finite things. No ... This is one of those trains that you don't bloody get off. This is one of those things that takes over your life and *forces* you to change" (quoted in Liddington, 1989: 230). Homeless even more, though hardly forced to be there.

The group decided to share individual concerns about the proposed action in a way that would become characteristic of Greenham decision making, and it was a far cry from the decision-making models and practices that occupy the IR literature. Everyone in the group aired views without interruption, without sarcastic responses from the audience, without finding herself engaged in a liberal dialogue or debate; indeed, without any comment whatsoever from the others. "We realized that if we were going to do this ... we *all* had to do it; but without bullying, without bad feeling. And so we did that for two *long*, *long* meetings. We just went round and everybody said what they felt" (Pettitt, quoted in Liddington, 1989: 231). Unanimity and full consensus were not necessary; nor was it deemed appropriate to vote or to let one among them become the leader and make the decisions. The resultant policy was the absence of policy: four chained themselves to the fence and others did something else.

The usual Greenham style of deciding built empathy for difference through exercises that encouraged participants to listen to each other and cooperate, at minimum, by refusing to interrupt or to force conformity on others. In a manner reminiscent of that village meeting Trinh (1989: 1) narrates, there was "no directing, no breaking through, no need for a linear progression which gives the comforting illusion that one knows where one goes." This style led to a subsequent disavowal of hierarchy and of "tried and true" authority, task assignments, habits of deference, and modes of compliance in favor of cooperative anarchy:

> At the peace camp each woman does what she thinks is necessary, so there are no rosters or lists of who has to do what ... This is very unfamiliar to some people, who exclaim in frustration, "why don't

they *organize* something?" To their credit, women at the camp have not given in to this demand but have created a space that allows many women to ask instead, "What do *I* want to do?" Some feel alienated and do not return, but others become much more autonomous and effective than they would if they merely followed other people's directives. (G. Kirk, 1989b: 264)

Arguably, from a position of "I"ness, those who stayed developed an owlish sweep of vision that could detect and turn back appeals to individualism:

when a group like SWP [Socialist Workers' Party] or Wages for Housework turned up and said, "This is how you should believe ...", women were just saying, "Well, hang on a minute. We want to get to the bottom of this. We want to find out what really happened." (Rebecca Johnson, quoted in Liddington, 1989: 284)

A US feminist who spent time at Greenham Common reported a shift in her sense of political method:

For me, participating in decision making with the Greenham Common women brought on culture shock. In contrast to our West Coast [USA] style of consensus, involving facilitators, agendas, plans, and formal processes, their meetings seemed to have no structure at all. No one facilitated, no agendas were set; everyone spoke whenever she wanted to and said what she thought. Where we valued plans and scenarios, they valued spontaneity, trusting in the energy of the group and the moment. Instead of long discussions about the pros and cons of any given plan, those women who wanted to do it simply went ahead, and those who didn't, did not participate ... I found a delicious sense of freedom and an electricity in discussions unhampered by formalities. The consensus process I had known and practiced seemed, in retrospect, overly controlled and controlling. Its rules and procedures seemed to impose the Censor under a new form. (Starhawk, 1990: 187)

An unorthodox, free-wheeling approach to organization, however, did not make for uniform happiness at the Camp. We cannot ignore or write-off shifts in subjectivity that tipped in the direction of defections:

I'm not going to do the nightwatch any more ... I am going to stop making excuses for other women ... I am incapable of doing nightwatch when I'm getting evicted, avoiding the rain, talking to visitors, watching for changes in the base, and trying to keep warm. (Newsletter quoted in Liddington, 1989: 277)

With no facilitation, louder and more vocal women tend to dominate discussions. Women who have fears, concerns, or alternate plans often felt unheard. (Starhawk, 1990: 187–8)

188

But, as some encampers left, others clambered on board:

> Because women who were in fact getting ready – were needing to go
> – and that would be the signal for them: "It's time to go". And they
> would go. And new women would come, because they'd heard about
> the wonderful action, or they'd heard about the terrible eviction ...
> So there were these cycles that happened maybe twice a year.
> (Rebecca Johnson, quoted in Liddington, 1989: 276)

Theirs was an initial act of sympathy that often honed into empathy.

One such "woman" who heard about a terrible eviction and came to
the Camp was Merly Antonelli:

> It wasn't until I saw the pictures on the telly of the Yellow Gate
> eviction in March '84 ... then it suddenly occurred to me, "No, this
> can't go [on]. No, No, you're not doing this. I'm sorry. No way." [A
> few days later, after viewing the film *Carry Greenham Home*, I saw
> Greenham] *was* a small community. Ok, fairly bizarre but – from my
> experience! – but there was nothing wrong with it ... These women
> were actually living in it [the countryside] and caring for the land.
> And then I saw the mess the bailiffs made – just *tearing* everything
> down. And then one woman setting light to her bender [a shelter
> made under bent tree boughs] in protest ... And I just thought, just,
> Yeah, it's like the last bit of defiance you've got. So I came down for
> three days. (Quoted in Liddington, 1989: 275)

She stayed for more than two years.

Another camper recalls leaving the Camp and returning for the
"strange" reason of finding a pregnancy the source of a new subjectivity:

> I remember sitting in a blockage and a woman, just a few yards away
> from me, was lying down, and she was pregnant – about six months
> pregnant. She was quite thin, and so her pregnancy really showed,
> because it was just a small, nice hump. And she was wearing dun-
> garees and a small T-shirt. And she took her dungarees off, and let
> her stomach just – like show to the sun. And that was when I really
> decided that I had come to Greenham again, and that women's
> actions were the way forward for *me*. Dunno; just sitting watching
> that stomach; I just made *so* many connections ... about patriarchy
> and male violence and nuclear weapons being male violence. I just
> thought, "It's so right. There's no way I'm ever going to doubt it ever
> again." (Quoted in Liddington, 1989: 265–6)

Of all the images of the Peace Camp, none, perhaps, is as powerful
as the picture of "women," link-armed, on a cruise missile silo at night,
police cars in crazy disarray below them. The campers defied the
security of the base and, in that simple act, laid bare the official
justifications for adding missiles to Europe so as to keep the Europeans

189

safe from other enemy Europeans in the USSR. Local homebred women straddled a no-man's-land to homestead on "men's" and "women's" assigned places in the Western Way of Security – "men" as "women's" protectors, "women" as safe at home – without reaching for final authority and control over the situation.

To get into the military base for that exercise, the campers scrambled over the fences. On another occasion, they cut the nine-mile perimeter, ten-foot-high fences simply to show that it could be done, that base security could very easily be breached. Camper Nina Hall remembers:

> We'd practised getting up on each other's shoulders. And we unravelled lots [of fence, after] our bolt-cutters had been taken. And cut a *massive* section down, because we went to quite a deserted place ... So we cut about 200 yards down ... All it is is just snipping at the side of the posts, and then these big sections just fall down ... It was just an amazing sense of relief and freedom ... to be able to see ... a space where it was, and to know that you personally were responsible for taking it down. (Quoted in Liddington, 1989: 270)

This politics "on each other's shoulders," and the "amazing sense of relief and freedom" as the unravelled wire ("thick wire mesh topped by several feet of barbed wire, all supported at frequent intervals by cement pylons ... ([t]en feet farther inside are more rolls of barbed wire, forming a tangled second barrier rather like those on the battlefields of World War I") [Snitow, 1988: 344–5]) "just falls down" around you, is the type of creative step that destabilizes gender expectations along the fences of defense. On the other side of those fences the official warriors of state are vulnerable, even though the warrior women emerging out of the shadows of an insecure base camp do not, this time at least, invade the camp: "As great sections of the fence tumbled to the ground, an isolated soldier inside the base ... tried to summon help on his radio – but so too did all the other squaddies. Soldiers panicked. Pandemonium reigned" (Liddington, 1989: 270).

Other struggles with this outpost of western security were ironic in less amusing ways. The base, it has been reported, unleashed a "dirty little war" to immunize these "women" enemies once and for all. In September 1984, the campers began experiencing unusual physical symptoms from mild headaches to bouts of paralysis, from pressure in the ears and vaginal bleeding to miscarriage, burning skin, depression, irritability, aggressiveness, panic, loss of short-term memory and of concentration. Gwen Kirk (1989a: 126) refers to the source of these symptoms as "zapping," that is, beaming microwaves or ultrasound from the military base to the Peace Camp:

Zapping interferes with brainwave patterns. It is silent and invisible, but the effects are strong and immediate ... It has been worst ... close to the missile silos, and it has often occurred when the convoys left the base or returned. Zapping also happened during large demonstrations and intermittently at other times. Women have been investigating this, doing tests around the base and collecting information from those affected. The government, military, medical profession, and the press have all either denied that zapping could be going on or refuse to take up the issue. They attribute women's symptoms to stress, hysteria, or a cynical attempt to grab the headlines.

Other "dirty little wars" were seemingly more fair but similarly immunizing. On the occasion of the "women" occupying a military sentry box on the base (August 1982), they were charged in the Newbury Magistrates' Court (the local district) with "behaviour likely to cause a breach of the peace," under legislation traced back to 1361. The Peace Campers decided to ignore this prenuclear piece of legislation and to base a defense on the 1969 Genocide Act, the relevant article (II) of which states that genocide refers, in part, to acts:

committed with intent to destroy, in whole or in part, a national, ethnical, racial or religious group, as such:

(a) Killing members of the group;
(b) Causing serious bodily or mental harm to members of the group;
(c) Deliberately inflicting on the group conditions of life calculated to bring about its physical destruction in whole or in part;
(d) Imposing measures intended to prevent births within the group.

(Quoted in Harford and Hopkins, 1984: 79)

The idea was to turn the case around by arguing that the deployment of cruise missiles violated tenets of this Act and that the accused were merely doing their duty to bring attention to the illegalities.[17]

Defense counsellors called expert witnesses to describe the genocidal consequences of a nuclear war, including E. P. Thompson and the Bishop of Salisbury. They encouraged the defendants to make related statements about their reasons for being at the Camp. One defendant told the court that "the presence of nuclear weapons on our soil is causing serious mental harm to many people ... women are afraid of having more children" (Harford and Hopkins, 1984: 80). Another said that "[c]ruise missiles will mean the death of me and my children and millions more like me across the world" (quoted in Liddington, 1989: 242). One of the "women" lawyers, who admitted thinking before the

191

trial that courtrooms are "frightening places ... [because] courts are all to do with the legitimate exercise of power ... [with] special ways of being polite (courtesy) and of being rude (sarcasm and bullying) that are almost uniquely male" (Jane Hickman, quoted in Cook and Kirk, 1983: 118–19), later said of the defendants:

> They gave all the wrong responses. They laughed, cheered and clapped. They didn't take half of it seriously ... It didn't mean that arguments were just put in expressive, emotional, feeling ways, though that was unusual enough. It was also seeing women make the court listen to arguments that were articulate, intellectually coherent and historically wise. Women did it by poems, by singing, and some cried while they spoke ... Everywhere there were flowers. Courtrooms hardly frighten me at all now. (Hickman, in Cook and Kirk, 1983: 118)

Eleven "women" were found guilty and received sentences of fourteen days or a fine of one hundred pounds and being bound over to "keep the peace" for one year. These sentences were themselves a sign that the Greenham Common campers triumphed in the legal system of the United Kingdom, for they were unusually light, "an attempt to damp down further publicity and support for the women" (Cook and Kirk, 1983: 119–20). Sometimes the transgressors were not charged at all for flagrantly breaking the law. In February 1983, thirty "women" brought the Greenham fence to London when they laid down in Downing Street while US Vice President George Bush was having dinner with Margaret Thatcher. Each was decorated with the symbols of life that had earlier hung on the military base fence. It was a stunning merger of metaphor and action. For posing this security threat to the prime minister, they received conditional discharges after having been charged with obstructing traffic.

Another set of legal actions centered around eviction notices – notices, which can be seen as ironic messages to vacate the politics of homelessness for proper apolitical spaces at "home." In one case the Newbury District Council succeeded in persuading a High Court judge to order eighteen "women" to leave the area of the Peace Camp. Forty other "women" added their names to the list during the hearing, which had the effect of forcing the judge to move the proceedings to a larger venue, outside of which "women" staged a protest carnival complete with juggler, monks from a nearby Buddhist center beating drums, and a band. The defendants argued that establishing a peace camp on a Commons was as lawful as holding a picnic there. What were the grounds for eviction in the one case and not in the other? How could it be legal to deploy nuclear missiles on a Commons and illegal for nonviolent "women" to camp beside them there? Like feminist legal scholars, these "women" were attempting to establish that there was an overrepresentation of existing power structures in the law and insufficient rule flexibility to allow "openness to points of view that otherwise would seem natural to exclude" (Bartlett, 1990: 832).

These arguments were heard enough to enable the courts to give light sentences or to look the other way when the Campers simply moved the Camp slightly from one government jurisdiction over the land to another. In this way the Peace Camp endured as "a magnificent, exotic stage set for effective political gestures" (Snitow, 1988: 350) until the cruise missiles began to leave. It was linked to other camps in an international network that took the Greenham Common women to the rest of Europe for protests and even to the US to sue Ronald Reagan and members of his administration for deploying missiles in Europe in violation of international and US constitutional law (the case was rejected at the US Appeals Court level because there was a lack of judicially discoverable and manageable standards to judge it).

The Camp failed in its main mission, one supposes, and succeeded in unexpected realms. It subverted the security-based strategic vision of international relations by showing that acts of everyday insecurity, borne of a collective endeavor to write insecurity differently, to homestead it with knowledges gained from leaving "secure" homes for "women," could unravel the security studies texts with incisive clarity. More than fifty articles by softliners on citizen-based defense could not have made this point as well. Relatedly, Greenham helped to shape the local Campaign for Nuclear Disarmament into "the only movement in Britain in which feminist argument and practice has become integrated into the mainstream of analysis" (Liddington, 1989: 279, quoting *New Statesman*, November 25, 1988).

It also demonstrated that a good peace camp could be like a good anarchic system, in the sense that the absence of governed places can make it possible to redefine politics to include activities we do not often study as IR, and people we think of as having no place there. This anarchy contrasts with the pseudo-anarchy of much IR theorizing, which governs all spaces with the sovereign voice of "man." Alexander Wendt (1992) suggests that anarchy is what states make of it. I think it is what we make of it, and some of us can make it responsive to alternative homesteadings. Rather than throw out anarchy as a false projection of masculine autonomy from "women," we can rehabilitate it to study breakdowns in the gender places of IR, where those evacuated from sight can negotiate their own standards and politics.

193

The Greenham Common Peace Camp also homesteaded aspects of third-wave feminist theory by reminding the postmodernists among us that one can become homeless in many ways while still retaining the ability to seize on the existence of something called women. Indeed, as of 1982, by agreement of many who were then in residence, the Camp became all women:

> They were saying they wanted to live and work together unhindered and unquestioned on half an acre of land. The rest of the world is a free for all ... no one suggested, "Thou shalt never speak to men again", or "All men in the peace movement are to be suspected of foul play until further notice from the women at Greenham." (Sarah H., quoted in Harford and Hopkins, 1984: 34, 33)

This decision created a stir and some "women" left the camp on the heels of it. Some say Greenham was then held together, in its most difficult moments, by lesbian energy (e.g., Snitow, 1988: 353), an energy that may tap what Monique Wittig (1989) has explained in "The Straight Mind" as being neither of "women" nor of "men," as we have come to define those terms in relation to one another through the phallus, but of "minoritary" subjectivity as a subversive multicentric or acentric rather than phallo-centric position.

Some responses to the assertion of a women's-only Greenham Common Peace Camp, however, also showed the Janus-faced aspects of homesteading. In order to homestead realist security on behalf of women, some "women" had to deny other subjectivities, identities, and loyalties or leave the farm, so to speak. Dorothy Thompson (1987) thinks the Camp regrettably reinforced a polarized view of "men" and "women." Camp attender Sybil Oldfield (1989: 217) remembers the effort in 1982 to cover the base fence with the little images of life on the other side, and intimates that it was all too womanly: "Absurd, perhaps, to have hoped that such emotion-laden icons might help to make peace-makers of the powerful. But for a little while we did hope and possibly there was a slight shift in British public opinion." She regrets that, owing to a lack of coordinating organization, the Camp became "a self-selected and unusual group of volunteers without dependants" (ibid.: 217). She especially regrets that the feminist angle on peace evolved into a feminist separatist angle: "[O]ne fascism cannot be defeated by another" (ibid.: 218). "Women" of color thought the Camp was the preserve of privileged white "women" who had husbands at home to watch the children or to bring in an income. Lesbians thought the Camp was not sufficiently open about its "women"-loving-"women" tendencies and sought to make lesbianism one of those linked issues of security that the campers publicized. All

told, it seems the campers did not achieve a standpoint of homelessness within inherited notions of "women" – women-only meant biological females only – though they did become creatively homeless
within the apolitical places that are usually assigned to women.

I was not there. Like the US feminist Ann Snitow (1988: 346):

> I had joined the women's liberation movement [around] 1970 to
> escape this very myth of the special altruism of women, our innate
> peacefulness, our handy patience for repetitive tasks, our peculiar
> endurance – no doubt perfect for sitting numbly in the Greenham
> mud, babies and arms outstretched, begging men to keep our chil-
> dren safe from nuclear war.

In fact, I vividly remember the scornful tone in my assistant profes-
sorial voice when I visited a friend in Fairfield, Pennsylvania – at that
time my "home" – and found her helping a beaded and sandaled
friend finish a peace quilt for Greenham Common.

Snitow visited the Camp and came to realize that "[i]f the women
were such nice little home birds, what were they doing out in the wild,
balking at male authority, refusing to shut up or go back home?"
(Snitow, 1988: 346). I was too mock tough for all that. Thus, all of this is
hearsay, secondarily sourced. Yet Greenham Common Peace Camp
looms now in my mind as that village meeting that carries on with the
mundanities of insecure life as it meets and decides (Trinh, 1989: 1–2).
It was an exercise at the margins of feminist legal methods in which
one questions "the legitimacy of the norms of those who claim to
speak, through rules, for the community" when, in fact, there are
"many overlapping communities to which one might look for
'reason'" (Bartlett, 1990: 855). It was part retreat for and manifesto of
Haraway's (1985) cyborgs. It was a chimera and a concreteness, a
postpeace, a move beyond metaphor, text, and strategic vision into
simultaneous insecurities, and into actions that, in this era, can neither
succeed fully nor fail fully.

It also looms as an imperfect and impossible "model of method" for
empathetic cooperation in the service of feminist homesteadings of
knowledge. It takes us around and about the fences of security in ways
that combine the feminist standpoint determination to incorporate the
actual dailiness of real women's experiences with some feminist postmodernist concern over valorizing received subject statuses. If we
think of Greenham as one among many relevant communities of
knowledge on how to rewrite IR, we take away from it the following
lessons.

First, the Greenham campers embraced a certain "life politics" that
eschewed the usual authority patterns and hierarchies of "normal"

liberal politics. Even the only-women strategy can be seen in this light: any action in international relations that is led by people in women's bodies cannot be the usual authority pattern, nor can it be capable of showing proper obeisance to hierarchy. Along with its multiple strategies to insecure the military base and its promises of security, Greenham fits Nancy Fraser's and Linda Nicholson's (1990: 35) sense of postmodern feminism as "pragmatic and fallibilistic," tailoring "its methods and categories to the specific task at hand, using multiple categories when appropriate and forswearing the metaphysical comfort of a single feminist method or feminist epistemology."

Pauline Rosenau (1992: 146) tells us that life politics takes the place in postmodern social movements of the modern quest for emancipation:

> Emancipatory politics is rejected because so much of what the old social movements designated as emancipatory (seeking justice, freedom from inequality and oppression), the affirmatives argue, turned out to be oppressive. Besides, any plan for emancipation implies a "general prescription, a coherent plan, a program."

Life politics is also a far cry from the models of rational, organizational, and bureaucratic politics that represent decision making in international relations. It is none too concerned to poll attitudes, beliefs, and other psychological dimensions of the campers. Satisficing simply does not enter the picture and uncertainty is hardly an impediment to be overcome.

Second, again like "affirmative post-modernists" (P. Rosenau, 1992: 145–6), the campers at Greenham Common did

> not always argue for the superiority of their own group but rather work[ed] toward solidarity across groups in areas of politics, culture, and the arts; they [sought] out joint issue-specific commitments that encompass[ed] various interests. But neither d[id] they shy away from normative stands. Formulating value positions that are broad and inclusive is a delicate task; it requires considerable diplomacy and an exchange of views that does not attribute dogmatic authority to anyone.

This approach enabled Greenham Common to become an epistemic community within feminism and within softline peace activism, "a vehicle for the development of insightful theoretical premises about the creation of collective interpretation and choice" (Adler and Haas, 1992: 368).

At this moment in the genealogy of IR, the field has some open spaces for plurality in methods and politics. It has an owlish vision of many ways to broaden its concepts and substantive areas of inquiry.

But, as I noted in the previous chapter, the third debate in IR has some blindspots. The process of writing a field for the twenty-first century requires unraveling many more fences, insecuring many chimeric securities, while resisting the temptation – and that is the difficult part – of invading the open spaces we create in order to fill everything up again. To stand in the borderlands of immunity and dis-ease, by virtue of considering the implications of feminist literatures, and the experiences of "women" in the interstices of "politics," is to be homeless by our western standards of identification as professionals, perhaps as men and women too. That is why we do not consciously stand in such places too often. It is easier to ask the outlaws to accommodate to the field than it is to listen, negotiate respectfully, and incorporate those "strange" views that would make a strategic return or move to some fixed and immobile home position out of the question. It is easier to think that feminism needs IR more than IR needs feminism, but this, like security, is a chimera.

Women cooperators in Harare

A rather different angle on security and homesteading surfaces when we move the venue of analysis from a "women's" peace camp in the United Kingdom to "women" working in producer cooperatives in Harare, Zimbabwe. The concerns of these people do not lie in the realm of military matters or international relations. Asked in 1988 to tell me what worries them in their lives, not one "woman" among the nearly 300 I spoke to mentioned the possibility that a nuclear exchange in Europe or elsewhere could ruin their lives, spoil the planet, have genocidal effects. Indeed, in eleven years of researching the political economy of Zimbabwean development, I have encountered only wry and parodic local comments on western and global security; periodically offered by "men," the remarks are to the effect that "You Americans will have a war someday with the Russians and blow each other up. Africa will be the superpower continent then."

As well, the "women" cooperators with whom I spent time were not overtly concerned about the security threat posed by a still apartheid-bound South Africa. They were concerned instead with paying their children's school fees, with lazy husbands drinking away the household income, with prices for their crops; now they are concerned with structural adjustment policies suggested by the World Bank and taken on board by the government of Robert Mugabe. These are their insecurities. They face an immune system that seems more amorphous and maybe more limited in scope than the one Greenham Common

197

women faced. And yet the ambitions of some of these "women" belie any notion we might have that security studies can be restricted to some ubiquitous possibility of war between states when one of the warring parties is western, or that writing IR in a postmodern era should replicate the modernist error of overlooking the international cooperation of distant-peripheral others.

Zimbabwe became independent from Rhodesia and from absentee-landlord England in 1980. President Mugabe, a self-proclaimed scientific socialist who is now liberalizing the economy, has since struggled to manage and change an inherited white-settler capitalism that is heavily dependent on mining exports and food grown by white commercial farmers (Zimbabwe also has a manufacturing sector that has contributed approximately 25 percent of Gross Domestic Product). Part of that admixture of management and change has been concern to integrate "women," who prior to independence were legal minors for life, into production, while taking care not to disrupt traditions in which women are seen as the backbone of the family. Producer cooperatives bridge "women's"-only homebound production of household clothes, food, and services – assignments inherited from traditional and colonial notions of "womanhood" – with the money economy associated with all types of modern development, socialist and capitalist.

The "producer societies," which the government urged on "women" in the first eight years of independence, range the gamut from food preparation outside the factories of Harare and Bulawayo, to uniform-making, to raising pigs and poultry. Each cooperative is directed from above to set itself up the same way, with an initial contribution by all members to cover start-up costs, followed by an election of official leaders – chair, vice chair, treasurer, and several committee members. Then the cooperative must register with the government and work to accumulate surpluses, otherwise known as profits, using those profits to improve the cooperative and to pay individual members. This is the stuff of capitalist storybooks. The moral is this: to tame the scourges of idleness and poverty, one must expand into unoccupied spaces of the economy and take them over – in a ladylike way.[18]

Despite the directives from above, I have maintained that cooperatives also provide spaces for people called women that, in the words of several with whom I spoke, enable subjects "to think our own thoughts," "to learn skills without fear," "to do things by ourselves without doubting" (Sylvester, 1991b). Indeed, if we think of knowledge as "produced by individuals in actual settings, and as organized by and organizing definite social relations" (D. Smith, 1990: 62), then these cooperators produce more than the material goods they seek to sell for group profit. They participate in producing and reproducing gender knowledge and power against the backdrop of previous and ongoing struggles, victories, and losses. All this production is ostensibly for local consumption, which means that their experiences with international relations seem indirect at best. However, a close look at their stories reveals an interweaving of local and distant, domestic and international, western and nonwestern into "knowledge-power cooperatives" that are barely visible in IR, but that contain important lessons on cooperating to ease the burdens of insecurity.

Consider the texture of life, as I saw and recorded it in the late 1980s. Two "all-women" cooperatives are planning their entry into international relations.[19]

There is a mood of anxious hope radiating from the small silk-making cooperative in the urban township of Mabvuku on the outskirts of Harare. Dressed in their good clothes, the members talk nervously among themselves as they await the arrival of a delegation from the European Community that will, perhaps, pronounce the words the "women" tell me they have been waiting for a year to hear – that Mabvuku and its sister silk cooperative in Glen Norah are worthy of a Z$200,000 grant to expand their operations. Meager wares, machinery, and inputs are on careful display. Nearly half the small room is taken up with cartons of graded silk cocoons. In one corner stands a rickety hand loom readied for a demonstration and a spinning wheel loaded with silk thread. Rudimentary wall hangings, greeting cards crafted from cocoon parts, and a few nicely made articles of silk clothing stand out on unpainted walls.

As I survey the surroundings, two European "women" arrive with great fanfare. These are the patrons of the cooperatives, the Greek "women" responsible for starting and funding the producer societies to the tune of Z$70,000 to Z$80,000 over a two year period. They seem to be the center of gravity here, and as one breathlessly greets me the other makes suggestions for improving the display. Nervous energy goes into last minute details.

A more typical day at the cooperative is busy but less frenetic:

> The silk worms eat so much that we have to struggle to find enough mulberry leaves to satisfy them. Every day of feeding season, five of us take a public bus into the suburbs. We go house to house looking for mulberry trees and asking permission to take some leaves. The people there think we are mad. We stuff our bags and return, where

199

another group spends the afternoon cleaning dust and water off the leaves – the worms are so fussy. With money from the European Community, we hope to get five hectares to plant our own trees and solve the problem of traveling so much.

I ask them why they joined the cooperatives in the first place.

We joined the cooperative to get away from being a housewife.

I joined because I like working with women and want women to keep their unity – men wouldn't do the hard work women do.

This is a good way to use your hands when you are uneducated.

Here we can help families and husbands, share some ideas and cooperate with others, produce, and work together to gain money and education and ideas.

For me it was poorness.

We want to work as African people and women want to work for pay – I'd leave this cooperative and work for pay if a European came along and offered me a job.

I ask them how successful they would say the cooperatives have been.

These cooperatives are not good yet because we have the problem of finding leaves and little production. But we have learned new skills of weaving and crochet and operate like a family. The Greek women have been kind in sharing skills and social workers from the Harare City Council help. We have learned to be self-disciplined, because of a regular work schedule, and if resources become available the project will prosper and we can hire more people. Then we'll make many things, like mulberry jam and tinned mulberries. The cooperatives will keep poultry and expand our weaving.

A more typical day is also filled with even grander expectations:

We'll build a factory in the future – an extended family – and employ men and women, although the women will manage it because the men know they have no knowledge of silk. We have many plans. It took the Ministry of Cooperatives so long to process our papers for registration that some of us were discouraged. Our possibilities for EEC funding were held up. Maybe now it will be OK.

But this is not a typical day:

Yes, yes, we understand you have been undergoing training [says one of the two male EEC representatives]. But what about the administration of these cooperatives if the two Greek women leave Zimbabwe?

What about establishing prices? Who does that?

Have you considered the costs of fencing your new land?

Have you had the land surveyed? Precisely how much land is required for your project?

Can you get the spinning equipment you need in Zimbabwe?

How will you market your products?

Can you compete in export markets?

The Greek "women" answer all the questions. The local "women" sigh. They tell me that they can neither read well nor do sophisticated mathematics. But they also say that it is best for Europeans to speak to each other about the funding because they know each other: "We think our own thoughts while they speak their own words."

A month later I interview one of the EEC representatives from that Mabvuku Inquisition:

> We haven't given out any aid to Mabvuku and Glen Norah because we're waiting for the government of Zimbabwe to put together a program proposal for us on this. All our funding requires evidence that the government is willing to help the project to succeed by following through on its promises for land or sales outlets. The relevant ministries have taken well over a year on this.
>
> We plan to fund the two silk cooperatives separately because we want them to compete. If you're not competitive, you'll fail in six months.
>
> It's good to have the Greek women involved. We calculate that their advice to the cooperatives is worth about Z$1,000 a month – they're saving us money.

A year later (1989) I return to the European Community office in Harare. The original evaluation team for the silk cooperatives has left the country:

> Ah, the silk cooperatives. You know them? Then you know that they are risky ventures. We funded them a while back, but I wouldn't ever have funded them myself. Silk is a new product in Zimbabwe and we don't know if there is a market. Plus I don't like the idea that the whole thing is held together by two European women. If they decide to leave Zimbabwe, the cooperatives will fall apart. I know that.

Then why did the EEC fund them?

> It was all so well orchestrated as mainly a Greek-to-Greek thing. That evaluating officer you spoke to last year was Greek you know. It was like family.

In 1990 I ask the Greek patrons of the cooperatives how the ventures are going:

> We still have a problem, [says the more commanding of the two], because the women are not mature enough to see the project as their own. But they will learn.

201

> I think the problem is with the government [the other says]. They
> often give us only a half-hour notice for a meeting at the Department
> of Cooperatives to go over the details of our operations. When I say I
> can't possibly come, I think they're happy. They know we will try to
> push them. The Department is rubbish because they have held up
> construction of the buildings for the cooperatives. It's difficult to
> produce in large quantities without proper buildings.

This story brings to the fore the local faces of people who are often
hidden in-between domestic and international cooperations in some
subterranean netherworld of "anarchic" order. These "women"
cooperators have one foot in a world resonant with neorealism, where
competition and market-like coordinations are imposed; one foot in a
nostalgic realm of used-to-be-household politics, where "women" had
petty managerial responsibilities and where never the twain of international and domestic supposedly met; and a hand in the till of service
and development regimes, where government and international
funds get funneled or not to the insecure cooperatives that some of
these agencies described to me as "disaster areas." This means that
"women" in the cooperatives are simultaneously inside and outside
international relations, inside and outside international-local regimes
of aid and development (neoliberal institutions), and inside and
outside security. It also means, as a result, that their situation warrants
attention as part of a gender-sensitive expansion of "insecurity"; for
these in-between places, these spots that postmodernists seek out and
praise as subversive of dominant order, are sources both of some
security and of new insecurity for these "women," especially at a time
of structural adjustment in Zimbabwe, when the market for luxury
items has fallen through the floor.

The cooperators express a sense of "cooperation" that is tied to a
particular sense of security and viability with minimal discord. A
cooperative is like a nurturant family: it teaches skills to its members
and nourishes their dreams of achievement, even if it is itself resource
poor. Although there can be discord in families and opportunities
aplenty for "women" to underachieve for themselves therein, the
notion that a family is a cooperative homesteads both "the family,"
preventing fissures that could lower the security and viability of the
group, and the government's sense of a "cooperative" as a space away
from families for modern economic production.

There is no levels-of-analysis barrier for these cooperators that pre-
cludes a family from being in the national sphere of capitalism. To
attain maximum security, however, a good cooperative needs a "European" donor or benefactor, an agency or person that can infuse

202

international capital and know-how into the family-cooperative and thereby boost its security quotient. One needs, in other words, resources from (re)so(u)rcerers international. Thus the EEC is eagerly courted, fearfully met, and silently handed over to European "women" to handle. Unlike the "women" at Greenham Common, the point in this story is not to unravel the fences of European (in this case economic) security, but to experience the security of western-mediated viability.

All the while that complicated insider–outsider relational links are being negotiated, the local Zimbabwean "women" in these silk cooperatives guard their own plans, their own ideas on how the prospective donor funds should be used. They do not sit inside the fences the EEC would like them to construct (to parcel off their land from the robbers of their industry outside), but rather they homestead the donor agendas with their thoughts about factories in the future with vertically integrated production. Similarly, instead of being dominated by the Greek patrons or turning stubborn about a local autonomy that must refuse cooperations international to be authentic, these "women" mine the international for what they need. Their owlish visions are somewhat strategic: one "woman" says point blank that she would leave the cooperative if a European came along with a better offer, seeing nothing contradictory in her sense of working as "African people" and working with Europeans. Her identity politics is liminal.

The tug of competing standards catches up the Greek patrons more than it catches up the "women cooperators." The patrons, who have permanent residency in Zimbabwe, face a certain loss of "legitimate" identity by working so closely with the African other in a country that tolerates considerable *de facto* segregation (of "cultures," the whites say). They court that slip from sympathy to empathy that can leave one a bit homeless in one's secure identity. Their responses to this condition are interesting. One Greek "woman," the wealthier of the two, pawns off the "women" cooperators as "not mature," a designation that enables her to maintain some autonomy from those she would assist to feel secure. Read: "I am apart from them." The second patron has seemingly become more comfortable with liminality and verbally defects from the "mature" group of Europeans and donors by asserting support for the "women" cooperators. She calls certain (re)so(u)rcerers "rubbish" because they are "women"-evading and "women"-autonomizing instead of cooperative-securing. Despite the differences in the two "women's" views, both steadily support the cooperatives without a defection, albeit with a certain western sense that the local "women" are secure while they are around. Their presence, therefore, is reasoned strategically. And, indeed, given the skills and expenses required to engage in silk production, the reasoning of the Greek "women" is not false. But one among them is slipping her guard.

The EEC microproject representatives, meanwhile, are insecurely on the horns of many dilemmas. They question the Greek "women's" relations to the other, particularly their willingness to protect weak cooperatives with personal funds, all the while knowing that those personal funds are saving the EEC money. They draw on a "Greek-to-Greek" (family) relationship in order to justify funding the cooperatives. All the while, they worry about being exploited by kith-and-kin (but seemingly always other) Greek "women" who may entrap EEC money and end up insecuring the delicate local-international project through a certain shiftlessness. Their concern comes as no surprise to those who realize that "women" – "family" members included – do not have homes in western scripts of public place.

The donors also worry about the business acumen of the Zimbabwean "women." They think of these "women's cooperatives" as nonproductive, unviable entities ("they are risky ventures") that must be made eligible for modern development through the western business way of security. Absent from their thoughts is the sense that the local "women" will be homesteaders in their own right – settlers for their own security and economic well-being. Therefore, in attitude, these EEC donors seem to re-source the historical inferiorizing process of "women" in Zimbabwe, even as they posture about assisting these "women" strategically to re-source themselves.

There are concerns on the part of the Zimbabwean cooperators too, but these seem to this western-subject-with-somewhat-cross-culturally-mobile-subjectivities as less guarded and girded for battle. If we had more of the power we interpret contextually as "politics for life," these "women" seem to imply, we could "do things by ourselves without doubting." Until then, they lead an unavoidable existence of contradiction as participants and spectators in the politics around them. The cooperators are determined to mine the new "women"-including narratives of work and to enter spaces between "woman," "family," "cooperatives," and "enterprises." They seem to be able to reconcile all the government directives with "thinking own thoughts." They embrace a family metaphor of security while insecuring the modern subject status of "being a housewife." They want to work with "women" and they want to "help families and husbands." Their reasons for joining the cooperatives do not always mesh with the official "surplus-generating" reasons that line the official texts, nor are their scriptings of themselves – as cooperating "family"-cooperators who also have important relations international–anticipated in IR texts.

To sift through these contradictions and hyphenations is to realize that cooperating cooperators are models both of strategic interaction and of decision making *sans* the discord that the neoliberal institution- alists posit as the operative incentive, and without the fear of misper- ceptions that Stein (1990) inserts into his considerations of cooperative context. Strategy for these "women" is cross-dressed as desire, dreams, hope, ambition, and positionality. It is at once apart from the all- encompassing Way of Life, vision of the world, or war-making, peace- striving rationality that we see in security studies, and part of the metanarrative of progress as a European-situated resource. The modern protean trickster promises security and can deliver only chim- eras. These "women" seem to know about tricksters: they want the security of (re)so(u)rcerers while refusing the oversupervision of those who would make them securely modern in ways that trick them out of their own thoughts and plans. More than the Greek "woman" who is still struggling with the sympathy–empathy transversal, more than the EEC representatives who speak confidently of what these "women cooperators" need to succeed, the "women" cooperators are the homesteaders.

Like many "women" elsewhere, the cooperators become experts at linkage in order to craft their homesteads. They embrace gender separatism in tandem with the strategy of "helping [gender mixed] families," sounding for all the world like radical feminists, on the one hand, and Marxist feminist helpers of proletarian men on the other. Simultaneously, they exhibit an eagerness to learn and progress equally with men – a resonance with liberalism. But even here, there is a doubleness in their message on equality: on the one hand, the cooperative is the family at its best rather than the family in which "women" must do all the hard work as housewives; on the other hand, in seeking meaning and identity for themselves, they are never out of ear-shot of those flawed families, never unempathetically dis- connected from the men who may drink away the household income, never fully secure. Their politics of emancipation is a life politics of negotiated hyphenations. They want to be "African people" and they want to be European-identified African women and they will be both. Instead of cooptation to any one subject category, they make many identities and cooperations possible by empathetically and strategi- cally moving among the "needed incompatibles."

All the "women" in this story are at home and somewhat homeless.

Their struggles are simultaneous. Their desires and daily lives are mestiza. Their operations are postmodern. To put all of this differently, P. Rosenau (1992: 154) argues that "Third World forms of post-modernism are intellectually contradictory" and, judging by the case at hand, I would agree. But I do not agree with her that these forms always reject western truth claims and "do not hesitate to assert their own truth and argue its superiority over any other." In this tiny case of cooperation in an IR-remote country and level of analysis, western resources (truths) are eagerly sought and *commingled with local truths* into an agenda for daily life *and* emancipation from an immanent dailiness that is disliked. If anything is superior over anything else in the minds of these particular Zimbabwean cooperators, it is the power of "women" reclaiming and redefining themselves in tandem (inter-dependence) with people who would help and hinder them.

The Greek "women" are the immediate helpers. Their homelessness comes in that edgy slide backward and forward around and, in one case, away from European expectations. The EEC helpers are edgy too. Finally persuaded by international "women" to help local "women," they are none too secure in that decision and take refuge in "family" ties. Indeed, all the identities come up all wrongly mestiza from the perspective of international political economy (IPE) – the donors by allowing "family" considerations to enter into funding decisions, the Greek patrons by (almost) forgetting their places as homesteaders for the imperial west, and the "women cooperators" by conflating cooper-atives with factories with families, the private with public, domestic dreams with international donor agendas.

Third-debate IR must engage such distant home-based homeless-ness, and notice the unusual "conversations" that produce it, in order to confront the complex issues of epistemology that mark a post-modern era. Although such linkages evade the field so far, we can see in this one case a plethora of IR-relevancies. There are: authority-patterns to investigate along the lines that Ferguson and Mansbach (1991) suggest; ensembles of space and time, of inside and outside, that IR postmodernists find fascinating; meanings of "cooperation" and "security dilemma" that are unexplored in IR theory; and provocative forms of anarchy among "women cooperators," who refuse to relinquish their own thoughts, and surrounding Greek "women" who are not in full identity sinc with self-interested Europeans in a third world country. In addition, this case echoes some western feminism and writes it own. It previews what we will hear when we (finally) consider IR-remote terrains as sources of valuable knowledge about how relations international-national-local-household work.

206

So, where are we?

We is on the road to being a plural "we" through feminist appreci-
ations of postmodern politics forming and unfolding in "strange"
corners of international relations. I have tried to suggest, through trips
to a peace camp and to "women's" cooperatives, that we must do more
to vitalize the field we think of as IR than hold debates among
ourselves. We must look with empirical, interpretative, genealogical
and owlish eyes at the *mises en scénes* before us, the tableaux, the
tapestries of gender relations at and around and in defiance of national
and international boundaries. We must listen with the ears of people
who can no longer go home once they hear, insecured together, aware
that all subalterns may not even be speaking to us as long as their
conversations and stories are mediated by a western-subject-centered
otherness (Spivak, 1988). We must cooperate – not to avoid our
insecurity dilemmas, but to create new ones that include but also take
us beyond our fixations on either–or constructs of conflict versus
cooperation, war versus peace, strategy versus death. Then we can
homestead without bringing the colonial cavalry with us, without
seeking to integrate homelessnesses into mock Renaissance places or
Renaissance places into a golden nostalgia for strategy as a Way of Life.
We can see strategy as multinodal, partial, and changeable plans of
action springing from many diverse sources, which intersect with
other plans to frame ongoing conversations.

Most of all, I have attempted to show that there are IR relevancies
"out there" that do not symmetrically mirror-image the security
imaginary we find in field-specific security studies. To see those relevancies, it helps if one relinquishes arrogant wizardly authority. It
helps to hold "dirty little wars" against feminism in abeyance and to
temper a drive to control and secure the thresholds of imagination and
geospace. It helps to hold the brush in one's trunk as one embarks and
to breathe *en plein air*.

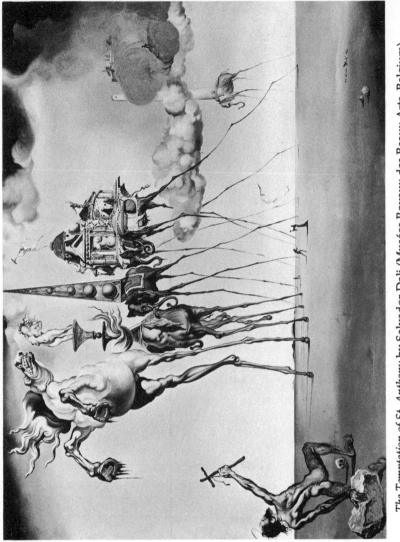

The Temptation of St. Anthony by Salvador Dali (Musées Royaux des Beaux-Arts, Belgium)

6 REPAINTING THE CANVASES OF IR

There are many topics in the conventional field of international relations that need to be held up to feminist critique and homesteading; all of them, in fact. While only scratching the surface here, my efforts to insecure the gendered texts of the field highlight the distortions and inaccuracies that result when we ignore or marginalize feminist scholarship. In this final chapter, I want to summarize the main points of my argument and explore ways to repaint a field without proving that if enough people take your side, you must be right.

The argument recalled

I have argued that the discipline of international relations is sorely bereft of gender awareness, despite more than twenty years of activities by feminists and those on behalf of whom they work – "women" – in the practical and theoretical endeavors of the field. One would hope that by now this point is becoming all too obvious, even hackneyed, and that we can therefore cease to make it in the near future and get on with the enormous task of rescripting-repainting IR. It appears, however, that there is still much to Simone de Beauvoir's (1952: 371) claim that "the world is defined without reference to her." Even though "we ourselves who are homeless constitute a force that breaks open the ice and other all too thin 'realities'" (Nietzche, 1974: 338), it is not yet time to drop our charge.

Before me is the Spring, 1992 issue of *Millennium*, one of the journals that first brought feminist contributions to the field. Andrew Linklater's piece, enticingly called "The Question of the Next Stage in International Relations Theory: A Critical-Theoretical Point of View," catches my eye. Linklater adds yet another dimension to the third debate by arguing that of all the current contenders for IR, "[c]ritical theory can best contribute to the next stage of international relations theory by exploring normative, sociological and praxeological questions about systems of inclusion and exclusion in world politics"

(Linklater, 1992: 97). This is a promising beginning, because feminists and people called women have been among those officially, but unconvincingly, excluded and rendered homeless. Indeed, Linklater argues that critical theory "begins with a prima facie commitment to human equality" (ibid.: 92) and emphasizes the possibilities in all situations for securing freedom from hypostatized forces through "open dialogue about the configuration of politics and society" (ibid.). These points resonate with all the feminist approaches that have surfaced in these pages.

Unlike others who have argued strongly on behalf of critical theory in the near past, however, such as Mark Hoffman (1987), Linklater maintains that critical theory requires more development before it can "possess a vision of international relations which ... can give direction to the field as a whole" (Linklater, 1992: 79). Critical theory has the normative purpose of facilitating "the extension of moral and political community in international affairs" (ibid.: 93). It is not averse to cultural diversity and difference within that project, but what is missing is an intellectual effort to move back and forth between the overarching critical-theoretical framework of emancipation and various perspectives of previously excluded groups. Again this sounds familiar. Feminists encourage IR to consider "perspectives of previously excluded groups," and some standpointers among us may look forward to an emancipatory finale to that process (although others will be more concerned to rescript ourselves as we rescript theories of emancipation). Feminism is also in the process of developing, moving across, between, and through the barriers of gendered nostalgias that resist insecuring.

When viewed against the backdrop of feminist concerns, Linklater's argument sounds feminism-friendly. But there is a formidable problem in his article that foreshadows yet another dialogue that will eclipse feminist concerns. Linklater mentions the diversity, the plural standpoints, that third-debaters bring to the field. He tells us "a profound challenge to orthodoxy has been posed by ... Marxism, critical theory, post-modernism, and now feminism" (ibid.: 77) and that "[w]hen this debate has run its course, critical social theory, post-modernism and feminism will have left an indelible impression upon the field" (ibid.: 78). He says that women are among the excluded groups whose individual perspectives must be taken into account in developing critical theory. Nonetheless, feminists, and the "women" they talk about, must be the illegitimate daughters of the really diverse ones because there is not one citation in Linklater's article to a feminist "woman." The postmodernists are cited. The critical theorists are

named. Feminist "women," however, have no names. How can femin-
ism leave an indelible impression on the field when femin*ists* are
absented from the literature?

The time has come, as my first point in outlining a course for IR, for
those who purport to update a field to do some serious home-work in
feminist theory instead of deferring this task to some future time. To
defer is to take refuge in a nostalgia that upholds the words of "men"
and relegates the words of "women" to the after hours of academic
work, to a hobby one never gets to. It will no longer do to say that one
is not adequately acquainted with feminist scholarship. The literature
is there to be read like every other strand of IR thinking, and it is
unprofessional to think that one need not read it to do good research.
The time has come to recognize "women" and feminists by naming us
rather than by winking at us as we walk by.[1]

One hopes that when this page has been found and read, the latest
"problem that has no name" will no longer exist. But feminist breaths
are not being held. It is apparent, as a second point of summation, that
gender cuts to the quick of this field. Despite feminist assurances that
to say "gender" is neither to mean "women" nor to attack "men" *qua*
people, despite Katherine Bartlett's able argument that feminist legal
methods bring the possibility of greater justice for all, to stand on the
gender precipice is, for many, to face the biggest fight imaginable,
something worse than usual battlefield combat. The imagined prospect is of utter loss (rather than gain, or loss and gain) of power,
control, authority, dominance, prestige, voice. Forever.

The debates of IR, therefore, are narrow and encrusting of a politics
in which "men" control knowledge and "women" are either out of
place altogether or are issued visitors' passes that enable us to leave
assigned homelands for temporary support roles in IR. Rosie Riveters
can temporarily enter IR through employment in war industries;
when the fighting men return, they must go "home" to domestic
duties "securely" lodged far from the sphere of citizensandstate and
war. "Women" can routinely enter IR as secretaries in the neoliberal
institutions of interstate cooperation; but they too must return "home"
each evening while the work of international relations continues at
diplomatic receptions and dinners (which other "women" often
prepare and serve from their homes). Statesmen, soldiers, decision
makers, and IR theorists – these are the makers of "men's" coherent
politics in international relations. "Women" are always of another
place. Our absence is required, must be invented, to enable the encod-
ing of international relations as masculine territory.

Unless one is a militant radical feminist, the idea of doing battle with

211

"men" for IR and killing them or the field dead in order to emancipate it is, however, utter nonsense. Most feminists want to share space, respect, and trust in a re-formed endeavor that will hear the can(n)on shots of the past without assuming that one canon is inevitable. Whether we call inclusion emancipation or merely the politics of mutual recognition that foreshadow the possibility of a method of empathetic cooperation, is a matter of dispute. We certainly want more than to be assigned the homelessness of homelands we did not freely negotiate for ourselves, and the passes that go with them, and less than a violent take-over. We want a different, difference-tolerant IR whose theories embed a range of mestiza consciousnesses and owlish sweeps of vision. The third point to reiterate is that we can take a variety of paths to achieve a difference-tolerant IR.

The liberal feminist path is the way of integration. It contains traps for the naive as well as some considerable strengths. On the plus side, liberal feminism strives mightily to assure women some rights to homesteads within canonical IR by pointing out the many ways we are on the inside through our support roles and yet are politically denied the keys to our houses out of habitual bias. The liberal feminist approach can also err by accepting the masculine canon as the baseline of the field and by valorizing home spaces within it that can never be free of the master's logic. We must remember, though, that attempts to integrate a field can be startlingly transformative if they disturb the settled homes of canonicals. Reconsider, in this light, the problematic of studying public opinion on foreign policy. To integrate "women" into the "public" can diminish our voices before the rule of the statistical mob. To become somewhat sensitive to this problem through feminist empiricist research can result in shattering "the public" as a measure of central tendency by revealing it as a site of diversity. It could also shatter one's sense of men and women. How does one justify the decision to designate a particular body one talks to, or voice one hears on the phone, as "man" or "woman" for the purposes of controlling for *gender* in one's research as opposed simply to controlling for biological sex? Should research subjects be asked to designate themselves as men or women? If so, what variation in their senses of gender would one be artificially guessing, tying down, and correlating? Pushing the issue of gender sensitivity means that we quickly reach the limits of some research strategies and find ourselves over the top. The lesson is that integration is risky. It can put a gloss on the practices of business as usual and it can be profoundly disruptive of them.

But liberal feminism is only one way to proceed. Other feminisms conjure up "new visions more consistent with a feminist standpoint of care, responsibility, and responsiveness" (Hirschmann, 1992: 247). These qualities are not easy to take into a field that operates on the principles of masculine standpoints. Indeed, "an approach that begins from women's experiences suggests that standard methods of theory will prove inadequate to the task at hand" (ibid.: 248). If we take the feminist standpoint perspective, integration is foiled as a form of emancipation for women in IR unless the field can change in response to the new visions. William Connolly (1988: 139) points out that "any particular settlement is potentially susceptible to disturbance," particularly if we do not hide "the political character of actual or ideal settlements behind a smokescreen of transcendental imperatives." But that is the rub: the political character of IR settlements has been smokescreened up to now by efforts to embed "women"-transcending principles in the field.

Postmodernism exposes the smokescreens, and the histories of the screens and the smoke, in brilliant, eye-opening ways. But postmodernist manifestations of IR can also beg the question of whether new-style "progressive" thinkers can have meaningful identities and question them too, or whether we really face a binary dilemma that pits various old-style allegiances against refusals of inherited subject statuses and the bodies of knowledge that promote them. To refuse makes some sense; but it also comes from a place that lacks empathy. I have argued that to have meaningful identities and to query them too situates us as appreciators of the many ways we stand in a space or moment of identity and look at other identity allegiances within ourselves and our context of knowledge with an empathetic–critical gaze. This gaze keeps us somewhat un-surefooted by defying the fixed "I." It also dispels fears about those who would colonize us by providing the resource of mobility that enables us to be many things at once, to be elephants and el(l)e-phants.

The empathetic cooperative gaze can divest IR's nostalgic gender settlements of power by infusing them with the knowledges that come from listening to and engaging canon-excluding and canon-including subjectivities. In listening, one becomes somewhat like a Kuhnian confronted with anomalies, and one shifts – not to a better and more encompassing theory, a sturdier home – but to a place of mobile subjectivity where basic questions can be rephrased in many tones. For example, instead of specifying how to study states through the voice of feminist theorizing, we ask how shifts in identity politics change our sagas of political authority and territory.

Point four has to do with feminist forms of homelessness. In these pages we have considered two types of feminist homelessness. One is that old "problem that has no name." It extends beyond bored house-wives in suburban lands of plenty to situations of discomfort and stultifying, chimerical "security" in homes assigned past the fences of recognized politics, outside international relations, and at the margins of political culture. In this nameless problem space, one is isolated from sociality, less by choice than by the expectations of society about properly divided turfs. The second type of feminist homelessness is an achieved standpoint that homesteads assigned places through a life politics of empathetic cooperation with difference. Rather than burning the homestead, or holding tight to fixed identity – whatever that may be – or to "a" research homespot, one engages in respectful negotiation, moving back and forth among multiple subjectivities that continually enlarge, combine, and gaze critically and empathetically at each other as one seeks out and takes seriously successive puzzles of inclusion and exclusion (see Sylvester, 1993a; 1993b).

Neither form of feminist homelessness – the fledgling sense that something is wrong with this homestead (and yet it all might be in my head – I'm too isolated to know), and the political embrace of homeless ontology as a basis for thinking of new homesteading approaches – is meant to refer to an existential condition. We are, in the West at least, all homeless in the same way that we are all insecure. But this con-dition has not generated an epistemology that enables the el(l)e-phants who paint to affect the "secure" and "separate" sense of ontology, the sense that we know who and what is of IR and who and what is "outside." A politically achieved standpoint of homelessness must supplement any existential condition of homelessness. That is, homelessness must be valorized as a venue for knowing and being.

Homelessness of all types is frightening to contemplate from a perspective of privilege. Why would someone in the guardhouses of IR want to shoot the can(n)on one last time, only to suffer angst and rush off to a therapy group for owls? My contention is that canonicals need not undergo profound conversion to feminism in order to parti-cipate in postmodern feminist ways of bringing life politics to IR. They need not dissolve themselves or reach desperately for "a" new consen-sus as the way forward. Canonicals, like everyone else, are already mestiza – at least half something other than their vested IR identity. The standpoint of homelessness is simply an awareness of the border-lands of identity one routinely traverses that is worked into a method for taking in and recording more about international relations than one has noticed before. It is also an awareness of and interpretative interest in the border-transgressing, discipline-disturbing "conver-sations" that take place in places that IR usually ignores (for example,

214

at and around Greenham Common). The method requires some willingness to extend recognition beyond one's backyard fence. Some will not want to do this. But those who resist will most likely want to speak their minds on the absurdity of the process. In doing so, those who are listening empathetically can incorporate the points raised by resisters so as to engage with those who refuse divesting engagements.

Analogously, I have argued against the postmodernist notion that "women" should renounce gender in order to be free to renounce all other modern instances of sovereign voice. If we throw out even false homes before searching through their spaces for hidden treasures, there is a possibility that we throw out those excluded ways of knowing before we have considered their merits and demerits for IR. As well, if we throw out all of standard IR thought, feminists miss the nuggets of wisdom that can keep us on our toes and away from the traps of wishful thinking. For example, mainstream depictions of prisoners with dilemmas teach us that some conditions may be more conducive to processes of empathetic cooperation than others. Hegemonic stability theory teaches us about potential problems in free-wheeling conversations that embrace disorder as a *modus operandi*.

By the same token, "women" do not want to use assigned homes as a base to homestead IR without some slippage or mobility of identity components on our end, or we will risk deceiving ourselves with insights that have been distorted by living only as visitors to IR. Thus a paradox: one does not want to vaporize the experiences of people who cannot afford to distance themselves from their assigned homes or who, as in the case of some Zimbabwean people called women, actually draw inspiration for transformed identity and practice from gender identity and solidarity; but at the same time, one cannot revel in gender homes because they may not really exist as meaningful foundations for the future. To negotiate this paradox, we need to give concepts like "gender" "flesh while maintaining analytic distance between them as heuristic devices, and the lived, material reality in and through which they echo and are refracted" (K. Jones, 1991: 123).

Postmodern theorizing, as a fifth point, encourages us to recognize and listen to others telling their stories about lived material realities. We can become empathetically related to those stories in an identity-refracting way that reveals repositories of exclusion in our subjectivities and insecures that which seems to hold fast. In such a process the relatively privileged white western feminist retains gender *and* comes out of her preoccupations with gender as a universal problematique.

The Zimbabwean "woman" experiences identity adjustment through a new-found inclusion on her terms of similarity and difference. The realist "man" is made aware of the many ways his theory is inappropriate and perhaps the areas of it that can be rehabilitated. Immune settlements are disturbed; gender is disturbed; theory is rewritten.

To reiterate, theorists rendered homeless from fixed and immobile research gazes by the process of empathetic cooperation do not wander the streets lost. Rather, there is a turn to sociality to keep some insecurity at bay. This is akin to the turn to cooperation under anarchy in neoliberal institutionalist theory. The turn to cooperation in postmodern feminism is possible, however, because there is a store of sociality to draw. We are connected in anarchy through the repetition of patterns of relationship and not through strictly voluntary agreements and contracts. We have subjectivities that shift and change, but we are also drawn into an attachment to the group with which we learn to empathize.[2] Nancy Hirschmann (1992: 253) argues that knowledge becomes "a conduit for relationship" rather than relationship guiding the search for knowledge. I think it cuts both ways, with relational memories serving to inspire epistemological processes and the search for knowledge leading to a sense of ontological homelessness that is compensated by relationships. None of this suggests an essential gentleness or caring in the relationships that spawn both homelessness and the turn to group attachment thereafter. Along with Arthur Stein (1990) and Robert Jervis (1988), I think that conflictual and cooperative relationships are two types of connections that are difficult to disentangle.

The seventh point to make is that empathetic cooperation leads to group homesteadings of a field as we move around the web of relations that simultaneously deconstruct our identities and reconstitute them in expansive ways. We homestead realism when we unravel the fences at Greenham Common. We homestead neoliberal institutionalism when we consider the relational bases of practice discussed in feminist psychoanalytic literature and the alternative cooperations that take place in marginalized spaces of IR such as Zimbabwe. When I say "homesteading," it is not to reiterate a nostalgia for the brutal colonizing process that forged the United States. It is not to find new natives to nativize and turn out nor is it to craft a general will that somehow transcends all the homeless positions but always leaves someone behind and displaced.[3] If homesteading is always a politics of disturbance that unsettles and plows up inherited turfs without planting the same old seeds in the field, then we must appropriate and rework the term so that it is less emblematic of heartless barbarism, nationalist primitivism, and universalist missions and more a heretical shifting that unravels some walls and makes other translucent, light, and movable.

Greenham Common is an example of homesteading as an unravelling-reworking process. At the camp, varied and nonconsensual circles of practice swirled around the common knowledge that all participants were interpreting life rather than destroying the instruments of deterrence and their wielders. In most cases, there was no party line to follow or general will to rehearse. Everyone involved had an interpretation of public life politics and a personal life politics that commingled in the damp British air. With the help of the nonhierarchical decision-making style, a range of borderland disturbing relationships transformed a walk for life into a mobile and always insecure homestead built through attachments to a group. There was a politics of recognition in Greenham's refusals to otherize the "men" they encountered behind the military fence. There was simultaneously a Janus-faced politics of disturbance unleashed by the controversial decision to make Greenham a women's camp. Both politics shook the foundations of everyone's sense of security. In these decisions one sees the simultaneities and contradictions of the late modern, postmodern era. And with that sight, the assurance that one always knows where one goes is tempered.

There is also a drama of unraveling and replanting at work among the "women" cooperators in Zimbabwe. These cooperators draw a sense of empowerment not only from sharing labor among themselves but from the empathy they interpret in the activities of cross-identified Greek patrons. Faced with an EEC effort to shape them into eligibility for western funding, the cooperators give the Greek "women" the say at the borderlands of unfamiliar georacial, geopsychological, and geohistorical spaces.[4] And yet these "women" themselves homestead all the donor agendas that overdefine them simply by "thinking our own thoughts." Cooperatives do not officially exist in Zimbabwe to facilitate the cacophony of "own thoughts" unless these thoughts coalesce into a strategy conducive to viable business. These cooperating "women," homeless in the texts of western business success and simultaneously homesteading "success' and "cooperation," take us a considerable distance toward understanding empathetic cooperative methods in situations where we cannot assume that the participants are equal in economic status, prestige, fluency, education, and so on. The gist of their method is to stand mestiza in a web of interactions in which one loses some voice but gains the resources necessary to continue to think thoughts. These "women" face dilemmas having to do with security, but they are not prisoners. They cooperate, but not within the context of IR-understood anarchy.

The last point I wish to make in this section is that notwithstanding my slavish adherence to a progression of points, simultaneous homesteadings do not add up to "a" homestead that science can enshrine. The notion that a theorist succeeds to the degree that s/he can stake a claim for universal truth – or pronounce a universal untruth – must be relinquished, and thus we must relinquish key aspects of the three discipline-defining debates of IR. Even the third debate, which has no clear-cut sides and more cross-referencing than the previous debates, can be a struggle for recognition in the sense of having "one's views recognized without recognizing the other" (Hirschmann, 1992: 252). Thus, Robert Keohane (1989b) recognizes feminist theorizing while nonrecognizing its agendas. Yale Ferguson and Richard Mansbach (1991) advocate studying authority patterns "out there" while nonrecognizing the gender-eclipsing authority patterns "in here." Linklater (1992) strikes some chords of postmodern feminism while neglecting to recognize those who have helped to write his tune.

The trouble with authority, says Kathleen Jones (1991: 119), "is that it discourages us from asking why? 'Why?' invites reflection, it evokes memory, it keeps the conversation going." Feminists ask why the field is constructed as it is and they challenge the authorities to enter a process of mutual recognition that will change it. At this juncture, I want to suggest a few directions that mutual recognition can take us in as we conjointly and empathetically cast owlish eyes and mestiza consciousness at the garishly painted landscapes of international relations.

Forming a conversation

The three debates that constitute the authority of IR have to do, in many of their permutations, with the question of whether international relations is an anarchy or a site of cooperation through institutional politics. This is not the only problematique in the field, but it is clearly the gist of the realist/idealist first debate, which Waltz brought squarely into the second debate, and which now reappears as the question of conceptual anarchy in the field (and nostalgic governancelessness in the world) versus various cooperations that could set us on a new path.

I have argued that a convention of cooperative autonomy from "women" runs through the IR literatures of the three debates and through the practices of statesman, which belies the very notion of anarchy. Others have reached a similar conclusion about the bank-ruptcy of anarchy by following a different route of argumentation. Cooperation comes in many costumes: it can be overt, as in the case of regimes formed to manage international trade, or it can be covert, as in the cooperative autonomy convention. We can be fooled into thinking that war is a sign of anarchy and we can be just as hoodwinked into thinking that cooperation is the antithesis of hostile relations, thus not seeing that when we refuse to reciprocate the work that "women" may do for regimes, there is gender hostility within cooperation. We have also considered the possibility that cooperation and anarchy coexist, the latter providing the structural bases and incentives for reciprocity in neoliberal institutionalism and for cooperative auton-omy from "women" in most of IR. As the field continually confronts the anarchy/cooperation problematique it evades the obvious: anarchy/cooperation is a web of relations more so than a polarity.

With that thought in mind, instead of maintaining the notion that we are studying international relations or international politics we may want to discuss the fact that our field is about "relations inter-national." That is, the field is about the myriad positions that groups assume toward one another across the many boundaries and identities that defy field-invented parameters. It is about "inters" of all sorts. Politics, by contrast, has often been the mode of relating very distantly, or of seeking to avoid relations, through rule-governed procedures and decision-making styles that constrain conversations. Think of the convention in liberal international politics to refuse "terrorists" access to diplomatic conversations. Think of electoral politics, which can be terribly strategic, adversarial, nonempathetic, prone to caricatures of relations, and prone to efforts to paint canvases in blacks and whites in an effort to appeal to blacks and whites and mestizas in the "public" or to defeat them.

Politics can be a conduit for relationships in a context where mutual recognition and respectful negotiation guide the process, and relations can bring forth politics. "Relations international" puts the emphasis directly on varieties of connection, including politics, across the lines, fences, wires, walls, imaginations, sound bites, politics, and immi-gration and customs guardhouses of the world. Some of these connec-tions are already well known from IR studies and are named as interdependence, war, balances, regimes and so on. Some of them, however, are less well known because they have been officially dis-connected; the *gendered* relations of our field stand as a case in point. Unless we begin with relations and query their forms, we are very likely to sally forth in this third debate trying, at best, to integrate

219

"women" and feminist concerns into the international in order to bring us into the few relations we do study. We will continue to put the cart before the horse by looking, first and foremost, for the international and then for the relations.

This emphasis on relations international is somewhat different from the emphasis on transnationalism that challenged realism in the 1970s (e.g., Pirages, 1978; Seymour Brown, 1974). Transnationalists rejected the anomie of realism as narrow, dated, and incomplete, and saw the real issues of international relations – energy, debt, pollution, population increases, shifts in comparative advantages, currency crises, third world underdevelopment – as undermining the wary state model of the world. The new arenas of politics wove economic activities into the fabric of system structure, constraining state autonomy, increasing the potential for cooperation (and mutual damage) in the system, and enhancing the roles of multinational corporations, common markets, commodity cartels, international trade regimes, and other nonstate actors. Transnationalists claimed that states were now so well integrated into global economic frameworks that it was sensible to speak of a transformed system. And yet, gender relations persisted untransformed, which must mean that important aspects of relations international did not change.

Relations international is also not the same as James Rosenau's (1990) sense of postinternational relations, for the simple reason again that the emphasis in that study is on the turbulent *international* trends that mark our system in this time. Changing relations affect the system, but I am not convinced that the changes Rosenau notes, such as the improvement of average people's skills, have altered the ways that relations of gender play out around the world and in our theories of the world. I am especially unconvinced that Rosenau's discussion of a bifurcated world with overlapping spheres of authority by sovereignty-free and sovereignty-bound actors presents us with a different way of viewing the international. In his postinternational relations, the international is dichotomous and once again the scene of conventional concerns with sovereignty. Improved skills or not, the message in Rosenau's work is that there are many ways to rearrange systems and still maintain a gender-sovereign system. "States persist – Men lead" (Sylvester, 1990a: 248). "Relations international" reverberates with the sounds of a polyarchic world and with the many cross-cutting subnationalisms that Rosenau highlights. But it takes the notion of going postinternational much farther.

Moving to relations international also lets us discover new interpretations of familiar signposts. I would argue, for instance, that the realist fascination with anarchy derives in part from conflating technological and political limitations to communication, that hindered relations international for much of the time up to the post-cold-war era, with a structural lack of governance in the system. Without the means to talk and listen regularly, the system seemed to miss the rudiments of "civilization." It was the wild state of nature recreated nostalgically "out there" as the realm of war. Even when conversation was evident in the international system – as in the conference mode of the Concert of Europe – it was subjected by realists to the presupposition of anarchic order and called the "balance of power" rather than the "discussion of power." The convention of anarchy was rehearsed and underscored through the first and second debates of IR, as we exaggerated, in liberal style, "certain human characteristics (those pertaining to separation and individualism) at the expense of others (those pertaining to connection and sociability), distorting the former, repressing the latter" (Hirschmann, 1992: 283).

We are no longer conversation-poor owing to weak transmission devices and officially marked polarities of structure, although we may be controlled by the managers of updated technologies and by the politics of lingering modern polarities of thought (Shapiro, 1990; Habermas, 1979). Emphasizing a range of relations breaks the stranglehold on the field of a certain interpretation of anarchy and replaces it with a sense of continuities and discontinuities of a different type, such as those having to do with gender relations over time and with the homesteading that took place through the anarchies of the Greenham Common Peace Camp. The emphasis on relations international also helps us to see that the conventions, treaties, and regimes of institutional IR have encrusted in the field some gendered assumptions about who or what is involved in reciprocity. When we look first at the international, we think of reciprocity as something that occurs between decision makers of states. When we put up the periscope and look for relations, we see the exploitation that passes for normal employee relations in some neoliberal quarters.

At the same time, the move to relations could be yet another totalizing effort – now all is relations and not old-style anarchy or cooperation – that would be at odds with a postmodern mood. The sense of relations that suffuses the method of empathetic cooperation, however, is not nativizing. It does not assume that one gender owns "relationship" by, for example, associating it with a maternal standpoint of care. Rather, it queries relations for their interlocking constraints and considers a more encompassing range of authority patterns than we have contemplated within standard IR. Also, it does

221

not assume that relations are derivative of liberal rights and contracts. "Relations" suggests acts of telling or recounting (to relate) and showing or establishing connections. Despite its common root, relations is not the same as relativism nor is it at total odds with the notion that ethical statements depend on the individuals and groups holding them. Relativism, as we usually think of the term, paradoxically denies that certain relationships may link or affect all our subjectivities. It reinvents a certain type of anarchy in the guise of disassociating from "others" by granting them rights to their idiosyncratic knowledge and practices. It sanctions total tolerance from a safe distance. It lets well-enough or simply enough alone to fall back into the trap of thinking we are alone and not in some relation of connection to separate knowers. Postmodern feminist method corrects this type of objectification and denies its power even while it encourages all of us to "consider the possibility that my views ... are hegemonic, oppressive, exclusive" (Hirschmann, 1992: 257).

With considerations of relations international in mind, we can redirect our attention to the three IR debates and consider the degree to which each of them is staged in a way that illuminates or denies the centrality of relations.

The first debate is all about establishing the international as a legitimate place for nonstatesmen to study and control. It reads as a dialogue (more so than a conversation) about the degree to which the international is the recreated place of nature beyond the socially contracted nation-state or the domestic political arena of liberal states writ large. For realists, the international was a place of citizensandstate escape from domesticity, a place where free-standing conquerors of the state of nature continued their struggles for dominance. For idealists, the international was the liberal national realm of politics on a larger scale, a place where gender-bound citizensandstates ruled their own affairs in a peaceful manner. This domestic analogy refused lessons on what constitutes the relations of domestic "democracy" for "women" within the nation and within the household. Given the gendered content of the debate we can say that although the politics of place was the real winner, we have inherited a distorted and partial sense of relations international because the two camps set masculine gender relations as the norm.

The texts of first-debate IR depended on sturdy nations to hold them up. Realists of the first debate had assumed that, with statesmen brokering the national realm of identity relations and the "out beyond" where these common understandings supposedly did not exist (and, therefore, where relations could exist only as accounts of suspicion), a nation would always go forth righteous. It could be confident that its mission was legitimate irrespective of how other nations chose to interpret it. Idealists drew more openly on one type of nation as the exemplar of the spirit of domestic cooperation that could be projected outward into a single international peace-lovingness. The democratic nation enveloped a group, not of strangers who could imagine themselves united into a community (Anderson, 1983), but of communities forged during the process of negotiating the social contract. These national communities could hatch an international social contract that would maintain official differences and yet collectively secure one another's existence around a shared foundation of democratic practices. In both the realist and idealistic scenarios, the international emerged as a by-product of nostalgia for a certain type of invented nation.

Today there is a nostalgia, says Connolly (1991: 463–4), for a politics of place that can amalgamate realism with its supposed foe of idealism to restore some "legitimate standards of collective action and the ability to identify them in one place." The nation was supposed to do this for us. It was the essential entity precursory to places international and it was supposed to act a certain way. Now the nation is, in many places, degenerating into virulent pockets of nationalism that operate to ward off particularistic "standards of collective action" at home. In the desperation to carve out and to define ethnically pure nations, in efforts to evict those who have "wrongfully" established homes in the pure nation, the nation is becoming homeless as an anchor of international relations. It is unhinged in the former Soviet Union and Yugoslavia, parodied in nationalist debates in (the now erstwhile) Czechoslovakia, in Canada, torched in Los Angeles, and fired at in China. For the moment it survives, but its miniaturization and civil wars may bode ill for texts of IR that depend on it.

The endangered nation may also bode ill for the "women" who are losing protection within it. Yet we must be careful to avoid nostalgias. The old nation celebrated in the first IR debate did not provide a "women"-negotiated home for "women." We remember debates within nations over whether "women" should vote or have equal rights with other citizens. We remember that colonized people did not have official nations and could not, accordingly, be at home in the national place of the colonizer nor in the nation-dependent international that was being carved out by the first debate. We remember that many people could only be visitors to international relations and, therefore, could only be visitors at best to a realist/idealist debate that took place among *bona fide* members of nations.

223

At this point we can insert stick figures for the people who were excluded from the first debate over IR. We can imagine what a process of empathetic cooperation could have produced by way of a theory of IR. Or we can consider glimmers of the silent other that appear in the metaphors and references of the realist/idealist texts. The other looms in E. H. Carr's (1962) allusions to a field borne in dissatisfaction with professional diplomats and in James Shotwell's (1929) assertion that the new attitude forcing its way in international politics is not for peoples in a semi-barbarous state. Rob Walker (1987) rereads the texts of realism and finds in them a community of diversity that has been ignored in the official stories of a field emergent. Connolly (1991: 468) finds realist/ idealist statements echoed in classical texts on democracy that rely on "feminine strategies to produce the superiority of masculine equiv- alences"; in the case of Schumpeter (1942), there are "pleasant associ- ations of an entirely extra-rational, very frequently sexual nature."

We are there. But the problem a postmodern feminist faces in taking some solace in these little discoveries is that the muted voices we hear are of the author studying and reporting his understanding of the other. Thus the priggish nun whose convent life denies her any knowledge of sex and any contact with "real world" problems, or the semi-barbarian who cannot be let in to idealism. These representations are dreamlike. We cannot simply excavate and recuperate lost voices in the texts and let these stand in for the living conversations that can render our inheritance less secure. That is why I have irreverently shifted the time dimension on the IR debates to accommodate conver- sations that feminists can have today.

But I am ahead of myself. Nation was the given for the first debate in IR and international was the place established for the national adven- ture "out there." In the second debate, science was the touchstone (although we remember Morgenthau's efforts to cast idealists as peace scientists) and the national/international divide was alternately asserted and denied – through scientific means. During the heyday of this debate, feminist theorizing was in full swing against the scientific rationalities that kept "women" in nostalgias of gender place. Tradi- tionalists, too, railed against science as a heartless and distant practice. The twains of feminism and IR's second-debate participants, however, did not meet. The scientists were only marginally concerned to incor- porate the various authority-challenging currents of the 1960s and 1970s into their research. Feminist theorists had other issues to con- sider and did not seek admission to IR's second debate in any direct way. Traditionalists could only see "women" as useful metaphors for what to avoid and what to court.

We remember of this debate that Klaus Knorr and James Rosenau (1969) painted relations between an IR scholar and his subject matter in words that evoked a gentle courtship process. We remember Hedley Bull (1969) suggesting that nuns and scientists have something prim in common. At the cusp of science and tradition we remember Graham Allison's (1969) models of decision making in the Cuban missile crisis against the backdrop of nostalgia in the US about Cubans and missiles and John Kennedy and his (all male) brightest. We know about our nostalgia for the tony times of Jackie in the White House against the cloth-coated Mrs. Khrushchev, and smooth Jack against a Soviet leader who pounded a shoe at the podium of idealism. The images are stark. The memories of "manned" space flights and good budgets for science and math in the schools lurk in the background.

The nation is, in the second debate, the starting point once again for international relations. This time, however, the nation is not always the unitary entity that it had been in realism and idealism. This nation has decision makers with operational codes and bounded rationality and organizational loyalties. In the second debate, however, science turns this into a fascinating point that still misses the gender point. There are a few more "women" in this moment of IR, as window-dressed models for Jackie wannabes to emulate and as secondary figures in the tales of some honeymoon cables. There are more "women" leaders about in India and Israel, but they seem to be anomalies. The second debate, no less than the first, is about "men" conducting relations with other "men," either directly or in the interstices of "anarchic" system structure.

Now we are in the throes of a third debate that could have emerged differently as an ongoing conversation had the field begun considering the voices of not-"men" (and others) and places of not-nation (like households) earlier in its history. Instead of struggling to come to terms with the perspectivists, paradigmatists, and relativists – many of whom do not seem to remember the names of feminist contributors to the field – we would be accustomed by now to inserting the word "why" and the phrases "for whom" and "where" into every theoretical discussion. We would be aware of the trouble with authority and with the pull of nostalgia for a time when "men" and "anarchy" and "nation-states" and the limited reciprocities of "men" supposedly secured the field.

The task before us now, however, is to homestead the third debate and its second- and first-debate remnants. We must take on the gendered anarchies and reciprocities of a field, freeing prisoners from manipulated dilemmas and refusing divisive levels of analysis that have us not-seeing the lessons on cooperative relations that third world cooperatives and first world peace camps can teach. I have attempted to provide the outlines of a process of empathetic cooperation as postmodern feminist method. To get concrete requires that the process simply begin, that the debaters of round three and the contributors without names agree to address each other's concerns in a spirit of colleagueship. How this will actually come about, I trust, is by repetitive feminist insistence that we be included on our terms, combined with arguments to the effect that the secure homes constructed by IR's many debaters are chimerical. For a while we will not be granted full recognition. Our terms will not be accepted by the many who are unfamiliar with our styles of critique and reconstruction. We will be told that we belong in women's studies or, for God's (-eyed) sake, somewhere other than here. Our demonstrations that the emperors of IR have little to wear at this point in time, that insecurity is ubiquitous, will be greeted quizzically. Other challengers will say that we are not doing it properly.

Throughout the discussions to come, we will remember that recognition is a hard-fought battle when one is among the excluded, and that debates and dialogues about emancipation can leave many people out of competent communication, scientific explanation, and recurrent patterns of law and logic. We remember momentary freedoms from hypostasized forces and feminist victories of communication that have been greeted with the backlash of gender nostalgia.

We postmoderns know that the fences and immune systems are fantastical. We know that they can be unraveled and immunomodulated by Chimera, the fire-breathing she-monster of Greek mythology, who has a lion's head, a goat's body, and a serpent's tail. And finally we know that her entourage includes easel-carrying elephants who paint *en plein air* in defiance of assigned homelessness in art (except as spindly bearers of "women" as temptations) and in defiance of metaphors that, by themselves, can move us only so far.

NOTES

Introduction: contestations and el(l)e-phants

1 *Millennium Journal of International Studies,* 17 (3) 1988. Editors: Rebecca Grant and David Long.

2 I am the guest editor of that Winter 1993 issue (vol. 18[1]).

3 At least that is what they look like to humans. Whether elephants think of abstractions versus realism is open to question. I thank Dick George for underscoring this point.

4 From a letter sent to me by "Elephant Person" Anita Schanberger from the Phoenix Zoo, January 22, 1991. Curiously, Ruby uses colors that please the human eye (reds, pinks, soft pastels). She also places a mark of "signature" at the bottom of each painting (the V-shaped stroke at the lower right). Both characteristics of her work invite questions about whether she has "our" sense of color and authorship or vice versus. For further information on Ruby, see D. George (1989) and Gilbert (1990).

5 For a discussion of the gender biases of US Homesteading Acts and the day-to-day activities of women homesteaders see Jones-Eddy (1992).

6 As I write this, a land controversy is unfolding in Arizona between the Navajo and Hopi, on the one hand, who are seeking to rectify injustices perpetrated on them by earlier government efforts to reserve places for them, and Arizonans whose private property may be affected by a new land deal. Many Arizona landowners claim that the US government has no right "to give away our land to Indians." Apparently, a collective amnesia has set in that has helped some to forget that native Americans were the "landowners" displaced in order to install private property rights.

7 See James Johnson (1993) for a similar appeal to respectful conversation across two strange bedfellows of IR, in that case, critical theory and rational choice.

8 W. J. T. Mitchell (1992: 15) says that a commonplace is "a half-truth, a premature generalization, an impression." "The West," for instance, has been a commonplace representation of inherent robustness that often smokescreened an imperial homesteading consciousness. It "never designates where it is, but only where it hopes to go, its 'prospects' and frontiers" (ibid: 13).

9 Following up on the commonplace as imperial consciousness (previous note), Mitchell (1992: 13–14) says: "For some time ... it has been evident that the Western empires have nowhere to go. We live not just in a

'postmodern' but a 'postcolonial' world, where the 'westering' imperative makes no literal or concrete sense ..." and where the commonplace is in question.

10 One woman we have not associated with international relations is Georgia O'Keeffe, the US painter. In the summer of 1938, the N. W. Ayer company approached O'Keeffe about undertaking a series of paintings in Hawaii that its client, Dole Pineapple, could use in advertisements. She took up the offer of this working vacation but broke with convention when she arrived on the islands by asking to stay in the workers' villages on the edge of the pineapple fields. Dole refused and thereafter the company and the artist had a "difficult" relationship that was, nonetheless, lucrative for Dole in the long run. O'Keeffe offered the company two paintings. Dole enthusiastically accepted one of them, a red ginger flower, and rejected her painting of a green papaya on the grounds that it was the product of a rival canning company. She had to paint a pineapple. When O'Keeffe returned to New York, Dole sent her a budding pineapple plant to paint so that their business agreement could be fulfilled. Dole included the subsequent painting in several annual reports and national magazine advertisements. (See Lisle, 1986: 302–5.)

11 We must bear in mind that "theoretical perspectives are rarely easy to categorize; schools of thought often blur together; they differ in coherence, parsimony and scope" (Deudney and Ikenberry, 1990: 2). Thus realism comes in "hard," "soft," structural, and statist varieties. And yet, realism tends to subsume most other schools of IR, not just because its variegations are multiple, but because it sets the pace in declaring itself autonomous from other standards, including, one supposes, the standards of "women" (see Sylvester, 1992a; Morgenthau, 1965).

12 The Tailhook Association scandal illustrates this point. During an annual gathering in Las Vegas, "women" naval officers reported that they were sexually assaulted and that commanding officers neither intervened to stop the harassment nor did they punish the offenders afterwards. Under pressure from the armed services committee of the US House of Representatives, on which the influential Congresswoman Patricia Schroeder sits, an investigation ensued and the offending officers were retired or reassigned (but have not been dishonorably discharged as yet from this "men's" club within relations international).

13 I am indebted to Ann Tickner for her very simple and elegant evocation of IR, especially the realists within it, as "white men in ties." Her analysis of gender in the field appears in *Gender in International Relations: Feminist Perspectives on Achieving Global Security* (1992).

14 Only one voice in the Lapid-inspired debate featured in the pages of *International Studies Quarterly*, 33 (3) 1989, even mentions feminism. See Biersteker (1989: 266).

15 The issue of *International Studies Quarterly* containing Ashley's and Walker's discussion on "Reading Dissidence/Writing the Discipline," 34, (3) 1990, is taken over entirely by postmodernist critiques of the field. In some of the contributions, mention is made of the marginal instances of women in international relations (e.g., Ashley and Walker, "Speaking the Language of Exile: Dissident Thought in International Studies": 259–68). But there is

no contribution to that special issue that focuses on the particular brand of marginality that has to do with gender in international relations. There is no contribution on feminist IR as a corrective dissidence. This "oversight" in a journal issue purporting to provide the field with insights into speaking the language of exile has elicited written criticism by the British feminist Marysia Zalewski (1993) and by two contributors to James N. Rosenau's *Global Voices: Dialogues in International Relations* (1993a) – the British IR scholar Steve Smith and myself. In addition, Roger Spegele (1992: 156) has taken exception to the way Ashley's and Walker's analysis sets up the possibility that "feminist positions which fail to play the game on their turf," that is, on the turf of postmodern dissidence, may be excluded or preempted.

16 One "dissident" who does demonstrate this recognition is David Campbell (1992).

17 Wendy Brown (1991) tells us about deciding rather than deriving as a mode of postmodern politics.

18 To claim a difference between postmodern feminism and feminist postmodernism is not uncontroversial. It is, as we will see in chapter 1, a feminist move that enables us to rescue feminism from the deconstructor's looming scalpel while recognizing that women are constructs – "our experience of our very subjectivity is a construct mediated by and/or grounded on a social discourse beyond (way beyond) individual control" (Alcoff, 1988: 416). Those who take the postmodern feminist path include Nancy Hirschmann (1992), Sandra Harding (1991), Teresa de Lauretis (1986), Jean Bethke Elshtain (1987), and Kathy Ferguson (1993).

19 There is a wide assortment of opinions on the characteristics of late modernity or postmodernity as an historical and cultural condition. See, for instance, Bauman (1992), Calinescu (1987), and Smart (1992).

20 Many of these qualities surface in the writings of Habermas (1987), Horkheimer (1974), and Bell (1974).

21 Pauline Rosenau (1992) might dispute the use of the term "emancipated," arguing that emancipation is a modern concern and "life politics" is more postmodern.

22 For gender-eclipsing shortcomings of humanist theory see Sylvester (1987, 1993b). For related shortcomings in Habermasian critical theory, see Narayan (1989).

23 A "boot camp" is a place that pounds the military way of life into civilian minds and bodies.

24 Evelyn Fox Keller (1985: 117) defines dynamic objectivity as:

> a form of knowledge that grants to the world around us its independent integrity but does so in a way that remains cognizant of, indeed relies on, our connectivity with that world. In this, dynamic objectivity is not unlike empathy, a form of knowledge of other persons that draws explicitly on the commonality of feelings and experience in order to enrich one's understanding of another in his or her own right.

Sketches of feminism's first wave in anticipation of chapter 1

1 Again, I remind the reader that I take the position here that women is not a natural category of existence and meaning but rather a contested subject status. I designate this by replacing women with "women" except where a

text or entire theoretical-epistemological tradition is known for accepting the existence of women unproblematically.

2 Robin Morgan (1989: 137–8) tells us that for the US:

> between 1940 and 1967, of the more than four hundred people who have been national-security managers, only one was a woman. Today, twenty years later, the State Department has only five female assistant secretaries (all with "soft" portfolios, such as Consumer Affairs, Communications, Protocol, and Narcotics Matters). Only three women have scrambled up anywhere near the real power circles and then just to the outer rim: Anne Armstrong, Jeane J. Kirkpatrick and Clare Boothe Luce, now deceased, were, as of October 1986, members of the President's Foreign Intelligence Advisory Board.

See her source: *Women's Foreign Policy Council Directory* (1987).

3 This oversight was later corrected to some degree in Wallerstein's introduction to J. Smith, Collins, Hopkins, and Muhammed (1988).

1 The palette of feminist epistemologies and practices

1 Women's struggles with individuation seem to come as young adults, when they must endeavor to differentiate themselves psychologically and sexually vis-à-vis their mothers.

2 For a discussion of women's bodies as ill-fitting the social body, see Kathleen Jones (1990).

3 Discussed in Judith Baer (1991).

4 One can question whether some of these characteristics are intrinsic or whether they mirror our commonplace amnesia about the *socially* constructed relations of mothering, a forgetting that is often accompanied by the tendency to equate "mothering" with "heterosexual relations" and with biology-based caretaking. West's list of defining characteristics also tips in the direction of premenopausal women. What happens to the quintessential female experience when a female cannot experience pregnancy, menstruation, and breast-feeding?

5 Read the account of her walk away from the Mormon church in *From Housewife to Heretic* (1981).

6 I am grateful to Shannon Stimson for reminding me of the humanist possibilities that lurk in some conversational logics.

7 Anne Sisson Runyan and V. Spike Peterson (1991: 96) point out that Keohane is aware of reifications in international relations that can forestall the ability to act, but he does not seem to appreciate the degree to which feminist standpoint "can be guilty of the same reification ... of women." Also see my response to his endorsement of feminist standpoint in Peterson (1989).

8 Kathy Ferguson (1993: 76) reminds us that Sara Ruddick's notion of preservative love is not essentialist in a biological way: "Mothers are not seen as inherently peaceful, but as beings whose work requires them to make *efforts* toward being peaceful." However, Ruddick tends to grant this struggle "a common 'woman space' that can serve as a foundational space for rendering lucid the experiences of those who inhabit it" (p. 77). This type of essentialism Ferguson calls universalizing.

9 Of course, one's subject status can simultaneously be made diffuse by feminist politics and maintained as a monolith by those who assert, often

with good liberal intentions, that women (*sans* inverted commas) comprise a bona fide group with special needs. When women is presented as monolith, the binary opposition of men/women remains intact and prevents relaxation into the many hyphenations that lie in-between or around the polarities. Even those who have slipped into hyphenated identities are not necessarily comfortable with them if they have a "sense of totally lacking roots or any space where one is at home in a relaxed manner" (Narayan, 1989: 266). Living on the cusp of the modern and postmodern eras means that the security of homeplace is sought with great determination and yet is insecured in ways that are often deemed threatening before the opportunities for new-style homesteadings are appreciated. I am grateful to an anonymous reader of this manuscript for Cambridge University Press for pressing me to consider these double-edges of relaxation.

10 In *The Science Question in Feminism* (1986a), Harding tended more toward a postmodernist position.

11 See Braidotti (1991, ch. 5) for a discussion of how "becoming woman" plays out as the nomadic mode in Gilles Deleuze's more feminist-sympathetic writings.

12 For a discussion of how "women" become homeless in this way and how bag-ladies are perceived by others, see Golden (1992).

13 See discussions in Hirschmann (1992), Hartsock (1983), and Flax (1983).

14 Irony is undoubtedly a good way of seeing tensions. Haraway (1985: 65) says that "[i]rony is about contradictions that do not resolve into larger wholes, even dialectically, about the tension of holding incompatible things together." Moreover, irony can be the wonderful moment when we become aware of the importance of "holding incompatible things together"; or it can be one way of leading up to that moment. What comes next, after we see the tension, is the issue for me and the point of introducing the concept of new-style homesteading.

15 Elsewhere (Sylvester, 1990b), I discuss anti-passive revolution, a term I am indebted to Christine Buci-Glucksmann (1980) for, as a type of bottom-up revolution of position that valorizes the plurality of differences necessary to mobilize an oppositional frontier against the state and its political mechanisms. Its meaning can be extended to include struggle against the makers of states and their mechanisms of oppressive-cooptative political economy.

2 The early field of IR – musings, assertions, debates, and (now) feminist interruptions

1 There is an effort in what follows to provide an evocative overview of the field of IR rather than a comprehensive literature review or depth summary of all theoretical traditions and subtraditions. Several good reviews of the field already exist (Holsti, 1985; Viotti and Kauppi, 1987; Dougherty and Pfaltzgraff, 1990; Tickner, 1992).

2 This particular conflict brings to mind, once again, the challenges involved in rethinking homespaces in postmodernity without resorting to modern homesteading projects that evacuate some so that a mythically pure,

dichotomously drawn group of unhyphenated selves can occupy the land. In the absence of a methodology that encourages postmodern forms of empathetic homesteading, this heinous form of nostalgia can be lamented but not readily challenged except through the instruments of war and weak international law.

3 See R. B. J. Walker (1993) for an enumeration of excisions from modern practices and theories of sovereignty.

4 We could, though, go back to the ancients. V. Spike Peterson (1992b) draws our attention to processes of women's subordination that took place in the shift from aristocratic kin-based social organization to centralized Athenian state authority. Phillip Windsor (1988: 452) says "all Western philosophy is a series of extended footnotes on Plato" and reminds us that women "are good enough to be the Guardians in domestic matters of *The Republic* ... [and] are not good enough to engage in the fundamental decisions of the *polis*. This means that private and domestic morality is different in kind from, and works at a level inferior to, that of public choice." To probe the ancients is simply beyond the scope of the challenge here. For a good overview, see Grant (1991).

5 Carol Miller (1991: 75) points out, however, that the Foreign Service also had difficulty accepting the new peace orientation of the times. She says: "The Foreign Office was placed in the awkward position of outwardly supporting the ideals of the League while at the same time essentially carrying on business as usual or at least, in the words of one Foreign Secretary, using 'a judicious mixture of the new League methods and "old diplomacy."'"

6 Indeed, Morgenthau dilutes his argument about the constancy of evil by claiming that the struggle for power is, at least in part, a consequence of the situational things people want and the constraints imposed by relationships:

> finding that his relations with his fellow-men contain at least the germs of ... conflicts of interest, man can no longer seek the goodness of his intentions in the almost complete absence of selfishness and of the concomitant harm to others but only in the limitations which conscience puts upon the drive toward evil. Man cannot hope to be good but must be content with being not too evil. (Morgenthau, 1946: 192)

Kenneth Waltz (1991: 35) claims, however, that even while partly locating the drive for power in a simple conflict of interests, Morgenthau "pulls toward the 'other root of conflict and concomitant evil' [Morgenthau, 1946: 192] – the *animus dominandi*, the desire for power. He often considers man's drive for power as a datum more basic than the chance conditions under which struggles for power occur." In either case, to enter my argument into the fray, Morgenthau does not do an adequate job of exploring either the nuances of "conflicting interests" (whose interests?) or of "human evil" in its gendered locations.

7 Shotwell (1929: 87) briefly mentions the US Federation of Women's Clubs in a discussion of mostly nameless members of publics who were against war in the interwar years.

8 Arthur Stein (1990: 9) makes a similar argument. He says that liberals

"readily recognize, and their arguments [about individuals] can and should be readily applicable to, states as actors." This means that realists who paint the state as a certain type of individual writ large have closet liberal tendencies. Idealists, of course, are openly liberal in orientation and cued into the individual rationality of men writ large through the exercise of national and international politics. This cusp of liberalism on which both realism and idealism stand is stronger than James Dougherty's and Robert Pfaltzgraff's (1990: 7) argument that realism is "basically conservative, empirical, prudent, suspicious of idealistic principles, and respectful of the lessons of history." It is also at odds with postmodernist tendencies to emphasize the plurality of community practices that defy the either/or cast of many theories of IR (Walker, 1987). There are pluralities in some areas of IR, but in the gender area realism and idealism are two chapters from one book of community practice. See Sylvester (1992a).

9 Peterson (1990), for instance, offers a *postpositivist* discussion of liberal individualist approaches to human rights.

3 The second debate in IR revisited by feminists

1 R. B. J. Walker's (1993) recent overview of the field contains some references to the excision of gender (and other considerations) from analyses of the second debate era.

2 For a discussion of the uneasy relationship between political protests in the US around the Vietnam war and the rise of science in IR, see James Rosenau (1993b).

3 Of course, neither Gilpin nor Wallerstein think of themselves as neorealists. Wallerstein comes out of the tradition of Marxist critique and Gilpin (1986: 302) starts "with individual state actors and seek[s] to explain the emergence and change of international systems." Terry Boswell and Mike Sweat (1991: 124) distinguish between systemic and realist theories of hegemony according to whether the world system as a whole is the unit of analysis or the nation-state. Robert Keohane (1986), however, thinks the divide between world-systems analysis and neorealism should be smudged, owing to the tendency in the world-systems camp to explain certain periods of change in the capitalist system with realist-like examples of armed conflict between states.

4 Again, there is no effort in what follows to provide a comprehensive overview of works in these areas. The texts highlighted merely illustrate tendencies that feminists need to address.

5 His sense of "institution" encompasses "persistent and connected sets of rules (formal and informal) that prescribe behavioral roles, constrain activity, and shape expectations" (Keohane, 1989a: 3).

6 One woman UN staff member told Gayle Kirshenbaum (1992: 18) that "[t]here is an untold, unwritten complicity between men in the organization [the UN] and men in governments." Between January and November 1990, governments nominated 454 candidates for internal positions in the UN and 126 of these were women. Moreover, of the 178 member states in the UN, only three were represented by women ambassadors in 1992.

233

7 The university where Jean Elshtain did her graduate training made no bones about its masculine mission in the early 1970s:

> Brandeis University has set itself to develop the whole man, the sensitive, cultured, open-minded citizen who grounds his thinking in facts, who is intellectually and spiritually aware, who believes that life is significant, and who is concerned with society and the role he will play in it. (Brandeis University Bulletin 1972–3: 11, quoted in Rich, 1979: 127)

4 The third debate in IR visited by feminists

1 Again, I am not striving to offer the reader a comprehensive review of the third debate, but rather to use specific works to illustrate broader themes. For good overviews of the third debate, see Ferguson and Mansbach (1991) and George and Campbell (1990).

2 There is an obligatory nod to be made here to the differences and similarities between these concepts. I think of postmodernism as beginning in architecture and the visual arts and as representing movement beyond modernism into nonlinearity and less function-based aesthetics. Post-structuralism seems to be a parallel concept in the social sciences and literature (e.g., Weeden, 1987). It is a move beyond structural linguistics and the types of closed-system analyses of social phenomena that marked IR's second debate and that either removed human agency to the analytic shadows or made of it an overconstructed Self. An important element in some feminist affinity with postmodernism rather than post-structuralism may have to do with a certain anti-empirical bent of post-structuralism. Some postmodernists have interest in the concreteness of daily life as an alternative to grand theory (P. Rosenau, 1992: n3). So do many feminists.

3 This is by no means the only way of thinking about deconstruction. Joan Scott (1989: 92) offers a Derridean understanding of the term as an analysis of the ways binary oppositions operate, with an eye to "reversing and displacing [their] hierarchical construction, rather than accepting [that construction] as real or self-evident or in the nature of things." Also see Derrida (1976; 1979) and Culler (1982).

4 Braidotti (1991: 3) argues that the response to this form of postmodernism that says it is skeptical and therefore negative is "the attempt to trivialize both the theoretical complexity and the subversive potential of post-structuralist philosophy, replacing them with a generalized nostalgia for humanistic goals."

5 Tom Biersteker (1989) makes a similar point when he suggests that Lapid is too sanguine about the degree to which everyone in the field has shifted to a postpositivist mode.

6 Flax later waffles on this point as she moves to distance feminist post-modernism from standpoint theorizing in her book, *Thinking Fragments* (1990). Hirschmann (1992: 318), however, picks up the argument where Flax stepped away:

> feminist standpoint epistemology is itself a postmodern strategy, or at least a strategy that coheres with certain ideas crucial to postmodernism, suggesting even that object relations and gender psychology *can*, if used in ways that avoid reductive claims to universal truth, be effective tools of both deconstructive and reconstructive strategies.

234

7 Gloria Anzaldua (1990a: xv) speaks of Chicanas making faces. It means:

> to put on a face, express feelings by distorting the face – frowning, grimacing, looking sad, glum or disapproving. For me, *haciendo caras* has the added connotation of making *gesto subversivos*, political subversive gestures, the piercing look that questions or challenges, the look that says, "Don't walk all over me," the one that says, "Get out of my face."

8 Ashley and Walker (1990a: 266) can shrug off this type of critique by shifting the emphasis away from voices: "all we can say is that we hope that the conduct of scholarship in the pages of this issue renders somewhat less effective another widely replicated and far more worrisome form of exclusion based not on physical limitations but on the supposed necessity of preserving institutional boundaries in the territorialization of political and scholarly life."

9 Braidotti (1991) believes, as noted earlier, that the crisis of late modernity has forced philosophy, once the home of rationality, to seek its feminine side in order to survive. This search is evident in the emphases on "becoming woman" that pepper some French postmodernist thinking. The most pernicious, in her view, is associated with the writings of Jacques Derrida, where the metaphorization of the feminine as the creative void or unconscious in the text enables endangered philosophers to name and assimilate "the feminine" to another falsely neutral mode of thinking.

10 Owls have, in the words of Webster's Dictionary, "large eyes." This is a quality postmodern feminists require in order to see the multistandpointed possibilities around us. At the same time, owls are said to be "birds of prey." The secret forces of President Mobutu Sese Seko of Zaire, that sweep the cities at night looking for dissidents, are called owls, and they are indeed preying. The tension in the meanings of "owl" should not be brushed aside. Seeing with large eyes is one thing. Crushing and silencing those one sees is another and, of course, that is not the postmodern feminist goal. The textual doubleness, the geospatial variation in interpretation serves as a warning about scope of vision.

11 Like Katharine Bartlett, Ferguson finds Linda Alcoff's concept of positionality useful as a way "to look at 'the moving historical context' within which different people [and feminisms] take up their relationship to constituted entities such as women and men" (1993: 158). But she underscores "the outcome of ... position*alizing* practice" (ibid.: 159) in order to draw attention to the identities one does (genealogically) as well as those one receives (and interprets) historically.

12 The fact that some citizensandstates have been led by "women" does not negate the point. As many feminists have indicated in many ways, when the territory is masculine a masculine world view can pay off for particular (and very, very few) women. They benefit from the gesture to equality and to nonhierarchical community relations that, in fact, is a way of fusing them, gratefully, to the citizensandstate. Thus, there can be clear limits on what "women" can bring to the political process as currently constituted.

13 Again, perhaps silences run deep because metaphors have been naturalized. Carolyn Merchant (1980) talks about a Pre-Enlightenment organicist metaphor in which the feudal commonwealth and then the state was a

235

prince writ large; indeed, Hobbes wrote that "sovereignty is an artificial soul" and, of course, accorded that soul to masculine nightwatchmen.

14 I have hijacked the word "immunomodulative" from Donna Haraway (1991: 209) who uses it in juxtaposition with the "magic bullet" type of medical thinking that prevailed until the 1980s. Immunomodulative designates some movement away from the idea that there is one strategic solution to a disease, but it retains a binary frame that can mask boundary conditions and interfaces. We should realize that the immunity narrative is unfinished as we "traffic across the specific cultural, biotechnical, and political boundaries that separate and link animal, human, and machine in a contemporary global world where survival is at stake" (ibid.: 229).

5 Feminist homesteadings of security and cooperation

1 Sean Lynn-Jones (1992) and Stephen Walt (1991) include peace studies issues in their discussions of security studies. Indeed, both call for a closer relationship and Lynn-Jones says, shades of Ferguson and Mansbach (1991): "The End of the Cold War allows for the *integration* of peace studies and security studies" (Lynn-Jones, 1992: 54 [emphasis added]). Although some peace studies analysts echo this call (Dunn, 1991), Elise Boulding (1992b: 1) says that "[s]ecurity strategists tend to create worst-case scenarios [while] [p]eace researchers explore best-case scenarios, looking for the emergent possibilities for peace building that exist in every human crisis." Edward Kolodziej (1992) argues that any "reductionist" collapse of war and peace dismisses the nuanced conceptions of security that may animate participants in a conflict.

2 There is a US-based Women in International Security organization headquartered at the University of Maryland. It is separate from the international security studies section of the International Studies Association, although the two memberships probably overlap.

3 Again, my discussion of these periods of security studies is intended to evoke epochal images rather than to inform the reader about the details of who said and did what when. The citations found throughout this chapter add up to a partial bibliography one can readily consult, along with the works of Meyer (1990), Haftendorn (1991), Nye and Lynn-Jones (1988), and Desch (1991), to learn those details. The reader should bear in mind, however, that I take liberties with the subfield of security studies by including some who might not wish to be there (e.g., perhaps Keohane) and by paying less attention to the firm lines demarcating the eras of subfield development than would others. Also, I use the term "strategic" in a broader sense than does Walt (1991).

4 See Roger Hurwitz (1989) for a poststructuralist analysis of the "social fictions" in game-theoretic constructions of strategy.

5 Walt (1991) thinks that this emphasis occurred after the Golden Age waned and the era of cold war "skirmishes" in the third world unfolded with a vengeance. Questions of linear boundary time aside, there is a marked continuity of thinking in the hardline, whether addressed to nuclear missiles or to those "dirty little wars" that could be substituted for the deadly wars of the nuclear age.

6 For a related discussion, see Richard Ashley (1989).

7 For another view of the mirror-image in strategic studies, see Timothy Luke (1989). Compare this to Barry Buzan (1987), who points out that at the level of rhetoric and propaganda, the USSR appeared to reject nuclear deterrence *in toto* years prior to the arrival of Gorbachev. Buzan laments the fact that the two superpowers did not come to terms on the importance of deterrence as a widely acknowledged stabilizing factor.

8 For additional illustrations of sexual imagery, see Klein (1989) and Cohn (1987).

9 This attitude was displayed more recently in the US during the 1991 Tailhook Association scandal that shook the Navy and spilled over to the other armed services (see Introduction, note 12). During a Congressional hearing on sexual harassment in the armed services, the question was raised of whether the prohibition of "women" in combat roles contributed to a sense that "women" were second-class members of the services, not worthy of the respect accorded real service members. General M. A. McPeak, Air Force chief of staff, expressed reluctance to order "women" into combat because "combat is about killing people. I have a very traditional attitude about wives and daughters being ordered to kill people" (*New York Times*, 26 July, 1992). With war naturalized as "man's" domain and "women" thereby kept from this terrible task, the General did not seem to notice that combat entails people called "men" killing people called "women" in distant places. As of April 1993, "women" in the US militaries have permission to participate in that and other combat practices, through the lifting of some restrictions on their scope of duty.

10 Inter-views emphasize communal and negotiated aspects of knowledge formation, the in-betweens that emerge when the researcher shares his/her views with the respondents while soliciting their views in group conversations rather than on an individual basis. For elaboration, see Sylvester (1991b; 1990c).

11 Mona Harrington (1992: 79) tells us that public opinion polls conducted during the Persian Gulf war found that "US women understood massive spending for the protection of an oil sheikdom and for Western access to oil supplies at advantageous price levels as displacing priorities such as day care for children, medical care for the elderly, drug rehabilitation programs, subsidies for heating fuel, and affordable housing." Since US public opinion polls consistently showed strong support for the Persian Gulf war, this deviance in the "public" is very telling.

12 Before moving on, we might say something about the out-of-fashion condemnatory softline of the left. It offers radical critiques of political economy, state, and capitalist world structure that maintain and reproduce strategism. "Rather than whisper into the ear of the prince, or affix him with a hearing aid, critics in this tradition would dispatch the whole princely class, seize the Winter Palace, and establish in its halls their own counterstrategic structure of revolutionary violence in defense of the people's state" (Klein, 1988a: 305). This approach slips on an agent–structure tension around the matters of where transformation commences and who is capable of providing agency for change. In this cauldron "women" can simply dissolve into "revolutionaries" who are not expected

to ask who among us is likely to gain most in a so-called people's state and whether prevailing forms of violence are generative as well as destructive (Sylvester, 1989). As in the classical Marxist tradition, the "women question" is a mentioned tension to be avoided (Luxemburg, 1971; Kaldor, 1981).

13 This situation is slowly changing. At the 1993 meetings of the International Studies Association in Acapulco, Mexico, there were two panels on masculinity in IR on which participants Steven Niva, Ralph Pettman, Steve Smith, and Rob Walker addressed issues of male sex–gender privileges. Not all are postmodernists.

14 See her *The Change: Women, Aging and the Menopause*. New York: Knopf, 1992.

15 For discussions of simultaneous struggles as revolutions in Zimbabwe, see Sylvester (1990b, 1994).

16 Under the "thirty-year rule," British state papers pertaining to actions at Greenham Common cannot be made public until early next century. Feminist historian Jill Liddington (1989: 221) is skeptical that they will be declassified even then. As she puts it, "[p]eace historians may have to wait until 2082 before they can begin to assess what impact *we* had on *them*: the British state and its NATO allies."

17 This was an interesting tactic to try because "only the Attorney General can bring a case under this law" and "he is hardly likely to bring a case ... against other members of the government" (Cook and Kirk, 1983: 116). The campers at Greenham tried to appropriate the Act for the protection of ordinary citizens, whose political activities, bodies, and minds were threatened by government security policy.

18 For background information on Zimbabwe see Sylvester (1991a; 1990d). For a discussion of the cooperative movement, see Sylvester (1991b).

19 My visits to cooperatives have been part of a larger study on the constitution of gender and work in Mashonaland, Zimbabwe, which has entailed inter-viewing, in addition to "women" cooperators, "women" factory workers, "women" peasant farmers, and "women" agricultural workers – nearly 300 in all – and 150 representatives of local and international agencies that support "women's" productive efforts in Zimbabwe.

6 Repainting the Canvases of IR

1 Perhaps IR needs to confront a cadre of Guerrilla Girls in order to learn this point. Guerrilla Girls is a group of artists formed in New York City in 1985 in order to publicize the fact that women artists are sorely underrepresented in galleries and art museums. Dressed in gorilla masks that call attention both to anonymity, to a fierce response to objectification, and to power, the Guerrilla Girls plaster certain areas of New York with posters (e.g. "Do Women Have to Be Nude to Enter the Metropolitan Museum of Art?" – a reference to the countless nudes that hang on the walls of art museums relative to paintings by women) and appear on TV talk shows. Their concerns are wide-ranging, but they tend to focus their most strenuous criticism on galleries whose displayed works are 90 percent by men.

2 Benjamin Barber (1984) also holds this view.

238

3 On this point, I disagree with Hirschmann (1992: 255) who tells us that the conversation is a way of attaining a general will that "allows individuals to see both their individuality and their commonality through their connections to others." I am skeptical of general will on the grounds raised by postmodernists who argue against the illusion of unity and totality. On this point see my article on "Unities and Disunities in Zimbabwe's 1990 Election" (1990d).

4 It is not as though the African "women" of Zimbabwe are unfamiliar with operating mestiza. With subjectivities and social expectations comprised of precolonial, colonial, and postcolonial elements, they must negotiate many inconsistencies and stand in many borderlands. The situation of dealing directly with agents of international relations, however, is new.

REFERENCES

Abray, Jane (1975), "Feminism in the French Revolution," *American Historical Review*, 80: 43–62.

Adler, Emanuel and Peter Haas (1992), "Conclusion: Epistemic Communities, World Order, and the Creation of a Reflective Research Program," *International Organization*, 46, 1: 367–90.

Aidoo, Agnes Akosua (1981), "Asante Queen Mothers in Government and Politics in the Nineteenth Century," in Filomina Chioma Steady, ed., *The Black Woman Cross-Culturally*. Rochester, VT: Schenkman Books: 65–78.

Alarcon, Norma (1990), "The Theoretical Subject(s) of *This Bridge Called My Back* and Anglo–American Feminism," in Gloria Anzaldua, ed., *Making Face, Making Soul: Haciendo Caras*. San Francisco: Aunt Lute: 356–369.

Alcoff, Linda (1988), "Cultural Feminism Versus Post-Structuralism: The Identity Crisis in Feminist Theory," *Signs*, 13, 3: 405–36.

Alexander, M. Jacqui (1991), "Redrafting Morality: The Postcolonial State and the Sexual Offences Bill of Trinidad and Tobago," in Chandra Mohanty, Ann Russo, and Lourdes Torres, eds., *Third World Women and the Politics of Feminism*. Bloomington: Indiana University Press: 133–52.

Alker, Hayward and Thomas Biersteker (1984), "The Dialectics of World Order," *International Studies Quarterly*, 28: 121–42.

Allison, Graham (1969), "Conceptual Models and the Cuban Missile Crisis," *American Political Science Review*, 63 3: 689–718.

  (1971), *Essence of Decision: Explaining the Cuban Missile Crisis*. Boston: Little, Brown and Co.

  (1988), "Testing Gorbachev," *Foreign Affairs*, 67, 1: 18–32.

Alonso, Harriet Hyman (1989), *The Women's Peace Union and the Outlawry of War, 1921–1942*. Knoxville: University of Tennessee Press.

  (1993), *Peace as A Women's Issue*. Syracuse: Syracuse University Press.

Anderson, Benedict (1983), *Imagined Communities: Reflections on the Origins and Spread of Nationalism*. London: Verso.

Anderson, Bonnie and Judith Zinsser (1988), *A History of Their Own: Women in Europe from Prehistory to the Present*, volume II. New York: Harper & Row.

Anzaldua, Gloria (1987), *Borderlands/La Frontera*. San Francisco: Spinsters/Aunt Lute.

  (1990a), "Haciendo caras, una entrada," in Gloria Anzaldua, ed., *Making Face, Making Soul – Horiendo Caras: Creative and Critical Perspectives by Women of Color*. San Francisco: Aunt Lute: xv–xxviii.

  ed. (1990b), *Making Face, Making Soul: Haciendo Caras*. San Francisco: Aunt Lute.

Aron, Raymond (1966), *Peace and War: A Theory of International Politics*, trans. Richard Howard and Annette Baker Fox. Garden City, NY: Doubleday.

Ashley, Richard (1981), "Political Realism and Human Interest," *International Studies Quarterly*, 25, 2: 204–36.

(1984), "The Poverty of Neorealism" *International Organization*, 38, 2: 225–86.

(1989), "Living on Border Lines: Man, Post-Structuralism, and War," in James Der Derian and Michael Shapiro, eds., *International/Intertextual Relations: Postmodern Readings of World Politics*. Lexington: Lexington Books: 259–321.

Ashley, Richard and R. B. J. Walker (1990a), "Speaking the Language of Exile: Dissident Thought in International Studies," *International Studies Quarterly*, 34, 3: 259–68.

(1990b), "Reading Dissidence/Writing the Discipline: Crisis and the Question of Sovereignty in International Studies," *International Studies Quarterly*, 34, 3: 367–416.

Axelrod, Robert (1984), *The Evolution of Cooperation*. New York: Basic Books.

Baer, Judith (1991), "Nasty Law of Nice Ladies? Jurisprudence, Feminism and Gender Difference," *Women and Politics*, 11, 1: 1–32.

Banks, Michael (1985), "Where We Are Now," *Review of International Studies*, 11: 215–33.

Barber, Benjamin (1984), *Strong Democracy: Participatory Politics for a New Age*. Berkeley: University of California Press.

Bartlett, Katharine (1990), "Feminist Legal Methods," *Harvard Law Review*, 103, 4: 829–88.

Bauman, Zygmunt (1992), *Intimations of Post-modernity*. London: Routledge.

Bell, Daniel (1974), *The Coming of Post-Industrial Society*. London: Heinemann.

Belenky, Mary Field, Blythe Clinchy, Nancy Goldberger, and Jill Tarule (1986), *Women's Ways of Knowing: The Development of Self, Voice, and Mind*. New York: Basic Books.

Bender, Jonathan and Thomas Hammond (1992), "Rethinking Allison's Models," *American Political Science Review*, 86, 2: 301–22.

Benhabib, Seyla (1992), *Situating the Self: Gender, Community, and Postmodernism in Contemporary Ethics*. New York: Routledge.

Bennett, Jane (1987), *Unthinking Faith and Enlightenment: Nature and the State in a Post-Hegelian Era*. New York: New York University Press.

Berkman, Joyce (1990), "Feminism, War, and Peace Politics: The Case of World War I," in Jean Bethke Elshtain and Sheila Tobias, eds., *Women, Militarism, and War: Essays in History, Politics, and Social Theory*. Savage, MD: Rowman & Littlefield, Inc.

Biersteker, Thomas (1989), "Critical Reflections on Post-Positivism in International Relations," *International Studies Quarterly*, 33, 3: 263–7.

Black, Naomi (1989), *Social Feminism*. Ithaca: Cornell University Press.

Bordo, Susan (1992), "Postmodern Subjects, Postmodern Bodies," *Feminist Studies*, 18, 1: 159–75.

Boserup, Esther (1970), *Women's Role in Economic Development*. London: Allen & Unwin.

Boswell, Terry and Mike Sweat (1991), "Hegemony, Long Waves, and Major

241

Wars: A Time Series Analysis of Systemic Dynamics, 1496–1967," *International Studies Quarterly*, 35, 2: 123–50.

Boulding, Elise, ed., (1992a), *New Agendas for Peace Research: Conflict and Security Reexamined*. Boulder, CO: Lynne Rienner.

(1992b), "Introduction: What is Possible," in *New Agendas for Peace Research: Conflict and Security Reexamined*. Boulder, CO: Lynne Rienner: 1–6.

Boxer, Marilyn and Jean Quataert (1987), *Connecting Spheres: Women in the Western World, 1500 to the Present*. Oxford: Oxford University Press.

Braidotti, Rosi (1991), *Patterns of Dissonance: A Study of Women in Contemporary Philosophy*. New York: Routledge.

Brink, Elsabe (1990), "Man-Made Women: Gender, Class and the Ideology of the *Volksmoeder*," in Cherryl Walker, ed., *Women and Gender in Southern Africa to 1945*. London: James Currey: 273–92.

Brock, Lothar (1992), "Security Through Defending the Environment: An Illusion?" in Elise Boulding, ed., *New Agendas for Peace Research: Conflict and Security Reexamined*. Boulder, CO: Lynne Rienner: 79–102.

Brock-Utne, Birgit (1985), *Educating For Peace: A Feminist Perspective*. New York: Pergamon Press.

(1989), *Feminist Perspectives on Peace and Peace Education*. New York: Pergamon Press.

Brown, Chris (1992a), "Marxism and International Ethics," in Terry Nardin and David Mapel, eds., *Traditions of International Ethics*. Cambridge: Cambridge University Press: 225–49.

(1992b), *International Relations Theory: New Normative Approaches*. New York: Columbia University Press.

Brown, Sarah (1988), "Feminism, International Theory, and International Relations of Equality," *Millennium*, 17, 3: 461–76.

Brown, Seymour (1974), *New Forces in World Politics*. Washington, D.C.: Brookings.

Brown, Wendy (1991), "Feminist Hesitations, Postmodern Exposures," *Differences*, 3, 1: 63–84.

Buci-Glucksmann, Christine (1980), "The State, Transition, and Passive Revolution," in Chantal Mouffe, ed., *Gramsci and Marxist Theory*. London: Routledge & Kegan Paul: 207–36.

Bueno de Mesquita, Bruce (1981), "Risk, Power Distributions, and the Likelihood of War," *International Studies Quarterly*, 25, 4: 541–68.

Bull, Hedley (1969), "International Theory: The Case for a Classical Approach," in Klaus Knorr and James N. Rosenau, eds., *Contending Approaches to International Politics*. Princeton: Princeton University Press: 20–38.

(1977), *The Anarchical Society: A Study of Order in World Politics*. New York: Columbia University Press.

Bundy, McGeorge (1983), "The Bishops and the Bomb," *New York Review of Books*, June 16: 3–8.

Butler, Judith (1990), *Gender Trouble: Feminism and the Subversion of Identity*. New York: Routledge.

Buzan, Barry, ed., (1987), *The International Politics of Deterrence*. New York: St. Martin's.

Caldicott, Helen (1984), *Missile Envy: The Arms Race and Nuclear War*. New York: William Morrow.

Calinescu, Matei (1987), *Five Faces of Modernity*. Durham, NC: Duke University Press.

Campbell, David (1992), *Writing Security: United States Foreign Policy and the Politics of Identity*. Minneapolis: University of Minnesota Press.

Carr, E. H. (1962), *The Twenty Years' Crisis: An Introduction to the Study of International Relations*. London: Macmillan.

Chaloupka, William (1990), "Immodest Modesty: Antinuclear Discourse, Lifestyle Politics, and Intervention Strategies," *International Studies Quarterly*, 34, 3: 341–52.

Chodorow, Nancy (1978), *The Reproduction of Mothering: Psychoanalysis and the Sociology of Gender*. Berkeley: University of California Press.

Cixous, Hélène (1976), "The Laugh of the Medusa," trans. Keith Cohen and Paula Cohen, *Signs*, 1: 875–93.

Clark, A. et al. (1984), *The Defense Reform Debate*, Baltimore: Johns Hopkins University.

Clark, G. and L. B. Sohn (1966), *World Peace Through World Law: Two Alternative Plans*. Cambridge, MA: Harvard University Press.

Cohn, Carol (1987), "Sex and Death in the Rational World of Defense Intellectuals," *Signs*, 14, 4: 687–718.

Collins, Patricia Hill (1990), "Learning from the Outsider Within: The Sociological Significance of Black Feminist Thought," in Mary Margaret Fonow and Judith A. Cook, eds., *Beyond Methodology: Feminist Scholarship as Lived Research*. Bloomington, IN: Indiana University Press: 35–59.

Connolly, William (1988), *Political Theory and Modernity*. Oxford: Basil Blackwell. (1991), "Democracy and Territoriality," *Millennium*, 20, 3: 463–84.

Cook, Alice and Gwyn Kirk (1983), *Greenham Women Everywhere: Dreams, Ideas and Actions From the Women's Peace Movement*. London: Pluto Press.

Corlett, William (1989), *Community Without Unity: A Politics of Derridian Extravagance*. Durham, NC: Duke University Press.

Culler, Jonathon (1982), *On Deconstruction: Theory and Criticism After Structuralism*. Ithaca, NY: Cornell University Press.

Dallery, Arleen (1989), "The Politics of Writing (the) Body, *Ecriture Féminine*," in Alison Jaggar and Susan Bordo, eds., *Gender/Body/Knowledge: Feminist Reconstructions of Being and Knowing*. New Brunswick, NJ: Rutgers University Press: 52–67.

Daly, Mary (1978), *Gyn/Ecology, The Metaethics of Radical Feminism*. Boston: Beacon Press.

de Beauvoir, Simone (1952), *The Second Sex*, trans. H. M. Parshley. New York: Vintage Books.

De Lauretis, Teresa (1986), "Feminist Studies/Critical Studies: Issues, Terms and Contexts," in Teresa De Lauretis, ed., *Feminist Studies/Critical Studies*. Bloomington: Indiana University Press. (1990), "Eccentric Subjects: Feminist Theory and Historical Consciousness," *Feminist Studies*, 16, 1: 115–50.

Delphy, Christine (1977), *The Main Enemy: A Materialist Analysis of Women's Oppression*, trans. Lucy ap Roberts. London: Women's Research and Resources Centre.

Der Derian, James (1989), "The Boundaries of Knowledge and Power in International Relations," in James Der Derian and Michael Shapiro, eds.,

International/Intertextual Relations: Postmodern Readings of World Politics. Lexington, MA: Lexington Books: 3–10.

(1990), "The (S)pace of International Relations: Simulation, Surveillance, and Speed," *International Studies Quarterly*, 34, 3: 295–310.

Derrida, Jacques, (1973), "Discussion," in *Nietzsche Aujourd'hui.* Paris: Union Générale d'Edition: 288–99.

(1976), *Of Grammatology*, trans. Gayatri C. Spivak. Baltimore: Johns Hopkins University Press.

(1979), *Spurs: Nietzsche's Style.* Chicago: University of Chicago Press.

(1981), *Positions*, trans. Alan Bass. Chicago: University of Chicago Press.

(1987), "Women in the Beehive: A Seminar," in A. Jardine and P. Smith, eds., *Men in Feminism.* New York: Methuen: 189–203.

Desch, Michael (1991), "Security Studies and the Social Sciences: An Agenda for the Future," Report on a workshop held at the University of Southern California, Los Angeles: Center for International Studies, University of Southern California.

Deudney, Daniel and G. John Ikenberry (1990), "Soviet Reform and the End of the Cold War: Explaining Large-Scale Historical Change," unpublished paper.

Di Stefano, Christine (1983), "Masculinity as Ideology in Political Thought: Hobbesian Man Considered," *Women's Studies International Forum*, 6, 6: 633–44.

(1990), "Rethinking Autonomy," paper presented at the 1990 annual meeting of the American Political Science Association, San Francisco.

Donnelly, Jack (1992), "Twentieth-Century Realism," in Terry Nardin and David Mapel, eds., *Traditions of International Ethics.* Cambridge: Cambridge University Press: 85–111.

Dougherty, James and Robert Pfaltzgraff (1990), *Contending Theories of International Relations: A Comprehensive Survey.* New York: Harper & Row.

Dubois, Ellen Carol (1978), *Feminism and Suffrage: The Emergence of an Independent Women's Movement in America 1848–1869.* Ithaca: Cornell University Press.

Dunn, David (1991), "Peace Research versus Strategic Studies," in Ken Booth, ed., *New Thinking About Strategy and International Security.* New York: Harper Collins.

Eakins, B. and G. Eakins (1976), "Verbal Turn-Taking and Exchanges in Faculty Dialogue," in B. Dubois and I. Crouch, eds., *The Sociology of the Language of American Women.* San Antonio, Texas: Trinity University Press.

Ebert, Teresa (1988), "The Romance of Patriarchy: Ideology, Subjectivity, and Postmodern Feminist Cultural Theory," *Cultural Critique* (Fall): 19–57.

Echols, Alice (1991), *Daring to Be Bad: A History of the Radical Feminist Movement in America, 1967–1975.* Minneapolis: University of Minnesota Press.

Eisenstein, Hester (1984), *Contemporary Feminist Thought.* London: Unwin.

Eisenstein, Zillah (1981), *The Radical Future of Liberal Feminism.* New York: Longman.

Elshtain, Jean Bethke (1981), *Public Man, Private Woman: Women in Social and Political Thought.* Princeton: Princeton University Press.

(1987), *Women and War.* New York: Basic Books.

(1988), "The Problem with Peace," *Millennium*, 17, 3: 441–50.

(1990a), "On Patriotism," in *Power Trips and Other Journeys: Essays in Feminism as Civic Discourse*. Madison, WI: University of Wisconsin Press: 163–80.

(1990b), "Realism, Just War, and the Witness to Peace," in *Power Trips and Other Journeys: Essays in Feminism as Civic Discourse*. Madison, WI: University of Wisconsin Press: 149–62.

(1992), "Sovereignty, Identity, Sacrifice," in V. Spike Peterson, ed., *Gendered States: Feminist (Re)Visions of International Relations Theory*. Boulder, CO: Lynne Rienner: 123–40.

Enloe, Cynthia (1989), *Bananas, Beaches, and Bases: Making Feminist Sense of International Relations*. London: Pandora.

Falk, Richard (1988), "Religion and Politics: Verging on the Postmodern," *Alternatives*, 13, 3: 379–94.

Faludi, Susan (1991), *Backlash: The Undeclared War Against American Women*. New York: Crown Publishers.

Fausto-Sterling, Anne (1985), *Myths of Gender*. New York: Basic Books.

Fedigan, Linda Marie (1986), "The Changing Role of Women in Models of Human Evolution," *Annual Review of Anthropology*, 15: 25–66.

(1982), *Primate Paradigms: Sex Roles and Social Bonds*. Montreal: Eden Press.

Ferguson, Kathy (1991), "Interpretation and Genealogy in Feminism," *Signs*, 16, 2: 322–39.

(1993), *The Man Question: Visions of Subjectivity in Feminist Theory*. Berkeley: University of California Press.

Ferguson, Kathy and Kirstie McClure (1991), "Politics/Power/Culture: Postmodernity and Feminist Political Theory (Preliminary)," *Differences*, 3, 1: iii–vi.

Ferguson, Yale and Richard Mansbach (1988), *The Elusive Quest: Theory and International Politics*. Columbia, SC: University of South Carolina Press.

(1991), "Between Celebration and Despair: Constructive Suggestions for Future International Theory," *International Studies Quarterly*, 35, 4: 363–86.

Firestone, Shulamith (1970), *The Dialectic of Sex: The Case for Feminist Revolution*. New York: Bantam Books.

Flax, Jane (1983), "Political Philosophy and the Patriarchal Unconscious: A Psychoanalytic Perspective on Epistemology and Metaphysics," in Sandra Harding and Merrill B. Hintikka, eds., *Discovering Reality: Feminist Perspectives on Epistemology, Metaphysics, and Philosophy of Science*. Dordrecht: D. Reidel: 245–81.

(1987), "Postmodernism and Gender Relations in Feminist Theory," *Signs*, 12, 4: 621–43.

(1990), *Thinking Fragments: Psychoanalysis, Feminism, and Postmodernism*. Berkeley: University of California Press.

Forcey, Linda Rennie, ed., (1989), *Peace: Meanings, Politics, Strategies*. New York: Praeger.

(1991), "Women as Peacemakers: Contested Terrain for Feminist Peace Studies," *Peace and Change*, 16, 4: 331–54.

Forsberg, Randall (1992), "Security Through Military Defense?" in Elise Boulding, ed., *New Agendas for Peace Research: Conflict and Security Reexamined*. Boulder, CO: Lynne Rienner: 67–78.

Foucault, Michel (1972), *The Archaeology of Knowledge*. New York: Pantheon Books.

(1982), "The Subject and Power," in Herbert Dreyfus and Paul Rabinow, *Michel Foucault: Beyond Structuralism and Hermeneutics.* Chicago: University of Chicago Press: 208–26.

Fox-Genovese, Elizabeth (1991), *Feminism Without Illusions: A Critique of Individualism.* Chapel Hill, University of North Carolina Press.

Fraser, Nancy and Linda Nicholson (1990), "Social Criticism without Philosophy: An Encounter between Feminism and Postmodernism," in Linda Nicholson, ed., *Feminism/Postmodernism.* New York: Routledge; 19–38.

French, Marilyn (1985), *Beyond Power: On Men and Women and Morals.* New York: Summit Books.

Friedan, Betty (1963), *The Feminine Mystique.* New York: W. W. Norton.

Friedberg, Aaron, (1992), "Is the United States Capable of Acting Strategically? Congress and the President," in Charles Kegley and Eugene Wittkopf, eds., *The Future of American Foreign Policy.* New York: St. Martin's Press: 95–111.

Fukuyama, Francis (1989), "The End of History," *The National Interest,* 16: 3–18.

Geddes, Patrick and J. Arthur Thomson (1890), *The Evolution of Sex.* New York: Scribner.

George, Alexander, (1974), "Adaptation to Stress in Political Decision Making," in G. Coelho, D. Hamburg, and J. Adams, eds., *Coping and Adaptation.* New York: Basic Books.

(1980), *Presidential Decisionmaking in Foreign Policy: The Effective Use of Information and Advice.* Boulder, CO: Westview Press.

George, Dick (1989), "Research at the Phoenix Zoo, 'Elephants: The Continuing Search for Better Ways to Care for Our Animals,'" *Arizoo,* November/December: 9–13.

George, Jim and David Campbell (1990), "Patterns of Dissent and the Celebration of Difference: Critical Social Theory and International Relations," *International Studies Quarterly,* 34, 3: 269–94.

Giddens, Anthony (1990), *The Consequences of Modernity.* Stanford: Stanford University Press.

(1992), "Uprooted Signposts at Century's End," *The Times Higher Education Supplement* (London), January 17: 21–2.

Gilbert, Bil (1990), "Once a Malcontent, Ruby Has Taken Up Brush and Palette," *Smithsonian Magazine,* December: 40–51.

Gilliam, Angela (1991), "Women's Equality and National Liberation," in Chandra Mohanty, Ann Russo, and Lourdes Torres, eds., *Third World Women and the Politics of Feminism.* Bloomington: Indiana University Press, 215–36.

Gilligan, Carol (1982), *In A Different Voice: Psychological Theory and Women's Development.* Cambridge, MA: Harvard University Press.

Gilpin, Robert (1981), *War and Change in World Politics.* New York: Cambridge University Press.

(1986), "The Richness of the Tradition of Political Realism," in Robert Keohane, ed., *Neorealism and its Critics.* New York: Colombia University Press.

(1987), *The Political Economy of International Relations.* Princeton: Princeton University Press.

Goetz, Ann Marie (1991), "Feminism and the Claim to Know: Contradictions in

Feminist Approaches to Women in Development," in Rebecca Grant and Kathleen Newland, eds., *Gender and International Relations*. Bloomington, IN: Indiana University Press. 133–57.

Golden, Stephanie (1992), *The Women Outside: Meanings and Myths of Homelessness*. Berkeley: University of California Press.

Goldstein, Joshua (1988), *Long Cycles: Prosperity and War in the Modern Age*. New Haven: Yale University Press.

(1991), "Reciprocity in Superpower Relations: An Empirical analysis," *International Studies Quarterly*, 35, 2: 195–210.

Gordon, Ann, Mari Jo Buhle, and Nancy Shrum Dye (1976), in Bernice Carroll, ed., *Liberating Women's History: Theoretical and Critical Essays*. Urbana, IL: University of Illinois Press: 75–92.

Gowa, Joanne (1986), "Anarchy, Egoism and Third Images: The Evolution of Cooperation and International Relations," *International Organization*, 40, 1: 167–86.

Grant, Rebecca (1991), "The Sources of Gender Bias in International Relations Theory," in Rebecca Grant and Kathleen Newland, eds., *Gender and International Relations*. Bloomington, IN: Indiana University Press: 8–26.

(1992), "The Quagmire of Gender and International Security," in V. Spike Peterson, ed., *Gendered States: Feminist (Re)Visions of International Relations Theory*. Boulder, CO: Lynne Rienner: 83–98.

Grant, Rebecca and Kathleen Newland, eds. (1991), *Gender and International Relations*. Bloomington, IN: Indiana University Press.

Greer, Germaine (1970), *The Female Eunuch*. New York: Bantam Books

(1992), *The Change: Women, Aging and the Menopause*. New York: Knopf.

Grieco, Joseph (1990), *Cooperation Among Nations: Europe, America And Non-Tariff Barriers to Trade*. Ithaca: Cornell University Press.

Haas, Ernst (1964), *Beyond the Nation-State*. Stanford: Stanford University Press.

Haas, Michael (1969), "A Plea for Bridge Building in International Relations," in Klaus Knorr and James N. Rosenau, eds., *Contending Approaches to International Relations*. Princeton: Princeton University Press: 158–76.

Haas, Peter (1990), *Saving the Mediterranean*. New York: Columbia University Press.

Habermas, Jürgen (1979), *Communication and the Evolution of Society*, trans. T. McCarthy. Boston: Beacon Press.

(1987), *The Philosophical Discourse of Modernity*, trans. Frederick Lawrence. Cambridge, MA: MIT Press.

Haftendorn, Helga (1991), "The Security Puzzle: Theory Building and Discipline Building in International Security," *International Studies Quarterly*, 35, 1: 3–17.

Halliday, Fred (1985), "A Crisis of International Relations?" *International Relations*, 8, 4: 407–12.

(1988), "Hidden From International Relations: Women and the International Arena," *Millennium*, 17, 3: 419–28.

Haraway, Donna (1978), "Animal Sociology and a Natural Economy of the Body Politics, Part I, A Political Physiology of Dominance," *Signs*, 4: 21–36.

(1985), "A Manifesto for Cyborgs: Science, Technology, and Socialist Feminism in the 1980s," *Socialist Review*, 15, 2: 65–108.

247

(1988), "Situated Knowledges: The Science Question in Feminism and the Privilege of Partial Perspective," *Feminist Studies*, 14, 3: 575–99.

(1989), *Primate Visions: Gender, Race and Nature in the World of Modern Science*. New York: Routledge.

(1991), "The Biopolitics of Postmodern Bodies: Constitutions of Self in Immune System Discourse," in *Simians, Cyborgs, and Women: The Reinvention of Nature*. New York: Routledge: 203–30.

(1992), "Otherworldly Conversations; Terran Topics; Local Terms," *Science as Culture*, 3 (part 1), 14: 64–98.

Harding, Sandra (1986a), *The Science Question in Feminism*. Ithaca: Cornell University Press.

(1986b), "The Instability of the Analytical Categories of Feminist Theory," *Signs*, 11, 4: 645–64.

(1987), "Introduction: Is There a Feminist Method?" in Sandra Harding, ed., *Feminism and Methodology: Social Science Issues*. Milton Keynes: Open University Press: 1–14.

(1989), "How the Women's Movement Benefits Science: Two Views." *Women's Studies International Forum*, 12, 3: 271–283.

(1991), *Whose Science? Whose Knowledge? Thinking From Women's Lives*. Ithaca: Cornell University Press.

Harford, Barbara and Sarah Hopkins eds. (1984), *Greenham Common: Women at the Wire*. London: Women's Press.

Hargrove, Erwin (1966), *Presidential Leadership: Personality and Political Style*. New York: Macmillan.

Harrington, Mona (1992), "What Exactly is Wrong with the Liberal State as an Agent of Change?" in V. Spike Peterson, ed., *Gendered States: Feminist (Re)Visions of International Relations Theory*. Boulder, CO: Lynne Rienner; 65–82.

Harris, Adrienne (1989), "Bringing Artemis to Life: A Plea for Militance and Aggression in Feminist Peace Politics," in Adrienne Harris and Ynestra King, eds., *Rocking the Ship of State: Toward a Feminist Peace Politics*. Boulder, CO: Westview Press: 93–114.

Harris, Adrienne and Ynestra King, eds. (1989), *Rocking the Ship of State: Toward a Feminist Peace Politics*. Boulder, CO: Westview Press.

Harrison, Faye (1991), "Women in Jamaica's Urban Informal Economy: Insights from a Kingston Slum," in Chandra Mohanty, Ann Russo, and Lourdes Torres, eds., *Third World Women and the Politics of Feminism*. Bloomington, IN: Indiana University Press: 173–96.

Hartsock, Nancy (1982), "The Barracks Community in Western Political Thought: Prolegomena to a Feminist Critique of War and Politics," *Women's Studies International Forum*, 5, 3/4.

(1983), "The Feminist Standpoint: Developing the Ground for Specifically Feminist Historical Materialism," in Sandra Harding and Merrill Hintikka, eds., *Discovering Reality: Feminist Perspectives on Epistemology, Metaphysics, Methodology and Philosophy of Science*. Dordrecht: D. Reidel: 283–310.

(1985), *Money, Sex, and Power: Toward A Feminist Historical Materialism*. Boston: Northeastern University Press.

Harvey, David (1989), *The Condition of Postmodernity: An Enquiry into the Origins of Cultural Change*. Oxford: Basil Blackwell.

Hawkesworth, Mary (1989), "Knowers, Knowing, Known: Feminist Theory and Claims of Truth," *Signs*, 14, 3: 533–57.

Herz, John (1951), *Political Realism and Political Idealism: A Study in Theories and Realities*. Chicago: University of Chicago Press.

Hirschmann, Nancy (1989), "Freedom, Recognition, and Obligation: A Feminist Approach to Political Theory," *American Political Science Review*, 83, 4: 1227–44.

(1991), "Feminism and Liberal Theory," *American Political Science Review*, 85, 1: 225–33.

(1992) *Rethinking Obligation: A Feminist Method for Political Theory*. Ithaca: Cornell University Press.

Hoffman, Mark (1987), "Critical Theory and the Inter-Paradigm Debate," *Millennium*, 16, 2: 231–49.

Holsti, K. J. (1985), *The Dividing Discipline: Hegemony and Diversity in International Theory*. Boston: Unwin Hyman.

Holsti, O. (1969), "The Belief System and National Images: A Case Study," in James Rosenau, ed., *International Politics and Foreign Policy: A Reader in Research and Theory*. New York: Free Press: 543–50.

Holsti, Ole and James Rosenau (1981), "The Foreign Policy Beliefs of Women in Leadership Positions," *Journal of Politics*, 43 (May): 326–47.

hooks, bell (1984), *Feminist Theory from Margin to Center*. Boston: South End Press.

(1990), *Yearning: Race, Gender, and Cultural Politics*. Boston: South End Press.

Horkheimer, Max (1974), *Critique of Instrumental Reason*. New York: Seabury.

Hughes, Diane Owen (1982), "Invisible Madonnas? The Italian Historiographical Tradition and the Women of Medieval Italy," quoted in Joan Kelly, "Early Feminist Theory and the Querelle de Femmes 1400–1789," *Signs*, 8, 1: 4–28.

Hurtado, Aida (1989), "Relating to Privilege: Seduction and Rejection in the Subordination of White Women and Women of Color," *Signs*, 14, 4: 833–55.

Hurwitz, Roger (1989), "Strategic and Social Fictions in the Prisoner's Dilemma," in James Der Derian and Michael Shapiro, eds., *International/Intertextual Relations*. Lexington, MA: Lexington Books: 113–34.

Irigaray, Luce (1977), "Women's Exile," *Ideology and Consciousness*. 1: 62–76.

(1985a), *Speculum of the Other Woman*, trans. Gillian C. Gill. Ithaca: Cornell University Press.

(1985b), *This Sex Which is Not One*, trans. Catherine Porter. Ithaca: Cornell University Press.

Jaggar, Alison (1983), *Feminist Politics and Human Nature*. Totowa, NJ: Rowman & Allenheld.

Jencks, Charles (1989), *What is Postmodernism?* London: St. Martin's Press.

Jervis, Robert (1969), "The Costs of the Quantitative Study of International Relations," in Klaus Knorr and James N. Rosenau, eds., *Contending Approaches to International Relations*. Princeton: Princeton University Press: 177–217.

(1978), "Cooperation Under the Security Dilemma," *World Politics*, 30, January: 167–214.

(1984), *The Illogic of American Nuclear Strategy*. Ithaca: Cornell University Press.

(1988), "Realism, Game Theory, and Cooperation," *World Politics*, 40, 3: 317–49.

Johansen, Robert (1987), "Global Security Without Nuclear Deterrence," *Alternatives*, 12, 4: 435–60.

Johnson, James (1993), "Is Talk Really Cheap? Prompting Conversation Between Critical Theory and Rational Choice," *American Political Science Review*, 87, 1: 74–86.

Johnson, Sonia (1981), *From Housewife to Heretic*. New York: Doubleday.

Jones, Ann Rosalind (1981), "Writing the Body: Toward an Understanding of *l'écriture féminine*," *Feminist Studies*, 7, 2: 247–63.

Jones, Kathleen (1990), "Citizenship in a Woman-Friendly Polity," *Signs*, 15, 4: 781–812.

(1991), "The Trouble With Authority," *Differences*, 3, 1: 104–27.

Jones, Kathleen and Anna G. Jonasdottir, eds. (1988), *The Political Interests of Gender: Developing Theory and Research With a Feminist Face*. New York: Sage Publications.

Jones-Eddy, Julie (1992), *Homesteading Women: An Oral History of Colorado, 1890–1950*. New York: Twayne Publishers.

Kaldor, Mary (1981), *The Baroque Arsenal*. New York: Hill & Wang.

Kaplan, Fred (1983), *The Wizards of Armageddon*. New York: Simon & Schuster.

Kaplan, Morton (1969), "The New Great Debate: Traditionalism vs. Science in International Relations," in Klaus Knorr and James N. Rosenau, eds., *Contending Approaches to International Relations*. Princeton: Princeton University Press: 39–61.

Keller, Evelyn Fox (1985), *Reflections on Gender and Science*. New Haven: Yale University Press.

Kelly, Joan (1982), "Early Feminist Theory and the Querelle des Femmes, 1400–1789," *Signs*, 8, 1: 4–28.

(1984), "Did Women Have a Renaissance?" in Catherine Stimpson, ed., *Women, History and Theory: The Essays of Joan Kelly*. Chicago: University of Chicago Press: 19–50.

Keohane, Robert (1984), *After Hegemony: Cooperation and Discord in the World Political Economy*. Princeton: Princeton University Press.

(1986), "Realism, Neorealism and the Study of World Politics," in Robert Keohane, ed., *Neorealism and its Critics*. New York: Columbia University Press: 1–26.

(1989a), *International Institutions and State Power: Essays in International Relations Theory*. Boulder, CO: Westview Press.

(1989b), "International Relations Theory: Contributions of a Feminist Standpoint," *Millennium*, 18, 2: 245–54.

King, D. K. (1988), "Multiple Jeopardy, Multiple Consciousness: The Context of a Black Feminist Ideology," *Signs*, 14, 1: 42–72.

Kirk, Gwyn (1989a), "Our Greenham Common: Feminism and Nonviolence," in Adrienne Harris and Ynestra King, eds., *Rocking the Ship of State: Toward a Feminist Peace Politics*. Boulder, CO: Westview Press: 115–30.

(1989b), "Our Greenham Common: Not Just a Place But a Movement," in Adrienne Harris and Ynestra King, eds., *Rocking the Ship of State: Toward a Feminist Peace Politics*. Boulder, CO: Westview Press: 263–80.

Kirk, Ilse (1988), "Images of Amazons: Marriage and Matriarchy," in Sharon MacDonald, Pat Holden, and Shirley Ardener, eds., *Images of Women in Peace and War: Cross-Cultural and Historical Perspectives.* Madison, WI: University of Wisconsin Press: 27–39.

Kirshenbaum, Gayle (1992), "Inside the World's Largest Men's Club," *Ms.*, 3, 2: 16–19.

Klein, Bradley (1988a), "After Strategy: The Search for a Post-Modern Politics of Peace," *Alternatives*, 13, 3: 293–318.

(1988b), "Hegemony and Strategic Culture: American Power Projection and Alliance Defence Politics," *Review of International Studies*, 14, 2: 133–48.

(1989), "The Textual Strategies of the Military: Or Have You Read Any Good Defense Manuals Lately?" in James Der Derian and Michael Shapiro, eds., *International/Intertextual Relations.* Lexington, MA: Lexington Books: 97–112.

(1990), "How the West was One: Representational Politics of NATO," *International Studies Quarterly*, 34, 3: 311–26.

Knorr, Klaus and James N. Rosenau (1969), "Tradition and Science in the Study of International Politics," in Klaus Knorr and James N. Rosenau, eds., *Contending Approaches to International Politics.* Princeton: Princeton University Press: 3–19.

Kohlberg, Lawrence (1981), *The Philosophy of Moral Development.* New York: Harper & Row.

(1984), *The Psychology of Moral Development.* New York: Harper & Row.

Kolodziej, Edward (1992), "Renaissance in Security Studies? Caveat Lector!" *International Studies Quarterly*, 36, 4: 421–38.

Krasner, Stephen (1985), *Structural Conflict: The Third World Against Global Liberalism.* Berkeley: University of California Press.

Kratochwil, Friedrich and John Ruggie, (1986), "International Organization: A State of the Art or an Art of the State," *International Organization*, 40, 4: 753–75.

Laird, R. F. and D. R. Herspring (1984), *The Soviet Union and Strategic Arms.* Boulder, CO: Westview Press.

Lapid, Yosef (1989), "The Third Debate: On the Prospects of International Theory in a Post-Positivist Era," *International Studies Quarterly*, 33, 3: 235–54.

Lebow, Ned (1981), *Between Peace and War: The Nature of International Crisis.* Baltimore: Johns Hopkins University Press.

le Doeuff, Michele (1991), *Hipparchia's Choice: An Essay Concerning Women, Philosophy Etc.* London: Basil Blackwell.

Levy, Marion J. (1969), "'Does It Matter If He's Naked?' Bawled the Child," in Klaus Knorr and James N. Rosenau, eds., *Contending Approaches to International Relations.* Princeton: Princeton University Press: 87–109.

Liddington, Jill (1989), *The Road to Greenham Common: Feminism and Anti-Militarism in Britain Since 1820.* Syracuse, NY: Syracuse University Press.

Liddington, Jill and Jill Norris (1978), *One Hand Tied Behind Us: The Rise of the Women's Suffrage Movement.* London: Virago.

Lindberg, Leon (1963), *The Political Dynamics of European Economic Integration.* Stanford: Stanford University Press.

Linklater, Andrew (1992), "The Question of the Next Stage in International Relations Theory: A Critical–Theoretical Point of View,"*Millennium*, 21, 1: 77–100.

Lisle, Laurie (1986), *Portrait of an Artist: A Biography of Georgia O'Keeffe*. New York: Washington Square Press.

Little, Richard and Steve Smith, eds. (1988), *Belief Systems and International Relations*. Oxford: Basil Blackwell.

Longino, Helen (1989), "Feminist Critiques of Rationality: Critiques of Science or Philosophy of Science?" *Women's Studies International Forum*, 12, 3: 261–9.

Lovejoy, Owen (1981), "The Origin of Man," *Science*, 211, 4480: 341–50.

(1984), "The Natural Detective," *Natural History*, 93, 10: 24–8.

Lugones, Maria (1990), "Playfulness, 'World'-Travelling, and Loving Perception," in Gloria Anzaldua, ed., *Making Face, Making Soul – Haciendo Caras: Creative and Critical Perspectives by Women of Color*. San Francisco: Aunt Lute: 390–402.

Luke, Timothy (1989), "'What's Wrong with Deterrence?' A Semiotic Interpretation of National Security Policy," in James Der Derian and Michael Shapiro, eds., *International/Intertextual Relations*. Lexington, MA: Lexington Books: 207–29.

Luxemburg, Rosa (1971), *Selected Political Writings*, edited by D. Howard. New York: Monthly Review Press.

Lynn-Jones, Sean (1992), "International Security Studies," *International Studies Notes*, 17, 1: 53–63.

Lyotard, Jean-Francois (1984), *The Post-Modern Condition: A Report on Knowledge*, trans. Geoff Bennington and Brian Massumi. Minneapolis: University of Minnesota Press.

McClelland, Charles and Gary Hoggard (1969), "Conflict Patterns in Interactions Among Nations," in James N. Rosenau, ed., *International Politics and Foreign Policy*, New York: Free Press: 711–24.

McClintock, Anne (1990), "Maidens, Maps and Mines: *King Solomon's Mines* and the Reinvention of Patriarchy in Colonial South Africa," in Cherryl Walker, ed., *Women and Gender in Southern Africa to 1945*. London: James Currey: 97–124.

MacDonald, Sharon, Pat Holden, and Shirley Ardener, eds. (1988), *Images of Women in Peace and War*. Madison, WI: University of Wisconsin Press.

McKeown, Timothy (1991), "A Liberal Trade Order? The Long-Run Pattern of Imports to the Advanced Capitalist States," *International Studies Quarterly*, 35, 2: 151–72.

MacKinnon, Catherine (1982), "Feminism, Marxism, Method, and the State: An Agenda for Theory," in Nannerl Keohane, Michelle Rosaldo, and Barbara Gelpi, eds., *Feminist Theory: A Critique of Ideology*. Chicago: University of Chicago Press: 1–30.

(1989), *Toward a Feminist Theory of the State*. Cambridge, MA: Harvard University Press.

Maghoori, Ray (1982), "Introduction: Major Debates in International Relations," in Ray Maghoori and Bennett Ramberg, eds., *Globalism Versus Realism: International Relations' Third Debate*. Boulder, CO: Westview Press.

Mahmoud, Fatima Babika (1986), "Women and Liberation, Fatima Babikar Mahmoud talks to Patricia McFadden," *Journal of African Marxists*, 8, January: 7–25.

Mandelbaum, Michael (1981), *The Nuclear Revolution: International Politics Before and after Hiroshima*. Cambridge: Cambridge University Press.

Martin, Biddy and Chandra Mohanty (1986), "Feminist Politics: What's Home Got to Do With It?" in Teresa de Lauretis, ed., *Feminist Studies/Critical Studies*. Bloomington, IN: Indiana University Press: 191–212.

Maugue, A. (1987), *L'Identité Masculine en Crise en Tournant du Siècle*. Paris: Rivages.

Mendlovitz, Saul and R. B. J. Walker, eds. (1987), *Towards A Just World Peace: Perspectives from Social Movements*. London: Butterworths.

Merchant, Carolyn (1980), *The Death of Nature: Women, Ecology, and the Scientific Revolution*. New York: Harper & Row.

Merton, Robert (1949), *Social Theory and Social Structure: Toward the Codification of Theory and Research*. Glencoe, IL: Free Press.

Meyer, Stephen (1990), "Revolutionary Changes in East–West Relations Should Revitalize the Field of Security Studies," *Chronicle of Higher Education*, February 7.

Mies, Maria (1986), *Patriarchy and Accumulation on a World Scale: Women in the International Division of Labour*. London: Zed Books.

(1988), "Introduction," in Maria Mies, Veronika Bennholdt-Thomsen, and Claudia von Werlhof, eds., *Women: The Last Colony*. London: Zed Books: 1–10.

Miller, Carol (1991), "Women in International Relations? The Debate in Interwar Britain," in Rebecca Grant and Kathleen Newland, eds., *Gender and International Relations*. Bloomington, IN: Indiana University Press: 64–82.

Millman, Maria and Rosabeth Moss Kanter, eds. (1975), *Another Voice: Feminist Perspectives on Social Life and Social Science*. New York: Anchor Books.

Milner, Helen (1992), "International Theories of Cooperation Among Nations: Strengths and Weaknesses," *World Politics*, 44, 3: 466–96.

Mitchell, W. J. T. (1992), "Postcolonial Culture, Postimperial Criticism," *Transition*, Issue 56: 11–19.

Modelski, George (1987), *Long Cycles in World Politics*. Seattle: University of Washington Press.

Mohanty, Chandra (1991), "Cartographies of Struggle: Third World Women and the Politics of Feminism," in Chandra Mohanty, Ann Russo, and Lourdes Torres eds., *Third World Women and the Politics of Feminism*. Bloomington, IN: Indiana University Press: 1–47.

Mohanty, Chandra, Ann Russo, and Lourdes Torres, eds. (1991), *Third World Women and the Politics of Feminism*. Bloomington, IN: Indiana University Press.

Moi, Toril (1985), *Sexual/Textual Politics*. New York: Routledge.

Molyneux, Maxine (1989), "Some International Influences on Policy-Making: Marxism, Feminism and the 'Woman Question' in Existing Socialism," *Millennium*, 18, 2: 255–64.

Morgan, Robin (1989), *The Demon Lover: On the Sexuality of Terrorism*. London: Methuen.

253

Morgenthau, Hans J. (1946), *Scientific Man Versus Power Politics*. Chicago: University of Chicago Press.

(1965), *Politics Among Nations: The Struggle for Power and Peace*, third edition. New York: Alfred Knopf.

Moschkovich, Judith (1981), "... But I Know You, American Woman," in Cherrie Moraga and Gloria Anzaldua, eds., *This Bridge Called My Back: Writings by Radical Women of Color*. Watertown, MA: Persephone Press: 78–84.

Moses, Claire Goldberg (1984), *French Feminism in the Nineteenth Century*. Albany: State University of New York Press.

Narayan, Uma (1989), "The Project of Feminist Epistemology: Perspectives from a Nonwestern Feminist," in Alison Jagger and Susan Bordo, eds., *Gender/Body/Knowledge: Feminist Reconstructions of Being and Knowing*. New Brunswick, NJ: Rutgers University Press: 256–72.

Nicholson, Harold (1942) quoted in *The Spectator* (London) January 23.

(1966), *Diaries and Letters, 1930–1939*, edited by Nigel Nicholson, London: Collins.

Nicholson, Linda, ed. (1990), *Feminism/Postmodernism*. London: Routledge.

Nicholson, Michael (1985), "The Methodology of International Relations," in Steve Smith, ed., *International Relations: British and American Perspectives*. London: Basil Blackwell: 56–70.

Nielson, Joyce, ed., (1991), "Introduction," in *Feminist Research Methods: Exemplary Readings in the Social Sciences*. Boulder, CO: Westview Press: 1–37.

Nietzsche, Friedrich (1974), *The Gay Science*, trans. Walter Kaufmann. New York: Vintage Books.

Nye, Joseph (1971), *Peace in Parts: Integration and Conflict in Regional Organization*. Boston: Little, Brown.

Nye, Joseph and Sean Lynn-Jones (1988), "International Security Studies: A Report of a Conference on the State of the Field," *International Security*, 12, 4: 5–27.

O'Brien, Mary (1981), *The Politics of Reproduction*. Boston: Routledge.

Offen, Karen (1988), "Defining Feminism Versus Post-Structuralism: A Comparative Historical Approach," *Signs*, 14, 1: 119–57.

Oldfield, Sybil (1989), *Women Against the Iron Fist: Alternatives to Militarism, 1900–1989*. Oxford: Basil Blackwell.

Olson, William and Nicholas Onuf (1985), "The Growth of a Discipline: Revised," in Steve Smith, ed., *International Relations: British and American Perspectives*. Oxford: Basil Blackwell: 1–28.

Organski, A. F. and Jacek Kugler (1980), *The War Ledger*. Chicago: University of Chicago Press.

Ornstein, Norman and Mark Schmitt (1992), "Post-Cold War 'Politics,'" in Charles Kegley and Eugene Wittkopf, eds., *The Future of American Foreign Policy*. New York: St. Martin's Press: 112–23.

Oye, Kenneth, ed. (1986), *Cooperation Under Anarchy*. Princeton: Princeton University Press.

Parpart, Jane (1986), "Class and Gender on the Copperbelt: Women in Northern Rhodesian Copper Mining Communities, 1926–1964," in Claire Robertson and Iris Berger, eds., *Women and Class in Africa*. New York: Africana: 141–60.

(1991), "Postmodernism: Can it Contribute to Gender and Development Theory and Practice?" paper presented at the annual meeting of the International Studies Association, Vancouver.

Pateman, Carole (1988), *The Sexual Contract*. Stanford: Stanford University Press.

Peterson, V. Spike (1989), "Clarification and Contestation: A Conference Report on 'Women, the State, and War': What Difference Does Gender Make?" Los Angeles: Center for International Studies, University of Southern California.

(1990), "Whose Rights? A Critique of the 'Givens' in Human Rights Discourse," *Alternatives*, 15, 3: 303–44.

ed., (1992a), *Gendered States: Feminist (Re)Visions of International Relations Theory*. Boulder, CO: Lynne Rienner.

(1992b), "Security and Sovereign States: What is at Stake in Taking Feminism Seriously?" in *Gendered States: Feminist (Re)Visions of International Relations Theory*. Boulder, CO: Lynne Rienner: 31–64.

Piaget, Jean (1965), *The Moral Judgement of the Child*. New York: Free Press.

Pierson, Ruth Roach (1988), "'Did Your Mother Wear Army Boots?': Feminist Theory and Women's Relation to War, Peace and Revolution," in Sharon MacDonald, Pat Holden, and Shirley Ardener, eds., *Images of Women in Peace and War: Cross-Cultural and Historical Perspectives*. Madison, WI: University of Wisconsin Press: 205–27.

Pirages, Dennis (1978), *Global Ecopolitics*. North Scituate, MA: Duxbury Press.

Pitkin, Hannah (1984), *Fortune is a Woman: Gender and Politics in the Thought of Niccolo Machiavelli*. Berkeley: University of California Press.

Plaza, Monique (1980), "'Phallomorphic Power' and the Psychology of 'Woman,'" *Feminist Issues*, 1, 1: 71–102.

Powell, Robert (1993), "Guns, Butter, and Anarchy," *American Political Science Review*, 87, 1: 115–32.

Power, Eileen (1975), *Medieval Women*. Cambridge: Cambridge University Press.

Presley, Cora Ann (1986), "Labor Unrest Among Kikuyu Women in Colonial Kenya," in Claire Robertson and Iris Berger, eds., *Women and Class in Africa*. New York: Africana: 255–73.

Putnam, R. D. (1988), "Diplomacy and Domestic Politics: The Logic of Two-Level Games," *International Organization*, 42 (Summer): 427–60.

Ranger, Terence (1979), *Revolt in Southern Rhodesia 1896–7*. London: Heinemann.

Reardon, Betty (1985), *Sex and the War System*. New York: Teacher's College, Columbia University.

Reilly, John (1992), "Public Opinion: The Pulse of the '90s," in Charles Kegley and Eugene Wittkopf, eds., *The Future of American Foreign Policy*. New York: St. Martin's Press: 124–32.

Rich, Adrienne (1979), "Toward a Woman-Centered University (1973–74)," in *On Lies, Secrets, and Silence: Selected Prose 1966–1978*. New York: W. W. Norton: 125–56.

Riley, Denise (1988), *"Am I That Name?" Feminism and the Category of "Women" in History*. Minneapolis: University of Minnesota.

Rorty, Amelie (1988), *Mind in Action: Essays in the Philosophy of Mind*. Boston: Beacon Press.

Rosenau, James, ed. (1986), "Before Cooperation: Hegemons, Regimes, and Habit-Driven Actors in World Politics," *International Organization*, 40, 4: 849–94.

(1990), *Turbulence in World Politics: A Theory of Change and Continuity*. Princeton: Princeton University Press.

ed., (1993a), *Global Voices: Dialogues in International Relations*. Boulder, CO: Westview Press.

(1993b), "The Superpower Scholar: Sensitive, Submissive, or Self-Deceptive?" in James Rosenau, ed., *Global Voices: Dialogues in International Relations*. Boulder, CO: Westview Press: 1–25.

Rosenau, Pauline (1992), *Postmodernism and the Social Sciences: Insights, Inroads, and Intrusions*. Princeton: Princeton University Press.

Rosow, Stephen (1990), "Forms of Internationalization: Representations of Western Culture on a Global Scale," *Alternatives*, 15, 3: 287–302.

Rossiter, Margaret (1982), *Women Scientists in America: Struggles and Strategies to 1940*. Baltimore: Johns Hopkins University Press.

Rothwell, Charles Easton (1973), "International Organization and World Politics," in Leland M. Goodrich and David A. Kay, eds., *International Organization: Politics and Process*. Madison, WI: University of Wisconsin Press: 23–38.

Ruddick, Sara (1983), "Pacifying the Forces: Drafting Women in the Interests of Peace," *Signs*, 8, 3: 471–89.

(1989a), *Maternal Thinking: Toward a Politics of Peace*. Boston: Beacon Press.

(1989b), "Mothers and Men's Wars," in Adrienne Harris and Ynestra King, eds., *Rocking the Ship of State: Toward a Feminist Peace Politics*. Boulder, CO: Westview Press: 75–92.

Rummel, Rudolph (1969), "Some Dimensions in the Foreign Behavior of States," in James N. Rosenau ed., *International Politics and Foreign Policy*. New York: Free Press: 600–21.

Runyan, Anne Sisson (1992), "The 'State' of Nature: A Garden Unfit for Women and Other Living Things," in V. Spike Peterson, ed., *Gendered States: Feminist (Re)Visions of International Relations Theory*. Boulder, CO: Lynne Rienner: 123–40.

Runyan, Anne Sisson and V. Spike Peterson (1991), "The Radical Future of Realism: Feminist Subversions of IR Theory," *Alternatives*, 16: 67–106.

Rupesinghe, Kumar (1992), "The Disappearing Boundaries Between Internal and External Conflicts," in Elise Boulding, ed., *New Agendas for Peace Research: Conflict and Security Reexamined*. Boulder, CO: Lynne Rienner; 43–64.

Sanjian, Gregory (1991), "Great Power Arms Transfers: Modeling the Decision-Making Processes of Hegemonic, Industrial, and Restrictive Exporters," *International Studies Quarterly*, 35, 2: 173–94.

Schelling, Thomas (1966), *Arms and Influence*. New Haven: Yale University Press.

Schumpeter, Joseph (1942), *Capitalism, Socialism and Democracy*. New York: Harper & Row.

Schwartz-Shea, Peregrine and Debra Burrington (1990), "Free Riding, Alternative Organization, and Cultural Feminism: The Case of Seneca Women's Peace Camp," *Women and Politics*, 10: 1–37.

Scott, Joan (1989), "Gender: A Useful Category of Historical Analysis," in Elizabeth Weed, ed., *Coming to Terms: Feminism, Theory, and Politics.* New York: Routledge: 81–100.

Shapiro, Michael (1990), "Strategic Discourse/Discursive Strategy: The Representation of 'Security Policy' in the Video Age," *International Studies Quarterly*, 34, 3: 327–40.

Shotwell, James (1929), *War as an Instrument of Policy: And Its Renunciation in the Pact of Paris.* New York: Harcourt, Brace & Co.

Singer, J. David, (1961), "The Level-of-Analysis Problem in International Relations," in Klaus Knorr and Sidney Verba, eds., *The International System: Theoretical Essays.* Princeton: Princeton University Press: 77–92.

(1969), "The Incompleat Theorist: Insight Without Evidence," in Klaus Knorr and James N. Rosenau, eds., *Contending Approaches to International Relations.* Princeton: Princeton University Press: 62–86.

(1979), *Correlates of War I: Research Origins and Rationale.* New York: Free Press.

Smart, Barry (1992), *Modern Conditions, Postmodern Controversies.* London: Routledge.

Smith, B. (1966), *The Rand Corporation: Case Study of a Non-Profit Advisory Corporation.* Cambridge, MA: Harvard University Press.

Smith, Barbara (1991), "The Truth that Never Hurts: Black Lesbians in Literature in the 1980s," in Chandra Mohanty, Ann Russo, and Lourdes Torres, eds., *Third World Women and the Politics of Feminism.* Bloomington, IN: Indiana University Press: 101–32.

Smith, Dorothy (1990), *The Conceptual Practices of Power: A Feminist Sociology of Knowledge.* Boston: Northeastern University Press.

Smith, J., J. Collins, T. Hopkins, and H. Muhammed (1988), *Racism, Sexism, and the World-System.* New York: Greenwood.

Smith, Michael Joseph (1986), *Realist Thought from Weber to Kissinger.* Baton Rouge: Louisiana State University Press.

Smith, Steve (1993), "Hegemonic Power, Hegemonic Discipline? The Superpower Status of the American Study of International Relations," in James Rosenau, ed., *Global Voices: Dialogues in International Relations.* Boulder, CO: Westview Press: 55–82.

Snitow, Ann (1988), "Holding The Line At Greenham Common: Being Joyously Political in Dangerous Times [Feb. 1985]," in Daniela Gioseffi, ed., *Women on War: Essential Voices for the Nuclear Age.* New York: Touchstone Books: 344–57.

Snow, D. (1989), "Stability and Soviet–American Relations: The Influence of Nuclear Weapons," in *Soviet–American Security Relations in the 1990s.* Lexington, MA: Lexington Books: 3–20.

Spegele, Roger (1992), "Richard Ashley's Discourse for International Relations," *Millennium*, 21, 2: 147–182.

Spivak, Gayatri, C. (1988), "Can the Subaltern Speak?" Cary Nelson and Lawrence Grossberg, eds., *Marxism and the Interpretation of Culture.* Urbana: University of Illinois Press: 271–313.

Starhawk (1990), *Truth or Dare: Encounters with Power, Authority, and Mystery.* San Francisco: Harper.

REFERENCES

Staudt, Kathleen (1987), "Women's Politics, the State, and Capitalist Trans-formation in Africa," in Irving Leonard Markovitz, ed., *Studies in Power and Class in Africa*. Oxford: Oxford University Press: 193–208.

Steady, Filomina Chioma (1987), "African Feminism: A Worldwide Perspective," in Rosalyn Terborg-Penn, Sharon Harley, and Andrea Rushing, eds., *Women in Africa and the African Diaspora*. Washington, D.C.: Howard University Press.

Stiehm, Judith (1989), *Arms and the Enlisted Woman*. Philadelphia: Temple University Press.

Stein, Arthur (1990), *Why Nations Cooperate: Circumstance and Choice in International Relations*. Ithaca: Cornell University Press.

Steinson, Barbara (1982), *American Women's Activism in World War I*. New York: Garland Publishing Inc.

Strange, Susan (1982), "*Cave! hic dragones*: a Critique of Regime Analysis," *International Organization*, 36, 2: 479–96.

Suganami, Hidemi (1989), *The Domestic Analogy and World Order Proposals*. Cambridge: Cambridge University Press.

(1990),"Bringing Order to the Causes of War Debates," *Millennium*,19,1: 19–36.

SWAPO Women's Solidarity Campaign (1986), "Class, Gender, and Race: Women in Namibia," *Journal of African Marxists*, 8, January: 43–73

Sweeney, James (1934), *Plastic Redirections in Twentieth-Century Painting*. Chicago: University of Chicago Press.

Sylvester, Christine (1987), "Some Dangers in Merging Feminist and Peace Projects," *Alternatives*, 12, 4: 493–509.

(1989), "Patriarchy, Peace, and Women Warriors," in Linda Rennie Forcey, ed., *Peace: Meanings, Politics, Strategies*. New York: Praeger: 97–112.

(1990a), "The Emperors' Theories and Transformations: Looking at the Field Through Feminist Lenses," in Dennis Pirages and Christine Sylvester, eds., *Transformations in the Global Political Economy*. London: Macmillan: 230–54.

(1990b), "Simultaneous Revolutions: The Zimbabwean Case," *Journal of Southern African Studies*, 16, 3: 452–75.

(1990c), "Interpreting the Discursive Practices of Zimbabwean Women Workers: Musings of Fieldwork and Feminism," paper presented at the annual meeting of the African Studies Association, Baltimore.

(1990d), "Unities and Disunities in Zimbabwe's 1990 Election," *Journal of Modern African Studies*, 28, 3: 375–400.

(1991a), *Zimbabwe: The Political Economy of Contradictory Development*. Boulder, CO: Westview Press.

(1991b), "'Urban Women Cooperators,' 'Progress,' and 'African Feminism' in Zimbabwe," *Differences*, 3, 1: 39–62.

(1992a), "Realists and Feminists Look at Autonomy and Obligation in International Relations," in V. Spike Peterson, ed., *Gendered States: Feminist (Re)Visions of International Relations Theory*. Boulder, CO: Lynne Rienner: 155–78.

(1992b), "Feminist Theory and Gender Studies in International Relations," for Special Issue of *International Studies Notes* on "The State of the Discipline," Winter: 32–8.

258

(1993a), "Homeless in International Relations? Women's Place in Canonical Texts and in Feminist Reimaginings," in Adam Lerner and Marjorie Martin, eds., *Reimagining the Nation*. London: Open University Press.

(1993b), "Reconstituting a Feminist-Eclipsing Dialogue," in James Rosenau, ed., *Global Voices: Dialogues in International Relations*. Boulder, CO: West-view Press: 27–53.

(1993c), ed. "Feminists Write International Relations," Special issue of *Alternatives*, 18, 1.

(1993d), "Riding the Hyphens of Feminism, Peace, and Place in Four- (Or more) Part Cacophony," *Alternatives*, 18, 1: 109–118.

(1994), "Simultaneous Revolutions and Exits: A Semi-Skeptical Comment on Zimbabwe," in Mary Ann Tetreault, ed., *Women and Revolution in Africa, Asia, and the New World*. Columbia, SC: University of South Carolina Press.

Taylor, A. J. P. (1965), *English History, 1914–1945*. London: Oxford University Press.

Taylor, Verta and Leila Rupp (1991), "Researching the Women's Movement: We Make Our Own History, But Not Just as We Please," in Mary Margaret Fonow and Judith Cook, eds., *Beyond Methodology: Feminist Scholarship as Lived Research*. Bloomington, IN: Indiana University Press: 119–32.

Thiele, Beverly (1986) in Carole Pateman and Elizabeth Gross, eds., *Feminist Challenges*. Boston: Northeastern University Press.

Thompson, Dorothy (1987), "Women, Peace and History: Notes for an Historical Overview," in Ruth Roach Pierson, ed., *Women and Peace: Theoretical, Historical and Practical Perspectives*. London: Croom Helm: 29–43.

Thompson, Kenneth (1960), "Toward a Theory of International Politics," in Stanley Hoffmann, ed., *Contemporary Theory in International Relations*. Englewood Cliffs, NJ: Prentice-Hall: 17–28.

Tickner, J. Ann (1988), "Hans Morgenthau's Principles of Political Realism: A Feminist Reformulation," *Millennium*, 17, 3: 429–40.

(1992), *Gender in International Relations: Feminist Perspectives on Achieving Global Security*. New York: Columbia University Press.

Tong, Rosemarie (1989), *Feminist Thought: A Comprehensive Introduction*. Boulder, CO: Westview Press.

Tooby, John and Irven DeVore (1987), "The Reconstruction of Hominid Behavioral Evolution Through Strategic Modeling," in Warren Kinzey, ed., *The Evolution of Human Behavior: Primate Models*. Albany: State University of New York: 183–237.

Tress, D. M. (1988), "Comment on Flax's Postmodernism and Gender Relations in Feminist Theory," *Signs*, 14, 1: 196–200.

Trinh, Minh-ha (1989), *Woman, Native, Other: Writing Postcoloniality and Feminism*. Bloomington, IN: Indiana University Press.

Tronto, Joan (1987), "Beyond Gender Differences to a Theory of Care," *Signs*, 12, 4: 644–63.

Van Allen, Judith (1976), "'Aba Riots' or Igbo 'Women's War'? Ideology, Stratification, and the Invisibility of Women," in Nancy Hafkin and Edna Bay, eds., *Women in Africa: Studies in Social and Economic Change*. Stanford: Stanford University Press: 59–86.

Verba, Sidney (1961), "Assumptions of Rationality and Non-Rationality in

Models of the International System" in Klaus Knorr and Sidney Verba, eds., *The International System: Theoretical Essays*. Princeton: Princeton University Press: 93–117.

Vincent, R. J. (1992), "The Idea of Rights in International Ethics," in Terry Nardin and David Mapel, eds., *Traditions of International Ethics*. Cambridge: Cambridge University Press: 250–69.

Viotti, Paul and Mark Kauppi (1987), *International Relations Theory: Realism, Pluralism, Globalism*. London: Collier Macmillan.

Vital, David (1969), "Back to Machiavelli," in Klaus Knorr and James N. Rosenau, eds., *Contending Approaches to International Relations*. Princeton: Princeton University Press: 144–57.

Walker, Alice (1983), *In Search of Our Mothers' Gardens*. San Diego: Harcourt Brace Jovanovich.

Walker, Cherryl, ed. (1990), *Women and Gender in Southern Africa to 1945*. London: James Currey.

Walker, R. B. J. (1987), "Realism, Change, and International Political Theory," *International Studies Quarterly*, 31, 1: 65–86.

(1989), "History and Structure in the Theory of International Studies," *Millennium*, 18, 2: 163–83.

(1992), "Gender and Critique in the Theory of International Relations," in V. Spike Peterson, ed., *Gendered States: Feminist (Re)Visions of International Relations Theory*. Boulder, CO: Lynne Rienner: 179–202.

(1993), *Inside/Outside: International Relations Theory as Political Theory*. Cambridge: Cambridge University Press.

Wallerstein, Immanuel (1974), *The Modern World-System I*. New York: Academic Press.

(1980), *The Modern World-System II*. New York: Academic Press.

(1991), *Geopolitics and Geoculture: Essays on the Changing World-System*. Cambridge: Cambridge University Press.

Walt, Stephen (1991), "The Renaissance of Security Studies," *International Studies Quarterly*, 35, 2: 211–40.

Waltz, Kenneth (1959), *Man, the State and War: A Theoretical Analysis*. New York: Columbia University Press.

(1979), *Theory of International Politics*. Reading, MA: Addison-Wesley.

(1991), "Realist Thought and Neorealist Theory," in Robert Rothstein, ed., *The Evolution of Theory in International Relations*. Columbia, SC: University of South Carolina Press: 21–38.

Weber, Cynthia (1990), "Representing Debt: Peruvian Presidents Balaunde's and Garcia's Reading/Writing of Peruvian Debt," *International Studies Quarterly*, 34, 3: 353–66.

Weeden, Chris (1987), *Feminist Practice and Poststructuralist Theory*. Oxford: Basil Blackwell.

Wendt, Alexander (1987), "The Agent-Structure Problem in International Relations Theory," *International Organization*, 41, 3: 335–70.

(1992), "Anarchy is What States Make of It: The Social Construction of Power Politics," *International Organization*, 46, 2: 391–425.

Wendt, Alexander and Raymond Duvall (1989), "Institutions and International Order," in Ernst-Otto Czempiel and James N. Rosenau, eds., *Global*

Changes and Theoretical Challenges: Approaches to World Politics of the 1990s. Lexington, MA: Lexington Books: 51–74.

West, C. and D. H. Zimmerman (1983), "Small Insults: A Study of Interruptions in Cross-Sex Conversations Between Unacquainted Persons," in Barrie Thorne, C. Kramarae, and N. Henley, eds., *Language, Gender, and Society.* Rowley, MA: Newbury House: 103–17.

West, Robin (1988), "Jurisprudence and Gender," *University of Chicago Law Review,* 55: 1–72.

Whitworth, Sandra (1989), "Gender in the Inter-Paradigm Debate," *Millennium,* 18, 2: 265–72.

Wight, Martin (1966), "Why Is There No International Theory?" in Herbert Butterfield and Martin Wight, eds., *Essays in the Theory of International Politics.* Cambridge, MA: Harvard University Press: 17–34.

Williams, Sherley Anne (1990), "Some Implications of Womanist Theory," in Henry Louis Gates, Jr., ed., *Reading Black, Reading Feminist: A Critical Anthology.* New York: Meridian Books: 68–75.

Windsor, Philip (1988), "Women and International Relations: What's the Problem?" *Millennium,* 17, 3: 451–60.

Wittig, Monique (1989), "The Straight Mind," *Feminist Issues,* 1, 1: 103–11.

Wolfers, Arnold (1960), "Statesmanship and Moral Choice," in Stanley Hoffman, ed., *Contemporary Theory in International Relations.* Englewood Cliffs, NJ: Prentice-Hall: 273–86.

Women's Foreign Policy Council Directory (1987), Mim Kelber, editorial director. New York: Women's Foreign Policy Council.

Wong, Nellie (1991), "Socialist Feminism: Our Bridge to Freedom," in Chandra Mohanty, Ann Russo, and Lourdes Torres, eds., *Third World Women and the Politics of Feminism.* Bloomington, IN: Indiana University Press: 288–96.

Wright, Michael (1982), "The New Marines: Life in the Pits," *San Francisco Chronicle,* June 27.

Yaeger, Patricia and Beth Kowaleski-Wallace (1989), *Refiguring the Father: New Feminist Readings of Patriarchy.* Carbondale, IL: Southern Illinois University Press.

Yankelovich, Daniel and Richard Smoke (1988), "America's New Thinking," *Foreign Affairs,* 67, 1: 1–17.

Yerkes, Robert (1930), "Mental Evolution in Primates," in E. V. Cowdry, ed., *Human Biology and Racial Welfare.* New York: Hoeber: 115–38.

Young, Iris (1985), "Humanism, Gynocentrism and Feminist Politics," *Women's Studies International Forum,* 8, 3: 173–83.

Young, Oran (1969), "Aron and the Whale: A Jonah in Theory," in Klaus Knorr and James N. Rosenau, eds., *Contending Approaches to International Relations.* Princeton: Princeton University Press: 129–43.

(1982), "Regime Dynamics: The Rise and Fall of International Regimes," *International Organization,* 36 (Spring): 277–97.

Zalewski, Marysia (1993), "Feminist Theory and International Relations," in M. Bowker and R. Brown, eds., *From Cold War to Collapse: Theory and World Politics in the 1980s.* Cambridge: Cambridge University Press.

Zinnes, Dina (1980), "Prerequisites for the Study of System Transformation," in Ole Holsti, P. Siverson, and A. George, eds., *Change in the International System.* Boulder, CO: Westview Press.

INDEX

CAMBRIDGE STUDIES IN INTERNATIONAL RELATIONS